THE EASIEST FRENCH VERB BOOK
(your one stop shop for French verbs)

Includes over 2,000 French verbs, their meanings, pronunciations, conjugations and more!

By Sharon Harrison & Lindsay Hope Kern

Copyright ©2010

Special thanks to Farah Chowdhury and Sandra Harrison
for their help in the process of this book.

© 2010

Table of Contents / Table des Matières   Page

Introduction	5
Abbreviations and Notes	6
Parts of Speech	7
Guide to French Pronunciation	10
The International Phonetic Alphabet	20
Verb Formation	23
Person and Number	25
Subject Pronouns	25
Tense and Mood	28
The Present Tense	29
The Past Tenses	30
The Present Perfect	30
The Past Perfect	30
The Future Perfect	30
The Imperfect	32
QUI The Recent Past and Temporal Expression	34
The Future	34
QUI The Near Future	34
The Conditional	35
The Conditional Perfect	35
The Subjunctive	36
The Past Subjunctive	38
The Imperative	39
QIU The Past Imperative	40
The Present Participle	41
The Difference between Present Participle and Gerund	42
Un peu du grammar The Prepositions	43
The Past Participle	44
Simple and Compound Tenses	45
Intransitive Verbs and Transitive Verbs	46
Other uses of Être as an Auxiliary Verb	48
Semi-auxiliary Verbs	48
Voice	49
Forming the Passive Voice	50
Forming the Interrogative	51
Forming the Negative	52
Classification of French Verbs	53

© 2010

Table of Contents / Table des Matières   Page

Pronominal Verbs	54
Types of Pronominal Verbs	54
Reflexive Verbs	54
Reciprocal Verbs	58
Idiomatic Verbs	59
Additional tenses and mood	60
Literary Tenses	61+
Passé Simple	-
Passé Antérieur	-
Imparfait du Subjonctif	-
Plus-Que-Parfait du Subjonctif	-
Seconde Forme du Conditionnel Passé	-
Review List of French Simple and Compound tenses and moods	66
Conjugations	68+
Regular Verbs, R's, *'s, and #'s	-
Irregular Verbs, A1-A67	-
French to English Verb Index	147
English to French Verb Index	191
Recommendations for learning French	241

Introduction

This book has been written to help you learn French verbs in the easiest and most direct way. You will learn French verb formation, all the French tenses and moods, grammar tips and the types of conjugations which we have condensed to 70 easily recognizable patterns all listed together. All the regular verb conjugations have been given special, snappy names in this book to help you identify them more readily in the indexes and commit them more easily to memory. Over 2000 verbs, their meanings and pronunciations are included. Whenever you look up a verb in the indexes (which you can do in both French and English), you'll see a page number (A1 to A67) which directs you to the page that shows how to conjugate the verb. On that page also is a list of all the verbs in this book conjugated the same way.

To help you learn pronunciation of the French verbs, we've used the International Phonetic Alphabet. IPA is a system of phonetic notation based on the Latin alphabet and used as a standardized representation of the sounds of spoken language. Using the IPA symbols as a guide, we've provided you with a phonetic transcription of the sounds they represent. This book has a list of all the IPA symbols (with their pronunciations) that the French language uses so you can pronounce any French words in a dictionary.

Keep in mind that any printed rules for pronunciation can, at best, be an approximate guide because there are sounds in one language that have no exact corresponding sounds in another. Obviously, as in English and other languages, you must be aware of and allow for regional variations in pronunciation, especially the vowels. Be that as it may, this book includes the most accurate and easy to comprehend pronunciation guide currently available in any English book on French verbs.

© 2010

Abbreviations / Abréviations

e.o.	each other
o.s.	oneself
s.o.	someone
sth	something
sing.	singular
pl.	plural
masc.	masculine
fem.	feminine
QIU	Quelque Imformation Utile (Some Useful Information)

PARTS OF SPEECH

Parts of Speech (Parties du Discours)

"Parts of speech" are the basic classifications of words used to compose sentences. A sentence is grammatically a word (Run!), or a group of words (I am running in the marathon next Sunday) that expresses a complete idea. You need to be able to recognize and identify different parts of speech to understand grammar explanations and use the proper word form where it belongs. Although word classifications can sometimes vary from one language to another, both French and English identify the same parts of speech.

Part of Speech	English Example	Exemple français
Noun (Nom) A noun describes a person, place, thing, idea, quality or action.	woman world tree kindness arrival	femme monde arbre bonté arrivée
Verb (Verbe) A verb describes a action (doing something) or a state (being something).	to do to give to take to be to believe	faire donner prendre être croire
Pronoun (Pronom) A pronoun is used as a substitute for a noun.	me we herself it theirs	moi nous elle-même il / elle les / leurs
Adjective (Adjectif) An adjective describes or qualifies a noun.	wise other green last necessary	sage autre vert dernier nécessaire
Article (Article) An article is a special type of adjective that introduces a noun and also limits or clarifies it. "A" and "an" are called indefinite articles; "the" is called a definite article.	a, an the	un, une la, le, les

© 2010

Part of Speech	English Example	Exemple français
Adverb (Adverbe) An adverb usually describes a verb. It tells how, when, where, how much.	slowly yesterday here less always	lentement hier ici moins toujours
Preposition (Préposition) A preposition usually comes before a noun, pronoun or noun phrase and joins them to some other part of the sentence. It shows the spatial, temporal or other relationship of its object to the rest of the sentence.	on in to by between	sur dans, en à par entre
Conjunctions (Conjonction) A conjunction joins two words, phrases, clauses or sentences together.	and but if because that	et mais si parce que que

Note that sometimes a word can be one part of speech in one sentence and another part of speech in a different sentence, depending on the context.

Noun
I had an inspirational <u>thought</u>.
J'ai eu une <u>pensée</u> inspiratrice.

Verb
She <u>thought</u> that she knew what to do.
Elle <u>pensait</u> qu'elle savait que quoi faire.

Adjective
They have <u>less</u> money than last year.
Ils ont <u>moins</u> d'argent que l'an dernier.

Adverb
Francois tends to sleep <u>less</u> in the summer.
Francois a tendance à dormir <u>moins</u> en été.

GUIDE TO FRENCH PRONUNCIATION

Guide To French Pronunciation

Firstly, a brief overview of vowels and consonants. A vowel is a sound that is pronounced through the mouth without obstruction of the lips, tongue or throat. In contrast, a consonant is a sound in which there are one or more points where air is stopped along the vocal tract.

Here are a few guidelines for pronouncing French vowels. (voyelles français):

Most French vowels are pronounced further forward in the mouth than their English counterparts.

Keep the tongue tensed throughout the pronunciation of the vowel.

French vowels are monophthongs which means that the vowel sound doesn't change during pronunciation.

Monophthongs are sometimes called pure or stable vowels. This is important to remember because in English, vowels are often dipthongs, types of vowels where two vowel sounds are connected in a continuous, gliding motion. In English, the vowels a, e, and i tend to glide into a y sound; the vowels o and u into a w sound.

afraid   (uh frayeed)
bought   (bawt)

In French, even though the sound may seem similar, strive to keep the vowel sound constant and not add an off-glide (a transition into the final, weaker part of a dipthong sound). Listen carefully to French speakers to learn the distinction and to reproduce the purer, more stable quality of French vowels.

The French vowels are a, e, i, o and u. As in English the letter y can be a vowel or a consonant. When y is a vowel, it's sound is similar to the y in the English word happy (ee). The vowels a, o, and u are sometimes called hard vowels; e and i are soft vowels. These terms relate to the hard and soft pronunciations that the consonants c, g and s have, depending on which vowels follow the consonant. In the combinations ca, co and cu and when c is the final letter of a word, the French c has a hard sound, like the k sound of c in the English word cat.

cacher (kah shay)   to hide
colis   (kaw lee)   parcel
cuire   (kweer)   to cook
sac   (sahk)   bag

In contrast, ce and ci have a soft sound, like the s in the English word sing.

cerner (sehr nay)   to surround
ciseler (see zuh lay) to chisel

The combinations ga, go and gu have a hard sound like the g in the English word good.

garder (gahr day)   to keep
gober   (gaw bey)   to swallow
guerre (gehr)   war

© 2010

Ge and gi are soft g's and pronounced as zh, similar to the sound of the s in the English word pleasure.

gentil　(zhawn tee)　kind
gilet　(zhee leh)　waistcoat

The s, although it has a hard and soft sound in French pronunciation, it has different rules than c and g. When s is the first letter of a word, when it occurs between a vowel and a consonant, or as ss, it is pronounced like the s in the English word sand.

sel　　(sehl)　　　salt
destin　(deh stahn)　fate
dessin　(day sahn)　drawing

However, when it occurs between two vowels, the French s has a sound similar to the z in the English word zoo.

réserver　(ray zehr vay)　to reserve

Vowels followed by m or n are often nasal. French nasal vowels (voyelles nasalles français) are sounds produced by expelling air through the mouth and nose without obstruction of the lips, tongue or throat. Nasal pronunciation is considerably different from the standard pronunciation of the same vowels. Nasal vowels occur when final or before another consonant, except for h, double m or a double n.

grimper　(grahn pay)　to climb
montage　(mohn tahzh)　assembly
brun　　(bruhn)　　brown
cent　　(sawn)　　a hundred

French Nasal Vowels	phonetic pronunciations
en, em, an, am, aon, aen	awn
in, im, yn, ym, ain, aim, ein, eim	ahn
un, um, eng, oin, oing, oint	ahn
ien, yen, éen	ahn
on, om	ohn
un	uhn

The French language also feature a number of vowel combinations that make a single vowel sound. In any other vowel combination that is not part of this grouping, the vowels should be pronounce separately.

Combination	Sound	
ai	eh	
au	oh	
eau	oh	
ei	eh	
eu	uh	(oeu in a few words)
oi	wa	
ou	oo	
ou	w	(when it precedes a vowel)

French also has three semi-vowels (les semi-voyelles), sounds produced by the partial obstruction of air through the throat and mouth.

The semi-vowels are:

-ill, -il   papillon   (pah pee yohn), travail (trah vahy)
y after a vowel   payer   (pay yay)
i before a vowel   papier   (pah pyay)

The sound is similar to y in the English word say.

ui, uî, uy   huit (weet), huître (wee truh), appuyer (ah pwee yay)

This sound is similar to the sound of the English adjective wee.

oi, oy   trois (trwah), voyage (vwah yahzh)

The sound is similar to the wa in the English word watch.

French Accents and Diacritical Marks

In French, there are three written accents used with vowels which can change their pronunciation. Note that although they can alter pronunciation, they do not indicate any special voice stress on the syllable where they occur.

The accents are:
(é) The accute accent (l'accent aigu), the most common, is used only over e. The é has a sound similar to the a in the English word l<u>a</u>te (l<u>ay</u>t), but without the off-glide

(à, è, ù) The grave accent (l'accent grave) is used mainly over e, giving it a sound similar to the e in the English word p<u>e</u>t (p<u>eh</u>t). When l'accent grave is used over a and u, it does not alter their pronunciation. It is used to distinguish homonyms (words that are spelled or sound alike, but have different meanings).

a	(ah)	- has	à	(ah)	- to, at
la	(lah)	- the, it, her	là	(lah)	- there
ou	(oo)	- or	où	(oo)	- where

(â, ê, î, ô, û) The circumflex accent (l'accent circonflexe) may be used over any vowel, and generally lengthens the sound of the vowel:

flâner	(fl<u>ah</u> nay)	- to stroll
rêver	(r<u>ay</u> vay)	- to dream
île	(<u>ee</u>l)	- island
côte	(k<u>oh</u>t)	- coast
sûr	(s<u>ew</u>r)	- sure

The diacritical marks are:

(ç) The cedilla (la cédille) is added to the letter c to modify its pronunciation. The hook placed under the consonant ç before the vowel a, o, and u shows that it is pronounced as s rather than k.

| français | (frawn <u>s</u>ay) | - French |
| je reçois | (zhuh ruh <u>s</u>wah) | - I receive |

The other diacritical mark is the dieresis (le tréma). This sign is placed over a vowel to indicate that the vowel is pronounced as a separate syllable from the preceding vowel.

| haïr | (ah <u>eer)</u> | to hate |
| Noël | (naw <u>ehl</u>) | Christmas |

© 2010

French Consonants (Consonnes françaises)

Generally, written consonants at the end of French words are silent. The usual exceptions are final c, f, l and r.

Here are a few guidelines for the pronunciation of French consonants:

They are pronounced further forward in the mouth than their English equivalents. The one exception is the French r which is pronounced in the throat. Keep the tongue tensed throughout pronunciation.

In English, words are often pronounced without opening the mouth at the end of the word similar to swallowing the final sound. In French, you must keep the mouth open to complete the sound.

The French consonants b, d, k, m, n, v and z are pronounced very much like their English counterparts. There are only a few important distinctions to learn. When b is followed by -s or -t, it is pronounced as p.

absenter	(ap sawn tay)	- to go away
obtenir	(awp tuh neer)	- to obtain

M and n are silent after a nasal vowel. The letter f is usually pronounced when it is at the end of a word. Sometimes the f sound is written as ph.

photographier (faw toh grah fyay) - to photograph

The French h is always silent which means that it is not pronounced and the word sounds as if it begins with a vowel. However, there are two categories of French h, h muet and h aspiré. With the h muet, elision and liaison are required.

homme	(awm)	- man
l'homme	(lawm)	- the man

Although h aspiré is silent, it functions more as a "phantom consonant". Elisions are not permitted and liaisons are not made before it.

halo	(ah loh)	- halo
le halo	(luh ah loh)	- the halo

The pronunciation of the French p is similar to the English, but without the aspiration. The letter q almost always occurs in the combination qu, and is pronounced similar to the English k.

quitter (kee tay) - to quit

In French, the consonant t has two sounds. The first is similar to the t in English, but remember to avoid any initial aspiration. The second pronunciation of t is similar to the s sound in the English word sea. This sound occurs in -tion and -tial combinations.

actionner	(ahk syaw nay)	- to activate
partial	(pahr syahl)	- biased

© 2010

The letter w occurs in words brought into French from other languages and is pronounced either like the v in the English word very, or as an English w.

wagon   (vah gohn) - car, truck, wagon
watt   (waht)   - watt

The French consonant j has the same sound as the French g before e or i, a sound similar to the s in the English word pleasure.

jaser   (zhah zay) - to gossip

The French l is quite different from its English counterpart. The tip of the tongue must touch the upper front teeth to pronounce it correctly. Pronounce it more tensely than the l of the English word fell. Double ll is often pronounced as a single l except in the combinations -ill, vowel plus -ill, or vowel plus final -il. In these combinations, it is pronounced similar to the y in the English word yet.

briller   (bree yay)   - to shine
batailler   (bah tah yay)   - to fight
détail   (day tay)   - detail

> **QIU**
> The same sound is sometimes represented by the letter y.
>
> payer   (pay yay)   - to pay
> voyelle (vwah yehl)   - vowel

The French r is nothing like the English r which is pronounced in the middle of the mouth. The Parisian pronunciation of the French r has been described as sounding like a gargle. Its pronunciation rules are a bit complex. When the r is final in one-syllable words, it is pronounced.

cher   (shehr) - dear
jour   (zhoor) - day

However, in words of more than one-syllable, the final r is usually silent. The final r of the infinitive verb ending -er is always silent, as is the final r of words of more than one-syllable ending in -ier.

parler   (pahr lay)   - to speak
dernier   (dehr nyay)   - last

Yet, there are exceptions to this rule. These common French words of more than one-syllable have the final r pronounced.

couleur   (kool uhr)   - color
hiver   (ee vehr)   - winter
obéir   (aw bay eer) - to obey

When a final -re has a vowel preceding it, it is pronounced as ehr.

f<u>aire</u>   (f<u>ehr</u>)   - to do / to make

It is always pronounced (eer) in the infinitive ending -ir.

ven<u>ir</u>   (vuh n<u>eer</u>)   - to come

When a final -re has no vowel before it, it has a ruh sound. In the International Phonetic Alphabet (I, P, A,) this is written simply as r. In the verb indexes, it is written phonetically as (ruh) to approximate the gargling sound of the French r.

attend<u>re</u>   (ah tawn d<u>ruh</u>)   to wait for

The letter x in French is pronounced as either ks or gz. The general rule is ex+vowel is pronounced as (egz), and ex+consonant is pronounced as eks

e<u>x</u>ister	(e<u>g</u> <u>z</u>ee stay)	- to exist
e<u>x</u>cuser	(e<u>ks</u> kew zay)	- to excuse
e<u>x</u>cellence	(eh<u>k</u> <u>s</u>eh lawns)	- excellence
e<u>x</u>istence	(eh<u>g</u> <u>z</u>ee stawns)	- existence

Consonant Combinations (Consonne de combinaisons)

The French ch combination is pronounced similar to the sh in the English word shine. The ch is never pronounced as the ch in the English word church.

enchanter	(awn shawn tay)	- to delight
acheter	(ash tay)	- to buy

However, there are a few words in French brought in from other languages in which ch is pronounced much similar to the k in the English word key.

choral	(kawr ahl)	- choral
chrome	(krohm)	- chromium

The French cc before the hard vowels, a, o, and u has a pronunciation similar to the k in the English word kitten, but again, without aspiration.

accabler	(ah kah blay)	- to overwhelm
accomplir	(ah kohn pleer)	- to accomplish

However, before the soft vowels, e and i, the French cc is pronounced as a ks sound.

accélérer	(ahk say lay ray)	- to accelerate
accepter	(ahk sep tay)	- to accept

The French sc combination has two possible pronunciations. Before the soft vowels, e or i, the pronunciation of sc is similar to s in the English word sing.

scinder   (sahn day)   - to split

However, when sc precedes the hard vowels, a, o, u, the two sounds are pronounced separately.

scander   (skawn day)   - to scan

The ph combination has a pronunciation similar to the ph in the English word photo.

photographier	(faw toh grah fyay)	- to photograph
orthographe	(awr taw grahf)	- spelling

The th combination is similar in pronunciation to the t in the English word tell, without aspiration. Never is it pronounced like the English th sounds in the or think.

théorie	(tay aw ree)	- theory
méthod	(may tawd)	- method

© 2010

The sound of French gn is similar to the sound of ny in the English word canyon, but with one important difference. The ny of the English canyon represents two separate sounds, each belonging to a different syllable (can yon). While, the French gn is a single sound. Note that gn is a nasal sound.

accompa<u>gn</u>er   (ah kohn pah <u>ny</u>ay)   · to accompany

However, when the French <u>gn</u> is before a final e, the pronunciations is something like (nyuh).

monta<u>gn</u>e   (mohn tah<u>n yuh</u>)   · mountain

Euphony in French Pronunciation

French is considered a very musical sounding language because it tends to flow from one word to the next without pause. This flow maintains euphony, meaning agreeable and harmonious sound. Where euphony does not occur naturally in the language, French requires that sounds be added or words altered. French does not like to have a word that ends in a vowel followed by a word that begins with a vowel sound. This pause created between two vowel sounds is called a hiatus. When this happens, the vowel at the end of the first word is dropped and replaced with an apostrophe (') to combine the two vowels. This is called elision. Elision means slide; essentially you are sliding two words together.

<u>je</u> arrive (<u>zhuh</u> ah reev)   becomes   j'arrive (<u>zh</u>ah reev)

Two other techniques used to maintain euphony are liaison and enchaînement. Although they both affect consonants, there is a subtle difference between them. Liaison carries the usually silent sound at the end of the first word onto the beginning of the second word.

vou<u>s</u> avez is pronounced (voo <u>z</u>ah vay) rather than (voo ah vay).

When the consonant sound at the end of a word is carried over to the next word and pronounced regardless of whether the next word begins with a vowel or mute h, this is called enchaînement as in.

ave<u>c</u> (ah veh<u>k</u>)   ave<u>c</u> elle (ah veh<u>k</u> ehl)

Whenever possible these techniques are used to increase the flow and musicality of the language. Another useful guideline is to try and give all syllables in a French word equal stress, with only a slight emphasis on the last syllable.

THE INTERNATIONAL PHONECTIC ALPHABET

The International Phonetic Alphabet

The International Phonetic Alphabet (IPA) is a system of phonetic notation used as a standardized representation of the sounds of spoken language. The most common uses of IPA are dictionaries and linguistics. Each unique IPA symbol represents a single sound. The IPA transcription of a word may have more or fewer letters than the regular spelling of the word; it's not a one letter/one symbol relationship. Silent letters are not transcribed. Once you learn these IPA symbols, you can refer to any French dictionary and know how to pronounce the words.

IPA	French	IPA	Pronunciation

Vowels

[a]	abaisser	[abese]	(ah bay say)
[ɑ]	sometimes called an open a, so-called because the sound is produce with the mouth wide open. The distinction between the a/ɑ sounds is being phased out of French speech.		
[ɛ]	mèttre	[mɛtr]	(meh truh)
[e]	écouter	[ekute]	(ay koo tay)
[ə]	abstenir	[apstənir]	(ap stuh neer)
[ø]	creuser	[krøze]	(kruh zay)
[i]	finir	[finir]	(fee neer)
[ɔ]	abroger	[abrɔʒe]	(ah braw zhay)
[œ]	cueillir	[kœjir]	(kuh yeer)
[u]	accoucher	[akuʃe]	(ah koo shay)
[y]	unir	[ynir]	(ew neer)
[o]	rose	[roz]	(rohz)
	appauvrir	[apovrir]	(ah poh vreer)

Semi-vowels

[ɥ]	appuyer	[apɥije]	(ah pwee yay)
[w]	voyager	[vwajaʒe]	(vwah yah zhay)
[j]	travailler	[travaje]	(trah vah yay)

Nasal Vowels

[ã]	vendre	[vãdr]	(vawn druh)
[ɛ̃]	pincer	[pɛ̃se]	(pahn say)
[ɔ̃]	consommer	[kɔ̃sɔme]	(kohn saw may)
[œ̃]	brun	[brœ̃]	(bruhn)

| IPA | French | IPA | Pronunciation |

Consonants

[b]	bourrer	[bure]	(boo ray)
[m]	accommoder	[akɔmɔde]	(ah kaw maw day)
[n]	naître	[nɛtr]	(neh truh)
[r]	arriver	[arive]	(ah ree vay)
[p]	pincer	[pɛ̃se]	(pahn say)
[k]	cacher	[kaʃe]	(kah shay)
[s]	sortir	[sɔrtir]	(sawr teer)
	durcir	[dyrsir]	(dewr seer)
[ʃ]	cacher	[kaʃe]	(kah shay)
[d]	dormir	[dɔrmir]	(dohr meer)
[t]	taxi	[takse]	(tahk say)
[f]	faire	[fɛr]	(fehr)
[v]	vendre	[vɑ̃dr]	(vawn druh)
[ʒ]	abroger	[abrɔʒe]	(ah braw zhay)
[g]	garantir	[garɑ̃tir]	(gah rawn teer)
[l]	lire	[lir]	(leer)
[z]	zébrer	[zebre]	(zay bray)

Nasal Consonant

[ɲ]	accompagner	[akɔpaɲe]	(ah kohn pah nyay)

Indicator of Forbidden Liaison

[']	le halo	[lɛ'alo]	(luh ah loh)

VERB FORMATION

Verb Formation
==============

The basic form of any verb in most languages is called the infinitive (l'infinitif). This is the "to..." form of the verb. To laugh, to sing, to do or to be anything all begins with the infinitive. The infinitive is the form of the verb that has no inflection to indicate person, number, mood or tense. This form is called the infinitive because the verb has not yet been limited or made "finite" by inflection. The system of verbal inflection is called conjugation (la conjugaison).

The five inflections are:

1) Person   Personne
2) Number Nombre
3) Mood   Mode
4) Tense   Temps
5) Voice   Voix

In English, the infinitive consists of two words; "to love", for example. In French the infinitive is a single word which consists of a stem and an ending. In the verb aimer (to love), aim is the stem and -er is the ending. All French infinitives will have one of these three endings, with -er being the most common.

-er (ay)   aimer   (ay may)   - to love
-ir (eer)   venir   (vuh neer)   - to come
-re (ruh)   attendre (ah tawn druh) - to wait for

A major difference between learning English verbs and learning French verbs is that English verbs have relatively few changes in their verb endings. French verbs are more complex because they require more ending variations to express the different forms of the verb. The ending of a French verb specifies person, number, mood, tense and voice. Conjugation is a matter of changing the verb endings. To conjugate French verbs, the changes in the endings have to agree with the subject (the person and number) and the tense (the timing) of the verb.

All regular verbs in the three conjugations have been given special names in this book for ease of reference and to help you remember them.

All regular -er verbs are called the Rs
All regular -ir verbs are called the stars *s
All regular -re verbs are called the bars #s

Person and Number (Personne et nombre)
French Subject Pronouns (Pronoms sujets)

The subject of a verb is the person or thing performing the action of that verb. Subjects are nouns and subject pronouns are used to replace them in a sentence.

Subject	Subject Pronoun
Colette lit.	Elle lit.
Colette is reading.	She is reading.
It is a travel guide to Spain.	Il est un guide de voyage en Espagne.
The book is a travel guide to Spain.	Le livre est un guide de voyage en Espagne.

You must understand subject pronouns to conjugate French verbs because the verb forms change to agree with them. The subject pronouns describe both the person and number of the subject in a sentence.

1st person refers to the person(s) speaking.
2nd person refers to the person(s) being spoken to.
3rd person refers to the person(s) being spoken about.

Each of these persons may be either singular or plural. All pronouns and verbs are classified according to these three persons.

The Subjects Pronouns (Pronoms sujets)

Person	Singular			Plural		
1st	je	(zhuh)	I	nous	(noo)	we
2nd	tu	(tew)	you	vous	(voo)	you
3rd	il	(eel)	He/it	ils	(eel)	they (mas.)
	elle	(ehl)	She/it	elles	(ehl)	they (fem.)
	on	(ohn)	one			

The only differences between the French 1st person singular "je" and the English "I" is that "je" is only capitalized when it begins a sentence, and "je" contracts to "j'" when it precedes a verb beginning with a vowel (j'espère - I hope) or a mute h (j'habite - I live). The second person subject pronoun has a marked difference. In English, that pronoun is always "you", no matter how many people are being addressed or what their relationship is to the speaker. French has two words for "you", tu and vous. You must understand the inportant distinctions between them to avoid unintentionally insulting someone. Tu is the familiar form. To address someone as "tu" demonstrates a closeness, or, at least, an informality.

Use tu when speaking to a:

friend
peer / colleague
relative
child
pet

Vous is both the plural and the formal way of addressing someone. When it is used in the singular, it maintains a distance or formality. Use vous when speaking to:

someone you don't know well
an authority figure
an older person
anyone to whom you wish to demonstrate respect

Remember that vous is also the plural form of you, and must be used when talking to more than one person, no matter what the relationship or circumstances. The tu/vous distinction can be problematic. Sometimes people follow the guideline of using whatever form a person uses to address them. This can be misleading. Someone in a position of authority may use "tu" with you, but that doesn't mean it would be acceptable to use "tu" with them. When in doubt use "vous", as it is preferable to show more respect than less. Allow the other person to suggest that you use "tu" with them. If you have been addressing someone as "vous" and think that the relationship is becoming less formal, there is a question you can use to make the change.

Simply ask: On peut se tutoyer?   Can we use tu with each other?
        (ohn puh suh tew twa yay)

> **QIU**
> Vous is always conjugated in the second person plural even when it refers to only one person.

The French third person singular pronouns il (he) and elle (she) are used as their English equivalents.

Il croit en les anges.   He believes in angels.
Elle se demande pourquoi il a fait cela. She is wondering why he has done that.

However, unlike English, both il and elle can also express "it". All French nouns are classified as either masculine or feminine. To replace them in a sentence, use the subject pronoun that agrees in gender. Therefore il not only refers to one male, but also expresses "it" when referring to a single masculine noun.

Les temps est élastique.   Time is elastic
Il peut passer lentement ou rapidement. It can pass slowly or quickly.

© 2010

Elle refers to one female (she) and also expresses "it" when the "it" is a single feminine noun.

La chanson est très populaire.	The song is very popular.
Elle est facile à chanter.	It is easy to sing

"On" is an indefinite pronoun and literally means one. "On" is listed with the personal pronouns because the French tend to use it more frequently for indefinite subjects than English speakers do.

On doit se lever maintenant.	One must stand up now.
On ne devrait pas poser de telles questions!	One should not ask such questions!

"On" can also be used as an informal replacement for we, you, they, someone, everyone and people in general.

On y va !	Let's go!
On a laissé tomber ses clefs de voiture.	Someone dropped his car keys.
On y danse.	People dance there.

QIU
On is a neuter singular pronoun. No matter what pronoun "on" replaces, "on" always takes a third person singular verb.

The first person plural subject pronoun nous is used the same as we in English.

Nous sortons dîner ce soir.	We're going out to dinner tonight.
J'espère que nous apprécions le repas.	I hope that we injoy the meal.

Unlike English, French has two third person plural subject pronouns which mean they, ils and elles. Ils is used for groups of men and mixed gender groups.

Mes frères jouent au football.	My brothers are playing football.
Ils auront faim à midi.	They will be hungry at midday.

Mes nièces et neveux viendront au spectacle, mais ils seront en retard.
My nieces and nephews are coming to the show, but they will be late.

Ils is also used for groups of masculine nouns,

Où sont les livres que j'ai achetés aujourd'hui ?	Ils sont dans le sac dans le hall.
Where are the books that I bought today?	They are in the bag in the hall.

and for groups of mixed masculine and feminine nouns.

Avez-vous vu la caméra et le trépied ? Oui, ils sont dehors.
Have you seen the camera and the tripod? Yes, they're outside.

Elles can only be used when every single person in a group is female.

Catherine et Marie vont en Egypte. Catherine and Marie are going to Egypt.
Elles partent à six heures du matin. They are leaving at six o'clock in the morning.

and for groups of feminine nouns.

Les fleurs sont magnifiques. The flowers are gorgeous.
Elles viennent du jardin de Tante Rose. They're from Aunt Rose's garden.

QIU
Even if a group consists of 200 women and only one man, you must still use ils. Ils and elles are pronounced exactly like il (eel) and elle (ehl) except when a liaison is needed.

Tense and Mood (Temps et mode)

Often there is some confusion regarding the difference between a tense and a mood. It is helpful to know that the French word for tense (temps) is also the word for time. The tense of a verb is its timing. Tense specifies when the verb's action or state of being occurs, how long it lasted and whether or not it was or will be completed. Mood expresses the feeling or attitude of the speaker towards the event or state the verb describes. Is the speaker stating a fact or offering an opinion? Is s/he considering a possibility or doubting an outcome? These feelings and attitudes are expressed through different verb moods.

French has seven moods that are divided into two categories, personal and impersonal. The personal moods are conjugated to agree with the subject pronouns. The impersonal moods are not conjugated to agree with any particular subject pronoun.

Personal Moods	Impersonal moods
The Indicative	The Infinitive
The Conditional	The Gerund
The Subjunctive	The Participle
The Imperative	

The indicative mood is the most frequently used mood. It indicates the speaker is relating a fact or making an assertion with the certainty of a fact.

The Present Tense (Présent)

The French present tense is in the indicative mood and is similar to the present tense in English with one important difference. In English there are three different verb forms to express the present:

I speak
I am speaking
I do speak

In French all three sentences can be translated by je parle (zhuh pahrl). Uses of the present tense:

1) to describe an action (or state of being) occurring in the present
   Fred habite Marseille.   Fred lives/is living in Marseille.

2) to describe habitual actions that are still true
   Chaque soir je prends le train pour aller au cinéma.
   Every evening I take the train to go to the cinema.

3) to express existing facts and perceived truths
   Rome est la capitale d'Italie.   Rome is the capital of Italy.
   La vérité est plus étrange que la fiction.   Truth is stranger than fiction.

QIU

French has an idiom "être en train de" + the infinitive of the verb to emphasize that something is happening right now.

Nous sommes en train d'écrire ce livre.
We are in the process of writing this book.

The Past Tenses (Temps passés)

The two most frequently used French past tenses are the imperfect (l'imparfait) and the present perfect (le passé composé). L'imparfait is a simple tense, which means it is composed of only one conjugated verb form. The French imperfect je parlais (zhuh pahr lay) translates as:

I spoke
I was speaking
I used to speak

Le passé composé is a compound tense, composed of two verb forms, an auxiliary verb and the past participle of the main verb. Even though le passé composé is a past tense, its grammatical name is the present perfect. Le passé compose, j'ai parlé (zhay pahr lay), translates as:

I spoke
I have spoken

Since le passé composé is a compound tense, it is always conjugated with either avoir (to have) or être (to be) as its auxiliary verb. An auxiliary is a verb that combines with the main verb to show differences in tense, person and voice.

Even though être literally means "to be", when it is used as an auxiliary verb to form compound tenses, it translates as "have".

avoir (ah vwahr) to have			être (eh truh) to be		
j'ai	(zhay)	I have	je suis	(zhuh swee)	I am
tu as	(tew ah)	you have	tu es	(tew ay)	you are
elle/il a	(ehl/eel ah)	she/he/it has	elle/il est	(ehl/eel ay)	she/he/it is
nous avons	(noo zah vohn)	we have	nous sommes	(noo sawm)	we are
vous avez	(voo zah vay)	you have	vous êtes	(voo zeht)	you are
elles/il ont	(ehl/eel zohn)	they have	elles/ils sont	(ehl/eel sohn)	they are

These two past tenses illustrate the important distinctions between an imperfect tense and a perfect tense. Perfect tenses do not mean perfect in an ideal sense. Perfect, in this sense, means finished or completed. All perfect tenses express actions that either are, had been, or will be completed. Have is in the present and completed is in the past meaning it is done now so it is "perfect".

    I have finished the article.
    J'ai fini l'article.

With a past perfect (le pluperfect) verb, the action had been completed in the past.

    I *had* finished the article last week.
    J'*avais* fini l'article la semaine dernière.

With a future perfect (futur antériur) verb, the action will be completed at a future time.

    I *will have* finished the article before Monday.
    J'*aurai* fini l'article avant lundi.

Although the past perfect and the future perfect tenses are not included in this book's conjugation tables, you should know how to conjugate them because they are frequently used. The French past perfect is formed using the imperfect of the auxillary verb of either avoir or être and the past participle of the main verb whereas the French future perfect is formed using the future of the auxillary verb of either avoir or être and the past participle of the main verb.

Examples with avoir

The past perfect (pluperfect)

j'avais fini	(zhah vay fee nee)	I had finished
tu avais fini	(tew ah vay fee nee)	you had finished
elle/il avait fini	(ehl/eel ah vay fee nee)	she/he/it had finished
nous avions fini	(noo zah vee ohn fee nee)	we had finished
vous aviez fini	(voo zah vee ay fee nee)	you had finished
elles/ils avaient fini	(ehl/eel zah vay fee nee)	they had finished

The future perfect

j'aurai fini	(zhoh ray fee nee)	I will have finished
tu auras fini	(tew oh rah fee nee)	you will have finished
elle/il aura fini	(ehl/eel oh rah fee nee)	she/he/it will have finished
nous aurons fini	(noo zoh rohn fee nee)	we will/shall have finished
vous aurez fini	(voo zoh ray fee nee)	you will have finished
elles/ils auront fini	(ehl/eel zoh rohn fee nee)	they will have finished

Examples with être

The past perfect

j'étais *arrivé/-(e)*	(zhay tay ah ree vey)	I had arrived
tu étais *arrivé/-(e)*	(tew ay tay ah ree vey)	you had arrived
elle/il était *arrivé/-(e)*	(ehl/eel ay tay ah ree vey)	she/he/it had arrived
nous étions *arrivé/-(e)s*	(noo zay tee ohn ah ree vey)	we had arrived
vous étiez arrivé/-*(e)(es)(s)*	(voo zay tee ay ah ree vey)	you had arrived
elles/ils étaient arrivé/-*(e)s*	(ehl/eel zay tay ah ree vey)	they had arrived

The future perfect

je serai arrivé(e)	(zhuh suh ray ah ree vay)	I will have arrived
tu seras arrivé(e)	(tew suh rah ah ree vay)	you will have arrived
elle/il sera arrivé(e)	(ehl/eel suh rah ah ree vay)	she/he/it will have arrived
nous serons arrivé(e)s	(noo suh rohn ah ree vay)	we will/shall have arrived
vous serez arrivé(e)(es)(s)	(voo suh ray ah ree vay)	you will have arrived
elles/ils seront arrivé(e)s	(ehl/eel suh rohn ah ree vay)	they will have arrived

© 2010

In contrast, imperfect tenses express actions or states that are not completed. The imperfect describes something which is ongoing, habitual, continuous. Even though something may have occurred in the past, if it was not finished or completed, it is considered imperfect. One very important use of the imperfect is to describe background information in a narration.

Le passé composé is used to express a specific event that occurred against that background.

Alors que je regardais (imperfect) par la fenêtre, j'ai vu (perfect) un accident de voiture.
When I was looking out of the window (the background continued over an indefinite period of time), I saw a car accident (a specific event).

The imperfect is also used:

to describe what occurred regularly in the past

Quand j'étais jeune, j'étudiais le ballet.
When I was young, I studied ballet.

to refer to a previous habitual action.

J'allais au parc tous les jours après l'école.
I went to the park every day after school.

to describe past conditions and states as well as past emotional reactions and attitudes.

Il neigeaït vendredi.
It was snowing on Friday.

Elle était très triste de les laisser.
She was very sad to leave them.

to express duration or a continuing event.

Il travaillait toute la matinée.
He worked all morning.

Elle tenait un journal quotidien.
She kept a daily journal.

in phrases where "used to...." occurs in English

Il jouait au football professionnel.
He used to play professional football.

In contrast, le passé composé is used:

to describe a past event that happened once

>Jacques a gagné le Tour de France.
>Jacques won the Tour de France.

to describe a finished, completed event.

>Enfin, ils *ont* fini le projet !   At last they *have* finished the project!

to describe a series of distinctly separate events.

>Elle est arrivée à Venise, a rencontrée un poète local, et a changé ses plans de voyage.
>She arrived in Venice, met a local poet, and changed her travel plans.

Note these important differences between l'imparfait and le passé composé.

L'imparfait	Passé composé
Event is repeated or habitual.	Event happened once.
Event is continuing, unfinished.	Event is completed, finished.
Description of past habitual actions, past emotional states, actions that were in the progress when something else happened	Description of a series of distinct and separate events.

Some frequently used verbs that express an attitude or a state rather than an action tend to use the imperfect more often than the perfect.

Here is a list of the most significant ones:

aimer	to love/to like
avoir	to have
croire	to believe
désirer	to desire / to want
espérer	to hope
être	to be
imaginer	to imagine
penser	to think
pouvoir	to be able to
préférer	to prefer
regretter	to regret
savoir	to know
sentir	to smell
vouloir	to want / to wish

> **QIU**
>
> French has two other past forms, the first is called the recent past (le passé récent). As you can say "I just" in English as in "I just saw Lillian". you can use the present tense of venir "to come" plus the preposition de plus the infinitive of the main verb to express something that just happened.
>
> Je <u>viens de</u> voir Lillian.   (Literal meaning "I <u>come from</u> seeing Lillian")
> I <u>just</u> saw Lilian.
>
> The other one is called a temporal expression. As you can say "ago" in English as in "I just saw Lillian 10 minutes ago", you always use the past tense of the verb and use il y a "it there has" and then add the amount of time that has passed since it happened.
>
> I saw Lillian 10 minutes <u>ago</u>.
> j'ai vu lillian <u>il y a</u> 10 minutes.   (Literal meaning "I have seen Lillian <u>it there has</u> 10 minutes)

The Future (futur)

As in English the future tense is used to express an action or state that will happen or exist.

  Les filles <u>chanteront</u> à un concert dimanche soir.
  The girls <u>will sing</u> in a concert Sunday evening.

The future can also be used:

in conditional clauses when the "if" clause is in the present

  Si vous travaillez dur, vous <u>réussirez</u>.
  If you work hard, you <u>will succeed</u>.

after quand (when), lorsque (when), dès que (as soon as) and aussitôt que (immediately) when a future action is meant

  <u>Quand</u> elle <u>partira</u> tout le monde lui donnera des fleurs.
  <u>When</u> she <u>leaves</u>, everyone will give her flowers.

> **QIU**
>
> French has another future form called the near future (le futur proche). Just as you can use "to go" in English as in "I' am going to do it tomorrow", you can use the present tense of aller "to go" plus the infinitive of the main verb to express future time or intention.
>
> Je <u>vais</u> le faire demain.
> I <u>am going</u> to do it tomorrow.

The Conditional (Conditionnel)

Remember the conditional is technically a mood rather than a tense.
This difference has no effect on its forms and uses, and it is included in the conjugation tables.
The French conditional has the same uses as in English:

to describe what would happen if a certain condition is met

    Si elle avait de l'argent, elle se déplacerait à Paris.
    If she had the money, she would move to Paris.

Note that the condition itself, the "si" clause is expressed in the imperfect (elle avait), the result (elle se déplacerait) is expressed using the conditional.

to convey the future from a past perspective

    Zacharie dit, Luc a dit qu'il devrait nous donner la télévision avant mercredi.
    Zacharie says, Luc said that he would have to give us the television by Wednesday.

Although the conditional perfect (conditionnel parfait) is not included in the conjugation tables, you should know its uses and how to conjugate it because it's frequently used in speaking and writng. The French conditional perfect is used to express actions that would have occurred if past circumstances had been different. The conditional perfect is often used for the result clause (the si clause) while the past perfect is used to express the unmet condition.

    Si j'avais su que tu venais, j'aurais fait un gâteau.
    If I had known you were coming, I would have made a cake.

Other uses of the conditional perfect are:

to express an unrealized desire in the past

    J'aurais aimé aller avec toi, mais j'ai dû rentrer.
    I would have liked to go with you, but I had to go home.

to report an unverified event, especially in the news

        Il y aurait eu un accident sur l'autoroute.
        There has allegedly been an accident on the motorway.

The French conditional perfect (also called the past conditional), is conjugated using the conditional of the auxiliary verb avoir or être and the past participle of the main verb. When the auxiliary verb is être, the past participle must agree with the subject. When avoir is used, the past participle usually agrees with its direct object.

Examples with avoir:

The conditional perfect

j'aurais fini	(zhoh ray fee nee)	I would have finished
tu aurais fini	(tew oh ray fee nee)	you would have finished
elle/il aurait fini	(ehl/eel oh ray fee nee)	she/he/it would have finished
nous aurions fini	(noo zoh ree ohn fee nee)	we would have finished
vous auriez fini	(voo zoh ree ay fee nee)	you would have finished
elles/ils auraient fini	(ehl/eel zoh ray fee nee)	they would have finished

Examples with être:

The conditional perfect

je serais arrivé(e)	(zhuh suh ray ah ree vay)	I would have arrived
tu serais arrivé(e)	(tew suh ray ah ree vay)	you would have arrived
elle/il serait arrivé(e)	(ehl/eel suh ray ah ree vay)	she/he/it would have arrived
nous serions arrivé(e)s	(noo suh ree ohn ah ree vay)	we would have arrived
vous seriez arrivé(e)(es)(s)	(voo suh ree ay ah ree vay)	you would have arrived
elles/ils seraient arrivé(e)s	(ehl/eel suh ray ah ree vay)	they would have arrived

---

QIU
There is no direct translation for the word "would" in French. The only way to express the concept is in the verb endng itself. How to express the concepts "could" and "should" is explained in the section on semi-auxiliary verbs.

The Subjunctive (Subjonctif)

The subjunctive, as the conditional, is technically a verb mood, but is treated as a tense and conjugated. The subjunctive is usually found in a dependent/subordinate clause introduced by que (kuh) or qui (kee). Que nous allions is an example of a dependent clause. Although a dependent clause contains a subject and a verb, it does not express a complete and therefore cannot stand alone as a sentence. In sentences where the subjunctive is used, the subject of the dependent clause is usually different from the subject of the independent/main clause.

Il est temps que nous allions
It is time that we go.

Use the subjunctive:

with verbs and expressions describing needs, wants, recommendations, informal orders and requests

Jean-Paul souhaite qu'elles partent maintenant.
Jean-Paul wishes that they leave now.

Lenka suggère que nous restions à l'Hôtel Oya à Prague.
Lenka suggests that we stay at The Hotel Oya in Prague.

with verbs and expressions indicating a subject's emotional reaction such as happiness, sorrow, fear, anger, surprise, regret, etc.

Il craint qu'elle ne parte.
He is afraid that she is leaving.

Nous sommes heureux que Simone vienne ce soir.
We're happy that Simone is coming tonight.

with verbs and expressions describing doubt, possibility and opinion

Je doute qu'ils viennent.
I doubt that they will come.

Il est possible que les investisseurs aiment l'idée.
It is possible that the investors like the idea.

with some impersonal statements

Il est impressionnant que Claudine parle sept langues.
It is impressive that Claudine speaks seven languages.

The following list of verbs do not take the subjunctive when they are used in the affirmative because they express what the speaker considers to be certain.

c'est que	it's that/because
connaître (quelqu'un) qui	to know (someone) that/who
croire que	to believe that
dire que	to say that
espérer que	to hope that
être certain que	to be certain that
être sûr que	to be sure that
il est certain que	it is certain that
il est clair que	it is clear/obvious that
il est évident que	it is obvious that
il est probable que	it is probable that
il est exact que	it is correct/true that
il est sûr que	it is certain that
il est vrai que	it is true that
il me (te, lui...) semble que	it seems to me (you, her/him...) that
il paraît que	it appears that
penser que	to think that
savoir que	to know that
trouver que	to find/think that
vouloir dire que	to mean that

However, when the verbs are used in the negative, they require the subjunctive.

Affirmative
Nous croyons que le monde est beau.
We believe that the world is beautiful.

Negative
Nous ne croyons pas que le monde soit beau.
We don't believe that the world is beautiful.

Even though you can use other conjunctions to form the subjunctive, que is usually the one included in conjugation tables. Although que has various meanings and uses, when used as a conjunction, it is equivalent to "that". In an English sentence such as, " I'm happy you're coming with us", using the conjunction "that" is optional. In French, you must always use que in such sentences.

Je suis heureux que tu viennes avec nous.
I am happy that you're coming with us.

Note that que contacts to qu' before a vowel or a mute h.

The French subjunctive has only four tenses; the present, the past, the imperfect and the pluperfect. In ordinary conversation and writing, only the present subjunctive and past subjunctive are used. It can be confusing because the present subjunctive can be used for events that actually happened in the past. What matters is when the event/state happened in relation to the main clause.

Note the difference between the following sentences.

1) Nous étions heureux que vous veniez dîner hier soir.
   We were happy that you came to dinner last night.

In the first sentence, even though the action referred to happened in the past, you use the present subjunctive because the two verbs occur at the same time.

2) Nous sommes heureux que vous soyez venu dîner hier soir.
   We are happy that you came to dinner last night.

In the second sentence, you use the past subjunctive because the event (you came to dinner) happened before the main verb (we are happy) occurred.

Use the present subjunctive for events/states that occur at the same time or after the main clause. Use the past subjunctive when the action/state of the verb in the subordinate clause (the verb that follows que) occurred before the action/state of the verb in the main clause. In these types of sentences, the main clause is in the present tense and the subordinate clause is in the past tense.

The French past subjunctive (le subjonctif passé) is formed using the present subjunctive of the auxiliary verb (avoir or être) and the past participle of the main verb. It is similar to the passé composé except that the auxiliary verb used is in its present subjunctive form. When the auxiliary verb is être the past participle must agree with the subject. When avoir is used, the past participle usually agrees with its direct object.

parler (regular verb)
j'aie parlé
tu aies parlé
elle/il ait parlé

nous ayons parlé
vous ayez parlé
elles/ils aient parlé

aller (être verb)
je sois allé(e)
tu sois allé(e)
il/elle soit allé(e)

nous soyons allé(e)s
vous soyez allé(e)(s)(es)
ils/elles soient allé(e)s

se laver (pronominal verb)
je me sois lavé(e)
tu te sois lavé(e)
elle/il se soit lavé(e)

nous nous soyons lavé(e)s
vous vous soyez lavé(e)(s)(es)
ils/elles se soient lavé(e)s

The extra e is used when the subject is feminine.
The s is added when the subject is plural.

The other two subjunctive tenses, the imperfect subjunctive (imparfait du subjunctif) and the pluperfect subjunctive (plus-que-parfait du subjunctif) are never used in spoken French. They are verb forms used only in literature, journalism and historical texts.

QIU

French has no future subjunctive. Even if the action will occur in the future, the present subjunctive is still

Je suis contente que tu <u>viennes</u> à Londres.
I am happy that you <u>will come</u> to London.

The Imperative (Impératif)

The French imperative mood is used to give orders or instructions. Think of it as expressing a demand that something happens or directing someone to do something.

  The imperative has only three forms:
  tu   - the second person familiar
  vous - the second person familiar plural and singular formal
  nous - the first personal plural

In all three forms, the imperative is the present tense of the verb minus its subject pronoun.
Use the imperative tu form when speaking to one person in casual circumstances.

<u>Viens</u> ici tout de suite !
<u>Come</u> here now !

Use the imperative vous form when speaking to more than one person or to one person in a more formal way.

<u>Donnez</u>-moi 5 poires s'il vous plaît.
<u>Give</u> me 5 pears please.

© 2010

Use the imperative nous form to give an order to yourself as well as to others. The nous form translates as "Let's".

Allons-y !
Let's go !

Écrivons !
Let's write !

Only four verbs have irregular imperative forms:

		tu		vous		nous	
avoir	(to have)	aie	(eh)	ayez	(eh yay)	ayon	(eh yohn)
être	(to be)	sois	(swah)	soyez	(swah yay)	soyons	(swah yohn)
savoir	(to know)	sache	(sahsh)	sachez	(sah shay)	sachons	(sah shee ohn)
vouloir	(to want)	------		veuillez	(voo yee ay)	-------	

Note that veuillez is the form used to request something.

<u>Veuillez</u> rendre le livre demain.
<u>Please</u> return the book tomorrow.

QIU

French has only one other imperative form, the past imperative (impératif passé). It is used to give a command for something that must be done before a certain time.

<u>Aie</u> écrit ce rapport à midi.
<u>Have</u> this report written by noon.

© 2010

The Present Participle (Participe Présent)

Even though the present participle is so named, it is not linked to any of the French present tenses. To form the present participle, take the first person plural of the present tense (the nous form) and replace the -ons endings with -ant. The present participle usually ends in -ant (awn). Be aware this verbs form is used less often than its English counterpart, the verb form that ends in -ing. Unlike English, the French present participle is not used to describe what someone is doing. In French you wouldn't say "Je suis lisant" for "I am reading". Instead you must use the present tense of the verb, "Je lis". The French present participle isn't used after another verb. To express "She likes reading", you must use the infinitive form of the verb, "Elle aime lire" (She likes to read). Unlike English, where the present participle can be used as a noun to describe an activity, as in the sentence "Seeing is believing", in French, you use the infinitive, "Voir, c'est croire" (to see, it is to believe).

However, the French present participle is versatile and can be used as a verb, gerund, adjective or noun. When the present participle is used as a verb or gerund, its form is always the same, except in the case of pronominal verbs which are explained in the section on reflexive verbs. These verbs keep the appropriate reflexive pronoun in front of the present participle; me coiffant (doing my hair), en nous levant (upon [us] getting up).

When the French present participle functions as a verb, it expresses an action that is still occuring at the same time, but not indispensably related to the action of the main verb.

<u>Pensant</u> qu'il est facile à faire, ils ont commencé le projet.
<u>Thinking</u> that it is easy to do, they began the project.

<u>Négligeant</u> leur conseil, Danielle est allée de toute façon.
<u>Ignoring</u> their advice, Danielle went anyway.

When the present participle expresses an action that is related to the main verb, it functions as a gerund (le gérondif) which nearly always follows the preposition en (awn).

It is used:
to describe an action that is related to and simultaneous with the action of the main verb.
In these sentences, en usually translates as "while" or "upon".

<u>En entendant</u> les nouvelles, il a sauté de joie.
<u>Upon hearing</u> the news, he jumped with joy.

Elle chante <u>en travaillant</u>.
She sings <u>while working</u>.

to explain how or why something happens. In such sentences, en usually translates as "by".

Nancy a obtenu le rôle <u>en auditionnant</u> la perfection.
Nancy got the part <u>by auditionning</u> so perfectly.

<u>En me levant</u> tôt, j'ai eu le temp du faire du yoga.
<u>By getting up</u> early, I had time to do yoga.

to replace a relative clause (a subordinate clause that modifies a noun)

>les étudiants <u>parlant</u> français (qui parlent français)
>students <u>who speak</u> French
>
>les enfants <u>venant</u> de l'île (qui viennent de l'île)
>children <u>who come</u> from the island.

Difference Between Present Participle and Gerund

The present participle modifies a noun; its gerund form modifies a verb. Notice the distinction between the two in the following sentences:

>1) J'ai vu Vivienne <u>sortant</u> de café.
>   I saw Vivienne <u>leaving</u> the cafe. (I saw her as she was leaving)

The noun Vivienne is modified, therefore sortant is the present participle.

>2) <u>En sortant</u> du café, j'ai vu Vivienne.
>   <u>While leaving</u> the cafe, I saw Vivienne. (I saw her as I was leaving)

The verb leaving is modified, therefore en sortant is the gerund form.

Note the gerund form is not included in conjugation tables.

Sometimes the French present participle is used as an adjective. As with other French adjectives, it usually follows the noun it modifies and must agree with the noun in gender and number.

un camarade amusant	des possibilités intéressantes
an amusing fellow	interesting possibilities

The French present participle can sometimes be used as a noun. The usual gender/number agreement rules for nouns apply.

un enseignant   - a teacher   (male)
les étudiantes - the students (female stundents)

QIU

In English, the present participle is often used after a preposition, for example; before leaving, after playing, without saying. In French, "en" is the only preposition followed by the present participle.

All other prepositions are followed by the infinitive form of the verb:

avant de partir - before leaving
aprés jouer   - after playing
sans dire   - without saying

Un peu de grammar

Sometimes in English, verbs require a preposition for the meaning of the verb to be complete, such as "to talk to", "to look after", ect. It is the same in French, but the prepositions required for French verbs are often not the same for the verbs required for their English equivalents. So some verbs that require a preposition in English at times, don't take one in French, and vice versa.
There are at least 50 French prepositions, not all of them have to follow a verb.

Á and de are the most used French prepositions.
à   (ah)   at/to
de (duh)   of/from

> I am learning to fish.   He is going to try to swim.
> J'apprends à pêcher.   Il va essayer de nager.

Some verbs have different meanings depending on whether they are followed by à or de.

parler à	to talk to
parler de	to talk about
venir à	to happen to
venir de	to have just (done sth)
profiter à	to benefit
profiter de	to make the most of
jouer à	to play a sport or game
jouer de	to play an instrument
penser à	to think about/of (on your mind)
penser de	to think about/of (opinion)
manquer à	to miss someone
manquer de	to neglect (to do sth)/to have lack (object/quality)

arriver (to arrive)
arriver + à   to manage / to succeed in

être (to be)
être + à   to belong to

The Past Participle (Participe Passé)

The French past participle is similar to its English counterpart which usually ends in -ed (resolved) -en (broken) and sometimes -t (burnt). Most of le participe passé endings are - é (ay), - i (ee) or - u (ew). There are three principal uses of the French past participle.

1) It is the second element of compound verb forms.

J'ai <u>résolu</u> le problème.
I have <u>resolved</u> the problem.

Audrey a <u>envoyé</u> l'article au sujet des oiseaux africains au Nouvel Observateur.
Audrey has <u>sent</u> the article on African birds to the Nouvel Observateur.

2) It is used with être to form the passive voice construction.

Le programme sera <u>suivi</u> par un entretien avec le directeur.
The programme will be <u>followed</u> by an interview with the director.

Son programme de santé est <u>fait</u> tous les jours.
Her fitness routine is <u>done</u> every day.

3) The French past participle may be used as an adjective, either on its own or with être.

<u>Déçu,</u> je suis rentré tôt.
<u>Disappointed,</u> I went home early.

Le lac <u>gelé</u> a scintillé.
The <u>frozen</u> lake glistened.

La sculpture est-elle <u>finie</u> ?
Is the sculpture <u>finished</u>?

<u>Écrite</u> au le 18ème siècle, l'histoire est aujourd'hui toujours d'actualité.
<u>Written</u> in the 18th century, the story is still relevant today.

QIU
When participe passé is used as an adjective or in the passive voice construction, it must agree in number and gender with the word it modifies. In the compound tenses, it may not need to agree.

Simple and Compound Tenses (Temps simples et temps composés)

Verb tenses are also categorized by their number of parts. Simple tenses (temps simples) consist of only one conjugated verb form. Remember this form consists of a stem to which different endings are added to specify time, mood, person and number. This ending must agree with the subject pronoun.

je pense	I think/am thinking
tu finissais	you finish/were finishing
nous attendrons	we will wait

In contrast, compound tenses (temp composés) consist of two parts; an auxiliary verb (verbe auxiliaire) and the past participle (participe passé) of the main verb. In English, the auxiliary verb used to form compound tenses is always have, as in "I have forgotten the most important part". English used to have a second auxiliary verb; "I be gone". "The hour is come", but this auxiliary has been phased out of the language. Remember that in French, all compound tenses are formed using either avoir (to have) or être (to be). Most verbs use avoir as their auxiliary verb. The exceptions that use être are all reflexive verbs and a number of frequently used verbs expressing motion or change of state.

These verbs are:

aller	(ah lay)	to go
arriver	(ah ree vay)	to arrive
descendre	(day sawn druh)	to go down
devenir	(duh vuh neer)	to become
entre	(awn tray)	to enter
monter	(mohn tay)	to climb/to go up
mourir	(moo reer)	to die
naître	(neh truh)	to be born
partir	(pahr teer)	to leave
passer	(pah say)	to pass
rester	(reh stay)	to stay
sortir	(sawr teer)	to go out
tomber	(tohn bay)	to fall
venir	(vuh neer)	to come

Many verbs that are derived from these verbs by adding a prefix may also use être as their auxiliary. For example:

verbs derrived from venir: advenir, intervenir, parvenir, provenir and survenir prefix re- redevenir, remonter, renaître, rentrer, repartir, resortir, revenir, etc.

However, some verbs derived from these verbs take avoir as their auxiliary. verbs derrived from venir: circonvenir, contrevenir, convenir, prévenir and subvenir transitive verbs: demonter, surmonter, dépasser, surpasser, etc.

The endings of these verbs depend on whether the subject is feminine, masculine or plural.

tomber (tohn bay) to fall

    Je suis tombé
        tombé<u>e</u>
    Tu es tombé
        tombé<u>e</u>
    Elle est tombé<u>e</u>
    Il est tombé
    Nous sommes tombé<u>s</u>
    Nous sommes tombé<u>es</u>
    Vous êtes tombé
        tombé<u>e</u>
        tombé<u>s</u>
        tombé<u>es</u>
    Ils sont tombé<u>s</u>
    Elles sont tombé<u>es</u>

The e is used when the subject is feminine. The extra s is added when the subject is plural.

QIU
Remember that even though the literal meaning of être is "to be" when it is used to form the compound tenses, être translates as "to have".

Je <u>suis restée</u> dans cette ville trop longtemps.
I <u>have stayed</u> in this town too long.

<u>Intransitive Verbs (Verbes intransitifs) and Transitive Verbs (Verbes transitifs)</u>

The verbs that use être as their auxiliary are intransitive, meaning that they do not take a direct object (a noun or pronoun directly affected by the verb).

Intransitive verbs include:

verbs which take an indirect object. Usually a preposition is used with indirect objects.

    Je <u>suis passé</u> à côté du parc.
    I <u>passed</u> by the park.

and verbs which have no object at all

    Elle <u>est arrivée</u> à l'improviste.
    She <u>arrived</u> unexpectedly.

Some of these verbs can also be as transitive verbs, meaning they do take a direct object. With transitive verbs, no prepositions are needed to connect the verb and its object. When these verbs are used transitively, they have a slight change in meaning and must use avoir as their auxiliary.

Examples of Intransitive and Transitive Uses of Some Common Être Verbs

descendre
Il est descendu.   He went downstairs. (intransitive)
Il a descendu la valise.   He took the suitcase down(stairs). (transitive)

monter
Je suis monté au toit.   I went up to the roof. (intransitive)
J'ai monté les livres.   I took the books up(stairs). (transitive)

passer
Nous sommes passés à côté de la roseraie.
We passed by the rose garden. (intransitive)

Nous avons déjà passés le portail.
We have already gone through the gate. (transitive)

rentrer
Ils sont rentrés.   They came home. (intransitive)
Ils ont rentré les chaises.   They brought the chairs indoors. (transitive)

retourner
Elle est retournée à Paris.   She has returned to Paris. (intransitive)
Elle a retourné la robe.   She returned the dress. (transitive)

sortir
Amélie est sortie.   Amélie went out. (intransitive)
Amélie a sorti les albums de photos. Amélie took the photo albums out. (transitive)

Other Uses of Être as an Auxiliary Verb

Être is also used as the auxiliary with all verbs that take reflexive pronouns. These verbs known as pronominal verbs (verbes pronominaux) are divided into reflexive, reciprocal and idiomatic.

Reflexive: Nous nous sommes amusés des histoires et plaisanteries.
             We entertained ourselves with stories and jokes.

Reciprocal: Ils se sont parlés.
             They talked to each other.

Idiomatic   Elle s'est interessée à sa proposition.
             She is interested in his proposal.

Semi-auxiliary verbs (Verbes semi-auxiliaires)

In addition to the two main auxiliary verbs, avoir and être, which are used with the past participle to form all compound tenses, French also has several semi- auxiliary verbs. These verbs function as "helping" verbs to the main verb in a sentence, helping to express nuances of time and mood. Semi-auxiliaries are followed by the infinitive of the main verb of the sentence. Since French doesn't have modal auxiliaries equivalent to the English ones (can, may, must, ought, shall, should, will and would), it is difficult to directly translate them. In French "could" and "would" can be used in both the present and past tenses with different meanings.

Examples of Some Common French Semi-auxiliary Verbs

pouvoir (present)
Nous pouvons utiliser votre aide.
We can use your help.

pouvoir (conditional)
Je pourrais manger une pizza entière maintenant.
I could (would be able to) eat a whole pizza now.

pouvoir (imperfect)
Elle pouvait jouer du piano à l'âge de trois ans.
She could play the piano when she was three.

pouvoir (conditional perfect)
Jules et Jim auraient pu venir plus tôt.
Jules and Jim could have (would have been able to) come earlier.

devoir (present)
Vous devez admettre que c'est une bonne idée.
You must admit it's a good idea.

devoir (conditional)
Ils <u>devraient</u> finir le projet bientôt
They <u>should/ought to</u> finish the project soon.

devoir (passé composé)
Il <u>a dû</u> oublier de l'amener.
He <u>must have</u> forgotten to bring it.

devoir (conditional perfect)
Nous <u>aurions dû</u> quitter la fête avant l'aube.
We <u>should have</u> left the party before dawn.

Voice (Voix)

Voice is one of the five factors involved in conjugating French verbs. Voice describes the relationship between a verb and its subject.

French has three voices:

1) the active voice (voix actif)

The active voice is used when the subject performs the action of the verb. Active is the most frequently used voice.

<u>J'apprends</u> le français.   <u>I am learning</u> French.
<u>Nous avons fini</u> nos devoirs.   <u>We finished</u> our homework.

2) the passive voice (voix passive)

The passive voice is used when the subject receives the action of the verb.

<u>Le français est étudié</u> par millions de gens.   <u>French is studied</u> by millions of people.
Nos <u>devoirs seront finis</u> avant neuf heures.   Our <u>homework will be finished</u> before nine.

3) the pronominal voice (voix prominale)

The pronominal voice is used when the subject performs the action of the verb on itself.

Nous <u>nous habillons</u>.   We're <u>getting dressed</u> (<u>dressing ourselves</u>).
Elle <u>se brosse</u> les dents. She's <u>brushing her</u> teeth.

Forming the Passive Voice

La voix passive is formed with a conjugated être verb plus the past participle of the main verb. In the passive voice the past participle functions more like an adjective than a verb and must agree in gender and number with the subject of the sentence, not the agent. Agent is a grammatical term for the participant that carries out the action in a situation. Agency in la voix passive is usually expressed by "par" (pahr) meaning "by"

	(subject)		(agent)
Cette	chanson	a été écrite	par Jacques Brel.
This	song	has been written	by Jacques Brel.

However, agency is sometimes expressed by "de" (duh) which, in these cases, also translates as "by". Mostly "de" is used when the verb in the passive voice expresses a state of being rather than an action.

	(subject)	(agent)
Elle	est admirée	de tout le monde.
She	is admired	by everyone.

Un peu de grammaire

French uses la voix passive for stylistic reasons such as to facilitate a transition between sentences or to accentuate a word by placing it at the end of a phrase or a sentence. Since la voix passive has a slightly formal, literary tone, French tends to use it less frequently than other voices. Here are some ways to avoid using the passive voice:

If the agent of the action is given, simply turn the sentence around to transform it into the active voice.

Instead of: Ce roman a été écrit par un professeur d'art.
    The novel was written by an art teacher.

    Use: Un professeur d'art a écrit ce roman.
        An art teacher wrote this novel.

If no agent is given, use the impersonal pronoun "on" as the subject of an active sentence.

Instead of: Un remède sera découvert un jour.
    A cure will be discovered someday.

Use: On découvrira un remède un jour.
    They will discover a cure someday.

If the action is habitual or normally in the present tense, keep the subject but replace the passive voice with a pronominal verb in the active voice.

Instead of: Le dîner est servi à huit heures.
    The dinner is served at eight o'clock.

    Use: Le dîner se sert à huit heures.
    (literally) The dinner serves itself at eight o'clock.

The passive voice construction has one more verb (the conjugated être verb) in it than the active voice construction.

© 2010

Forming the Interrogative (Interrogatif)

The interrogative is the form used to ask questions. There are three ways of forming the French interoggative:

1) intonation

The most simple way to ask a question in French is raising your voice at the end of a statement. Just changing the tone of your voice indicates you're asking a question.

Vous parlez français ?   Do you speak French?

2) inversion

Another common question form is to invert the verb and the subject. In this form a hyphen is inserted between the verb and its subject.

Parlez-vous français ?   Do you speak French?
Parle-t-elle français ?   Does she speak French?

An extra t is added between the verb and the pronoun when the verb ends in -a or -e. In the plural, this t must be pronounced whereas normally the -ent would be silent.

Parlent-ils français ?   Do they speak French?

In le passé composé, it is the avoir or être verb that is inverted, not the past participle.

A-t-il vécu en France ?   Did he live in France? (literal: Has he lived in France?)
As-tu reçu mon cadeau ?   Did you receive my gift? (literal: Have you recieved my gift?)

3) est-ce que

Est-ce que (esk kuh) is a phrase placed in front of a sentence to make it a question.
It is comparable to using "do" in English to form a question.

Est-ce que vous parlez français ?   Do you speak French? (Literal: Is this that you speak French)
Est-ce que ta soeur parle français ?   Does your sister speak French?

In this construction the word order is not inverted. Normally only pronouns can be inverted whereas the est-ce que form can be used with both noun and pronoun subjects.

Forming the Negative (Négatif)

The negative construction has two parts in French; ne (nuh) which goes before the verb and pas (pah) which goes after the verb. This ne contracts to n' before a verb beginning with a vowel or mute h.

  Je ne veux pas rester ici. I don't want to stay here.
  Ils n'aiment pas les surprises. They don't like surprises.

In the compound tenses, as in English, the negative is applied to the auxiliary verb.

Geneviève n'est pas partie à destination de Provence. Geneviève has not left for Provence.

When using inversion to form a question, the two parts of the negative construction surround the verb and the pronoun.

Ne souhaitez-vous pas aller avec elle ? Do you not wish to go with her?

Here is a list of all the French negatives:

ne ...aucun(e)	no/none/not any
ne ...jamais	never
ne ...guère	hardly/barely/scarcely
ne ...ni ...ni	neither ...nor
ne ...nulle part	nowhere
ne ...pas	not/don't
ne ...pas du tout	not at all
ne ...personne	no one/nobody/not anyone/not anybody
ne ...plus	no more/no longer/not anymore
ne ...que	only
ne ...rien	nothing/not ...anything
ne ...nul(e)	no/not any
ne ...pas un(e)	no/not one
ne ...pas un(e) seul(e)	not a single
ne ...pas encore	not yet/still
ne ...pas toujours	not always
ne ...nullement	not at all
ne ...aucunement	not at all
ne ...pas que	not only
ne ...pas seulement	not only
non seulement	not only
ne ...quiconque	no one

ne ...point not/not at all (equivalent of ne ...pas in literary/formal)

seulement only (is the same as ne ..que but do not add the ne with seulement)
    Example: J'ai seulement un livre. I only have one book.

ne ... It is used to imply a negative meaning with SOME verbs.
   Mostly used in written French.
   Example: Je ne peux sortir. I can't go out.

Plus and jamais can be used with one another and with the negative words rien, aucun and personne.

combination of negatives:

>plus before rien
>Elle ne font plus *rien*   she no longer does *anything*
>
>plus before personne
>Je n'y rencontre plus *personne* maintenant   I no longer meet *anyone* there now
>
>jamais before rien
>Ils ne nous donnent jamais *rien*.   they never give us *anything.*
>
>jamais before persponne
>Je n'y recontre jamais *personne*.   I never meet *anyone* there.
>
>jamais before aucune
>Je ne vois jamais *aucune* perfection.   I never see *any* perfection.
>
>plus before aucun
>Je n'ai plus *aucun* argent.   I don't have *any* money anymore.
>
>plus before jamais
>Je ne peux plus *jamais* lui parler.   I can *never* talk to him anymore.

Classification of French Verbs (Classification de verbs français

Regular Verbs (Verbes réguliers)
The majority of French verbs are regular meaning that the stem (the part of the verb before its ending) does not change when conjugated. After learning how to conjugate a regular -er, -ir, or -re verb, simply apply the pattern to all verbs in that conjugation. Remember that for ease of reference and to help you remember them, all regular verbs in the three conjugations have special names in this book.

Here they are again in review:
All regular -er verbs are called the Rs.
All regular -ir verbs are called the stars (*s).
All regular -re verbs are called the bars (#s).

Irregularities in -er Verbs
Although aller is the only verb ending in -er that can be classified as a truly irregular verb, there are some groups of verbs ending in -er that deviate from the normal conjugation pattern. However, the variations are minimal and only occur to facilitate pronunciation.

Irregular Verbs (Verbes irréguliers)
Irregular verbs are verbs whose conjugation patterns do not follow one of the three groups of regular verbs. In this book, they are not Rs, stars or bars. These verbs have irregularities in their conjugations which apply to only a minority of verbs, and, in some cases, only to a single verb.

Pronominal Verbs (Verbes pronominaux)

Pronominal verbs are verbs that must be conjugated with a reflexive pronoun (pronom réfléchi). The reflexive pronouns correspond to the subject pronouns.

Subject Pronouns		Reflexive Pronouns		
je	I	me/m'	(muh)	myself
tu	you	te/t'	(tuh)	yourself
il	he/it (masc.)	se/s'	(suh)	himself
elle	she/it (fem.)	se/s'	(suh)	herself
on	one	se/s'	(suh)	oneself/itself
nous	we	nous	(noo)	ourselves
vous	you	vous	(voo)	yourself/yourselves
elles	they (fem.)	se/s'	(suh)	themselves (both masc and fem.)
ils	they (masc.)			

Me, te, and se contract to m', t' and s' before a vowel, before a mute h and before the indirect object pronoun "y" (ee) which can be used to replace a previously mentioned place (there) or object (it).

Reflexive pronouns are used only with pronominal verbs, and must always agree in number and gender with the subject of the sentence. A reflexive pronoun is placed directly before the verb, for example, Je me dépêche - I hurry myself. This placement before the verb occurs in every tense except the imperative where it follows the verb and is attached by a hyphen:

Dépêchez-vous !   Hurry! (literal: Hurry yourself !)   Dites-moi! Tell me!

Types of Pronominal Verbs (Types de verbes pronominaux)

There are three types of pronominal verbs:

reflexive verbs   (verbes réfléchis)
reciprocal verbs   (verbes réciproques)
idiomatic verbs   (verbes idiomatiques)

Reflexive Verbs
Reflexive verbs are so called because the action reflects back on the subject of the sentence. These verbs can be regular, irregular or stem-changing and still must be conjugated according to their infinitive endings. What makes them reflexive is that they are always preceded by a reflexive pronoun

which indicates that the subject of the verb is acting on itself. The subject and object of the verb are the same. English verbs don't usually require an explicit reflexive marker (such as myself, herself, ourselves, etc.) if the meaning can be inferred from the sentence. When someone says, "I wake up" or "I sit down", you understand that he or she is talking about him/herself. French is more explicit. These same actions must be expressed by using a reflexive pronoun and translate as follows:

Je me réveille.   I wake myself up.
Je m'assieds.   I sit myself down.

© 2010

Reflexive verbs can also be used as infinitives:

 Je vais me réveiller à 7h 00. I'm going to wake myself up at 7:00.
 Je vais m'asseoir maintenant. I'm going to sit myself down now.

Any kind of personal accident tends to be included in this category of pronominal verbs.

 se couper - to cut oneself
 se casser le doigt de pied - to break one's toe.

QIU
French pronominal verbs can be recognized by the se/s' which precedes the infinitive.
se réveiller (suh ray vay yay) - to wake o.s. up

Examples of Pronominal Verbs in Simple and Compound Tenses

Simple Tense
je me réveille	I wake (myself) up
tu te réveilles	you wake (yourself) up
elle/il se réveille	she/he/it wakes (herself/himself/itself) up
nous nous réveillons	we wake (ourselves) up
vous vous réveillez	you wake (yourself/yourselves) up
elles/ils se réveillent	they wake (themselves) up

In the compound tenses, as with all verbs that use être as their auxiliary, the endings of reflexive verbs depend on whether the subject is feminine, masculine or plural.

Compound Tense
Je me suis réveillé	I woke (myself) up
réveillé<u>e</u>	
Tu t'es réveillé	you woke (yourself) up
réveillé<u>e</u>	
Elle s'est réveillé<u>e</u>	she/it woke (herself/itself) up
Il s'est réveillé	he/it woke (himself/itself) up
Nous nous somme réveillé<u>s</u>	we woke (ourselves) up
réveillé<u>es</u>	
Vous vous êtes réveillé	you woke (yourself/yourselves) up
réveillé<u>e</u>	
réveillé<u>s</u>	
réveillé<u>es</u>	
Ils se sont réveillé<u>s</u>	they woke (themselves) up
Elles se sont réveillé<u>es</u>	they woke (themselves) up

The extra e is used when the subject is femminine.
The s is added when the subject is plural.

© 2010

In the imperative form, the reflexive pronoun te becomes toi.

Réveille-<u>toi</u> maintenant ! - (<u>You</u>) wake up now!

<u>Réveillons-nous</u> à midi ! - <u>Let's wake up</u> at noon!

In the negative forms, the ne is placed before the reflexive pronoun.

<u>Simple Tense</u>	<u>Compound Tense</u>	<u>Imperative</u>
Je <u>ne</u> me réveille <u>pas</u>.	Je <u>ne</u> me suis <u>pas</u> réveillé.	<u>Ne</u> te réveille <u>pas</u> !
I am <u>not</u> waking up.	I <u>didn't</u> wake up.	<u>Don't</u> wake up !

Une peu de grammaire

Although all pronominal verbs use être as their auxiliary verb to form the compound tenses, the past participles do not always agree in gender and number with the subject of the sentence as they must when conjugating the common "être verbs". With pronominal verbs, the past participle agrees when the reflexive pronoun is the direct object i.e. the direct object and subject are the same.

Elle s'est réveillée à 7 heures. - She woke up at 7 o'clock.

However, when the reflexive pronoun is the indirect object, the participle does not agree.

	(indirect object)		(direct object)	
Nous	<u>nous</u>	sommes préparé	<u>un repas</u>	délicieux.
We prepared	<u>ourselves</u>	a delicious	<u>meal</u>.	

For these reflexive verbs, the reflexive pronoun is always an indirect object so the past participle does not agree with it.

s'acheter	to buy (for o.s.)
se demander	to wonder
se dire	to tell (to o.s./e.o.)
se donner	to give (to e.o.)
s'écrire	to write (to e.o.)
se faire mal	to hurt (o.s.)
s'imaginer	to imagine/think
se parler	to talk (to o.s./e.o.)
se plaire (à faire)	to enjoy (doing...)
se procurer	to obtain (for o.s.)
se promettre	to promise (o.s./e.o.)
se rendre compte	to realize
se rencontrer	to meet (e.o.)
se rendre visite	to visit (e.o.)
se ressembler	to resemble (e.o.)
se sourire	to smile (at e.o.)
se téléphoner	to call (e.o.)

Many reflexive verbs can also have a non-reflexive use, meaning they can be used to express performing the action of the verb on someone or something else.

Reflexive
Je me lave les mains.
I am washing my hands.

Non-reflexive
Je lave la voiture.
I am washing the car.

Ils se sont habillés pour l'opéra.
They dressed (themselves) for the opera.

Ils ont habillé les mannequins pour la vitrine.
They dressed the mannequins for the window display.

When a reflexive verb is made non-reflexive, the auxiliary verb changes from être to avoir. Conversely, verbs that are not generally used as reflexives can be made reflexive by adding a reflexive pronoun.

Non-reflexive
Elle promène le chien.
She is walking the dog.

Reflexive
Elle se promène.
She is taking a walk.

Nous avons acheté un nouvel ordinateur pour toi.
We bought a new computer for you.

Nous nous sommes acheté un nouvel ordinateur.
We bought ourselves a new computer.

Reciprocal Verbs (Verbes réciproques)

Reciprocal verbs express a reciprocal action between subjects. In other words, two or more subjects do something interactively.

Nous nous comprenons.   We understand each other.
Les soeurs se ressemblent.   The sisters look like each other.

As with reflexive verbs, the past participle of reciprocal verbs agrees in gender and number with any reciprocal pronouns that function as a direct object.

Nous nous sommes compris.   We understood eachother.

The reciprocal pronoun can also function as an indirect object with a direct object pronoun.

Elles se sont écrit souvent.   They write to each other often.

Here is a list of some common reciprocal verbs:

s'adorer	to adore one another
s'aimer	to love (e.o.)
se comprendre	to understand (e.o.)
se connaître	to know (e.o.)
se détester	to hate (e.o.)
se dire	to tell (e.o.)
se disputer	to argue with (e.o.)
se donner	to give to (e.o.)
s'écrire	to write to (e.o.)
s'embrasser	to kiss (e.o.)
se parler	to talk to (e.o.)
se promettre	to promise to (e.o.)
se quitter	to leave (e.o.)
se regarder	to look at (e.o.)
se rencontrer	to meet (e.o.)
se rendre visite	to visit (e.o.)
se ressembler	to resemble (e.o.)
se retrouver	to meet (e.o.)
se sourire	to smile at (e.o.)
se téléphoner	to telephone (e.o.)
se voir	to see (e.o.)

Reciprocal verbs can also be used without the reflexive pronouns to express a non-reflexive meaning.

Reciprocal   Non reciprocal
Nous nous aimons.   Nous aimons Paris.
We love each other.   We love Paris.

Idiomatic Verbs (Verbes idiomatiques)

Idiomatic verbs are verbs that take on a different meaning when the reflexive pronoun is added. They do not describe reflexive or reciprocal actions. With idiomatic verbs, the se/s' pronoun is an integral and inseparable part which distinguishes them from their non-idiomatic meanings. This can be confusing. Consider the difference in meaning when idiomatic pronominal verbs are used with or without a reflexive pronoun.

Idiomatic	Non-pronominal meaning
Je m'appelle Jacqueline.	J'appelle Jacqueline.
My name is Jacqueline.	I'm calling Jacqueline.
Tu te trompes.	Tu me trompes.
You are mistaken.	You are deceiving me.

With idiomatic verbs, the past participle always agrees with the subject. Here is a list of the most commonly used French idiomatic pronominal verbs and their non-pronominal meanings.

	Pronominal	Non-pronominal
s'en alley	to go away	to go
s'amuser	to have a good time	to amuse
s'appeler	to be named	to call
s'approprier	to appropriate	to suit/to adapt to
s'arrêter de	to stop (o.s.)	to stop s.o. or sth else
s'attendre à	to expect	to wait for
se demander	to wonder	to ask
se débrouiller	to manage/to get by	to disentangle
se dépêcher	to hurry	to send quickly
se diriger vers	to head toward	to run/to be in charge of
s'éloigner	to move (o.s.) away	to move sth else away
s'endormir	to fall aseep	to put s.o. to sleep
s'ennuyer	to be bored	to bother
s'entendre	to get along with	to hear
se fâcher	to get angry	to make angry
se figurer	to imagine/picture	to represent/to appear
s'habituer à	to get used to	to habituate s.o. to
s'inquiéter	to worry	to alarm
s'installer	to settle in (to a home)	to install
se mettre à	to begin to	to put/to place
se passer	to happen	to pass
se perdre	to get lost	to lose
se rendre compte de	to realize	to account for
se réunir	to meet/get together	to gather/to collect
se sentir	to feel	to smell
se tromper	to be mistaken	to deceive
se trouver	to be located	to find

Additional Tenses and Moods

Although the pluperfect, the future perfect and the conditional perfect have been included in the section on tense and mood, the uses of these with reflexive verbs have not yet been shown.

Here are examples of their conjugation:

The pluperfect
je *m'*étais amusé(e)	(zhuh *may tay* ah mew zay)	I had amused *myself*
tu *t'*étais amusé(e)	(tew *tay tay* ah mew zay)	you had amused *yourself*
elle/il *s'*était amusé(e)	(ehl/eel *say tay* ah mew zay)	she/he/it had amused *her/him/itself*
nous *nous* étions amusé(e)s	(noo *noo* zay tee ohn ah mew zay)	we had amused *ourselves*
vous *vous* étiez amusé(e)(s)	(voo *voo* zay tee ay ah mew zay)	you had amused *yourselves*
elles/iles *s'*étaitent amusé(e)s	(ehl/eel *say tay* ah mew zay)	they had amused *themselves*

The future perfect
je *me* serai amusé(e)	(zhuh *mah* suh ray ah mew zay)	I will have amused *myself*
tu *te* seras amusé(e)	(tew *tah* suh rah ah mew zay)	you will have amused *yourself*
elle/il *se* sera amusé(e)	(ehl/eel *suh* suh rah ah mew zay)	she/he/it will have amused *her/him/itself*
nous *nous* serons amusé(e)s	(noo *noo* suh rohn ah mew zay)	we will/shall have amused *ourselves*
vous *vous* serez amusé(e)(s)	(voo *voo* suh ray ah mew zay)	you will have amused *yourself/selves*
elles/ils *se* seront amus(e)s	(ehl/eel *suh* suh rohn ah mew zay)	they will have amused *themselves*

The conditional Perfect
je *me* serais amusé(e)	(zhuh *mah* suh ray ah mew zay)	I would have amused *myself*
tu *te* serais amusé(e)	(tew *tah* suh ray ah mew zay)	you would have amused *yourself*
elle/il *se* serait amusé(e)	(ehl/eel *suh* suh ray ah mew zay)	she/he/it would have amused *her/himself*
nous *nous* serions amusé(e)s	(noo *noo* suh ree ohn ah mew zay)	we would have amused *ourselves*
vous *vous* seriez amusé(e)(s)	(voo *voo* suh ree ay ah mew zay)	you would have amused *yourself/selves*
elles/ils *se* seraient amusé(e)s	(ehl/eel *suh* suh ray ah mew zay)	they would have amused *themselves*

LITERARY TENSES

Literary Tenses (Temps littéraires)

French has five tenses that are used only in certain types of formal narrative such as historical texts, journalism and literature to narrate in a classic style that is slightly detached from the present. They are never used in spoken French. Even though the literary tenses are disappearing in modern written French, you will still encounter the passé simple in formal contemporary writing.

The five literary tenses are:

1) Passé simple

   This is the literary simple past tense and is also known as the past historic. Its non-literary equivalent is the passé compose. The distinction is that passé simple expresses an action that is complete and has no relationship to the present; the passé composé shows some relationship to the present.

   Passé simple   Passé composé
   La fille parla.   La fille a parlé.
   The girl spoke.   The girl has spoken.

2) Passé antérieur

   This is the literary compound past tense. Its non-literary equivalent is the pluperfect.
   All actions that occur before another action are described as being anterior. The passé antérieur expresses an action that occurred just prior to the action of the main verb which is expresses by the passé simple. The passé antérieur is formed using the passé simple of the auxiliary verb avoir or être and the past participle of the main verb.

   Passé antérieur   Pluperfect
   Quand elle eut parlé, nous écoutâmes.   Quand elle avait parlé, nous écoutá.
   When she had spoken, we listened.   When she had spoken, we listened.

3) Imparfait du subjonctif

   This is the literary simple past subjunctive. Its non-literary equivalent is the present subjunctive. The subtle difference is in the imperfect subjunctive, both the main clause and the subjunctive cluase (that she spoke) are in the past tense while in the present subjunctive, the subordinate clause (that she speak) is in the present tense.

   Imparfait du subjonctif   Subjunctive

   J'ai voulu qu'elle parlât.   J'ai voulu qu'elle parle.
   I wanted her to speak.   I wanted her to speak.
   (I wanted that she spoke)   (I wanted that she speak)

4) Plus-que-parfait du subjonctif

This is the literary compound past subjunctive. Its non-literary equivalent is the past subjunctive. With this form the distinction is even more subtle. The nuance is the action is in the remote past and has no relationship to the present (that she had spoken), whereas the past subjunctive expresses a slight relationship to the present (that she has spoken). The plus-que-parfait du subjonctif is formed using the imperfect subjunctive of the auxiliary verb avoir or être and the past participle of the main verb.

Plus-que-parfait du subjonctif

J'aurais voulu qu'elle eût parlé.
I would have wanted her to speak.
(I would have wanted that she had spoken)

Past subjunctive

J'aurais voulu qu'elle ait parlé.
I would have wanted her to speak.
(I would have wanted that she has spoken)

5) Seconde forme du conditionnel passé

This is the literary conditional past. Its non-literary equivalent is the conditional perfect. In the examples below, using the conditional perfect, second form emphasizes that I didn't buy it; using the non-literary conditional perfect implies it was more of a missed opportunity. The second forme du conditionnel passé is formed using the imperfect subjunctive of the auxiliary verb avoir or être and the past participle of the main verb. This form of the conditional perfect is an unusual verb as it is the literary equivalent of the conditional perfect and can be mistaken for the pluperfect subjunctive because they are conjugated the exact same way.

Seconde forme du conditionnel passé

Si je l'eus vu, je l'eusse acheté.
If I had seen it, I would have bought it.

Conditional perfect

Si je l'avais vu, je l'aurais acheté.
If I had seen it, I would have bought it.

© 2010

Although you will probably never need to conjugate the literary tenses, you should be able to recognize them. First you must be able to recognize the passé simple and imparfait du subjonctif of the auxiliary verbs avoir and être because they are used to form the compound literary tenses.

passé simple of avoir

je	eus
tu	eus
elle/il/on	eut
nous	eûmes
vous	eûtes
elles/ils	eûrent

passé simple of être

je	fus
tu	fus
il/elle/on	fut
nous	fûmes
vous	fûtes
ils/elles	furent

imparfait du subjonctif of avoir

je	eusse
tu	eusses
il/elle/on	eût
nous	eussions
vous	eussiez
elles/ils	eussent

imparfait du subjonctif of être

je	fusse
tu	fusses
elle/il/on	fût
nous	fussions
vous	fussiez
ils/elles	fussent

All -er verbs take these endings for the passé simple and the imparfait du subjonctif. Take off the final -er and replace it with the appropriate ending.

passé simple of aimer

je	aim*ai*
tu	aim*as*
elle/il/on	aim*a*
nous	aim*âmes*
vous	aim*âtes*
ils/elles	aim*èrent*

imparfait du subjonctif of aimer

je	aim*asse*
tu	aim*asses*
elle/il/on	aim*ât*
nous	aim*assions*
vous	aim*assiez*
elles/ils	aim*assent*

There are only two exceptions. With verbs ending in -ger, take off only the final -r. With verbs ending in -cer, change the c to a ç (cédille).

All the *s and #s have these endings for the passé simple and imparfait du subjonctif.
Take off the final -ir or -re and replace it with the appropriate ending.
Some irregular -re and -ir verbs have these endings for the passé simple.

passé simple of finis   imparfait du subjonctif entendre

je   finis   je   entendisse
tu   finis   tu   entendisses
il/elle/on finit   il/elle/on entendît
nous   finîmes   nous   entendissions
vous   finîtes   vous   entendissiez
ils/elles   finirent   ils/elles   entendissent

All other -ir and -re verbs have these endings. The difference is that with some irregular -ir and -re
verbs, the stem of the verb can also change.

passé simple of vivre   imparfait du subjonctif of vivre

je   vécus   je   vécusse
tu   vécus   tu   vécusses
il/elle/on vécut   il/elle/on vécût
nous   vécûmes   nous   vécussions
vous   vécûtes   vous   vécussiez
elles/ils   vécurent   elles/ils   vécussent

passé simple of obtenir   imparfait du subjonctif of offrir

je   obtins   je   offrinsse
tu   obtins   tu   offrinsses
il/elle/on obtint   elle/il/on offrînt
nous   obtînmes   nous   offrinssions
vous   obtîntes   vous   offrinssiez
ils/elles   obtinrent   elles/ils   offrinssent

© 2010

Here in review is a list of French simple and compound tenses/moods:

Simple Tenses (Temps simples)

Present	(Le présent)
Imperfect	(L'imparfait)
Future	(Le futur)
Conditional (present)	(Le conditionnel)
Subjunctive (present)	(Le subjonctif)
Past historic	(Le passé simple)
Present participle	(Le participe présent)
Infinitive	(L'infinitif)
Imperfect subjunctive	(L'imparfait du subjonctif)
Imperative	(L'impératif)

Compound Tenses (Temps composés)

Present perfect	(Le passé composé)
Pluperfect	(Le plus-que parfait)
Future perfect	(Le futur antérieur)
Conditional perfect	(Le conditionnel passé)
Past subjunctive	(Le subjonctif passé)
Past anterior	(Le pass antrieur)
Past participle	(Le participe passé)
Past infinitive	(L'infinitif passé)
Past imperative	(L'impératif passé)
Pluperfect subjunctive	(Le plus-que-parfait du subjonctif)
Conditional second form	(Le seconde forme du conditinnel passé)

Verb Tenses Sorted by Mood

The Indicative Mood (L'indicatif)

Simple Tenses

The present indicative	(Le présent de l'indicatif)
The imperfect	(L'imparfait de l'indicatif)
The past historic	(Le passé simple)
The future	(Le futur)

Perfect Tenses

The present perfect	(Le passé composé)
The pluperfect of the indicative	(Le plus-que-parfait de l'indicatif)
The past anterior	(Le passé antérieur)
The future anterior	(Le futur antérieur)

Other Tenses

The recent past (Le passé récent)

The near future (Le futur proche)

© 2010

The Subjunctive Mood (Le subjonctif)
The present subjunctive   (Le subjonctif)
The imperfect subjunctive (L'imparfait subjonctif)
The past subjunctive   (Le subjonctif passé)
The pluperfect subjunctive   (Le plus-que-parfait du subjonctif)

The Imperative (L'impératif)
The imperative   (L'impératif)
The past imperative   (L'impératif passé)

The Conditional mood (Le conditionnel)
The conditional   (Le conditionnel)
The past conditional   (Le conditionnel passé)
The second form of the conditional   (Le seconde forme du conditionnel passé)

Non-Finite Forms
The present participle   (Le participe présent)
The past participle   (Le participe passé)
The auxiliary verb   (Le verbe auxiliaire)
The infinitive   (L'infinitif)
The past infinitive   (L'infinitif passé)

© 2010

THE CONJUGATIONS

R's

CONJUGATING THE Rs

Remember all regular -er verbs are called the Rs in this book. All Rs follow the same conjugation pattern. Take off the final -er and replace it with the appropriate ending to agree with the subject pronoun. The exceptions are the conditional and the future. For the conditional and the future, keep the final -er and add the appropriate ending to the verb.

PARLER (pahr lay)
to speak

Présent
je parle   zhuh pahrl
tu parles   tew pahrl
il/elle parle   eel/ehl pahrl
nous parlons   noo pahr lohn
vous parlez   voo pahr lay
ils/elles parlent   eel/ehl pahrl

Passe composé
j'ai parlé   zhay pahr lay
tu as parlé   tew ah pahr lay
elle/il a parlé   ehl/eel ah pahr lay
nous avons parlé   noo zah vohn pahr lay
vous avez parlé   voo zah vay pahr lay
elle/ils ont parlé   ehl/eel zohn parh lay

Futur
je parlerai   zhuh pahr luh ray
tu parleras   tew pahr luh rah
elle/il parlera   ehl/eel par luh rah
nous parlerons   noo pahr luh rohn
vous parlerez   voo pahr luh ray
elles/ils parleront   ehl/eel pahr luh rohn

Impératif
parle !   pahrl
parlez !   pahr lay
parlons !   pahr lohn

Conditionnel
je parlerais   zhuh pahr luh reh
tu parlerais   tew pahr luh reh
il/elle parlerait   eel/ehl pahr luh reh
nous parlerions   noo pahr luh ree ohn
vous parleriez   voo pahr luh ree ay
il/elle parleraient   eel/ehl pahr luh reh

Subjonctif
que je parle   kuh zhuh pahrl
que tu parles   kuh tew pahrl
que il/elle parle   kuh eel/ehl pahrl
que nous parlions   kuh noo pahr lee ohn
que vous parliez   kuh voo pahr lee ay
que ils/elles parlent   kuh eel/ehl pahrl

Imparfait
je parlais   zhuh pahr leh
tu parlais   tew pahr leh
elle/il parlait   ehl/eel pahr leh
nous parlions   noo pahr lee ohn
vous parliez   voo pahr lee ay
elles/ils parlaient   ehl/eel pahr leh

Participe présent
parlant   pahr lawn

Participe passé
parlé   pahr lay

CONJUGATING THE STARS *s

Remember all regular -ir verbs are called the *s in this book. All *s follow the same conjugation pattern. Take off the final -ir and replace it with the appropriate ending to agree with the subject pronoun. For the conditional and the future, keep the final -ir and add the appropriate ending to the verb.

FINIR (fee nee)
to finish

Présent
je fin<u>i</u>   *zhuh* fee n<u>ee</u>
tu fin<u>is</u>   *tew* fee n<u>ee</u>
elle/il fin<u>it</u>   *ehl/eel* fee n<u>ee</u>
nous fin<u>issons</u>   *noo* fee n<u>ees</u> s<u>ohn</u>
vous fin<u>issez</u>   *voo* fee n<u>ees</u> s<u>ay</u>
ils/elles fin<u>issent</u> *eel/ehl* fee n<u>ees</u>

Conditionnel
je finir<u>ais</u>   *zhuh* fee neer eh
tu finir<u>ais</u>   *tew* fee neer eh
elle/il finir<u>ait</u>   *ehl/eel* fee neer eh
nous finir<u>ions</u>   *noo* fee neer ee ohn
vous finir<u>iez</u>   *voo* fee neer ee ay
ils/elles finir<u>aient</u> *eel/ehl* fee neer eh

Passé composé
j'**ai** fin<u>i</u>   *zhay* fee n<u>ee</u>
tu **as** fin<u>i</u>   *tew* **ah** fee n<u>ee</u>
elle/il **a** fin<u>i</u>   *ehl/eel* **ah** fee n<u>ee</u>
nous **avons** fin<u>i</u>   *noo* **z**ah **vohn** fee n<u>ee</u>
vous **avez** fin<u>i</u>   *voo* **z**ah **vay** fee n<u>ee</u>
ils/elles **ont** fin<u>i</u> *eel/ehl* **z**ohn fee n<u>ee</u>

Subjonctif
que je fin<u>isse</u>   *kuh zhuh* fee n<u>ees</u>
que tu fin<u>isses</u>   *kuh tew* fee n<u>ees</u>
que elle/il fin<u>isse</u>   *kuh ehl/eel* fee n<u>ees</u>
que nous fin<u>issions</u>   *kuh noo* fee n<u>ees</u> ee ohn
que vous fin<u>issiez</u>   *kuh voo* fee n<u>ees</u> ee ay
que ils/elles fin<u>issent</u> *kuh eel/ehl* fee n<u>ees</u>

Futur
je finir<u>ai</u>   *zhuh* fee neer ay
tu finir<u>as</u>   *tew* fee neer ah
il/elle finir<u>a</u>   *eel/ehl* fee neer ah
nous finir<u>ons</u>   *noo* fee neer ohn
vous finir<u>ez</u>   *voo* fee neer ay
elles/ils finir<u>ont</u>   *ehl/eel* fee neer ohn

Imparfait
je fin<u>issais</u>   *zhuh* fee n<u>ees</u> eh
tu fin<u>issais</u>   *tew* fee n<u>ees</u> eh
elle/il fin<u>issait</u>   *ehl/eel* fee n<u>ees</u> eh
nous fin<u>issions</u>   *noo* fee n<u>ees</u> ee ohn
vous fin<u>issiez</u>   *voo* fee n<u>ees</u> ee ay
ils/elles fin<u>issaient</u> *eel/ehl* fee n<u>ees</u> eh

Impératif
fin<u>is</u> !   fee nee
fin<u>issez</u> !   fee n<u>ees</u> ay
fin<u>issons</u> !   fee n<u>ees</u> ohn

Participe présent
fin<u>issant</u>   fee nee sawn

Participe passé
fin<u>i</u>   fee nee

© 2010

#'s

CONJUGATING THE BARS #s
Remember all regular -re verbs are called the #s in this book. All #s follow the same conjugation pattern. Take off the final -re and replace it with the appropriate ending to agree with the subject pronoun. The exceptions are the conditional and the future, just take off the final -e and add the appropriate ending to the verb.

ATTENDRE (ah tawn druh)
to wait for

Présent
j'attends — zhuh ah tawn
tu attends — tew ah tawn
il/elle attend — eel/ehl ah tawn
nous attendons — noo zah tawn dohn
vous attendez — voo zah tawn day
ils/elles attendent — eel/ehl zah tawnd

Conditionnel
j'attendrais — zhuh ah tawn dreh
tu attendrais — tew ah tawn dreh
il/elle attendrait — eel/ehl ah tawn dreh
nous attendrions — noo zah tawn dree ohn
vous attendriez — voo zah tawn dree ay
ils/elles attendraient — eel/ehl zah tawn dreh

Passe composé
j'ai attendu — zhay ah tawn dew
tu as attendu — tew ah ah tawn dew
il/elle a attendu — eel/ehl ah ah tawn dew
nous avons attendu — noo zah vohn ah tawn dew
vous avez attendu — voo zah vay ah tawn dew
ils/elles ont attendu — eel/ehl zohn ah tawn dew

Subjonctif
que j'attende — kuh zhuh ah tawnd
que tu attendes — kuh tew ah tawnd
que il/elle attende — kuh eel/ehl ah tawnd
que nous attendions — kuh noo zah tawn dee ohn
que vous attendiez — kuh voo zah tawn dee ay
que ils/elles attendent — kuh eel/ehl zah tawnd

Futur
j'attendrai — zhuh ah tawn dray
tu attendras — tew ah tawn drah
il/elle attendra — eel/ehl ah tawn drah
nous attendrons — noo zah tawn drohn
vous attendrez — voo zah tawn dray
ils/elles attendront — eel/ehl zah tawn drohn

Imparfait
j'attendais — zhuh ah tawn deh
tu attendais — tew ah tawn deh
il/elle attendait — ell/ehl ah tawn deh
nous attendions — noo zah tawn dee ohn
vous attendiez — voo zah tawn dee ay
ils/elles attendaient — eel/ehl zah tawn deh

Impératif
attends ! — ah tawn
attendez ! — ah tawn day
attendons ! — ah tawn dohn

Participe présent
attendant — ah tawn dawn

Participe passé
attendu — ah tawn dew

© 2010

A1

ABATTRE (ah bah truh)
to destroy

Présent		Conditionnel	
j'abats	ah bah	j'abattrais	ah bah treh
tu abats	ah bah	tu abattrais	ah bah treh
il/elle abat	ah bah	il/elle abattrait	ah bah treh
nous abattons	ah bah tohn	nous abattrions	ah bah tree ohn
vous abattez	ah bah tay	vous abattriez	ah bah tree ay
ils/elles abattent	ah baht	ils/elles abattraient	ah bah treh

Passe composé		Subjonctif	
j'ai abattu	ah bah tew	j'abatte	ah baht
tu as abattu	ah bah tew	tu abattes	ah baht
il/elle a abattu	ah bah tew	il/elle abatte	ah baht
nous avons abattu	ah bah tew	nous abattions	ah bah tee ohn
vous avez abattu	ah bah tew	vous abattiez	ah bah tee ay
ils/elles ont abattu	ah bah tew	ils/elles abattent	ah baht

Futur		Imparfait	
j'abattrai	ah bah tray	j'abattais	ah bah teh
tu abattras	ah bah trah	tu abattais	ah bah teh
il/elle/ abattra	ah bah trah	ils/elles abattait	ah bah teh
nous abattrons	ah bah trohn	nous abattions	ah bah tee ohn
vous abbatrez	ah bah tray	vous abattiez	ah bah tee ay
ils/elles abattront	ah bah trohn	ils/elles abattaient	ah bah teh

Impératif		Participe présent	
abats !	ah bah	abattant	ah bah tawn
abattons !	ah bah tohn		
abattez !	ah bah tay	Participe passé	
		abattu	ah bah tew

Here is a list of all the verbs in this book that follow the same conjugation pattern.

battre	(bah truh)	to beat
combattre	(kohn bah truh)	to fight
débattre	(day bah truh)	to discuss
ébattre (s')	(ay bah truh)	to frolic
rabattre	(rah bah truh)	to shut / to pull down
rebattre	(ruh bah truh)	to reshuffle

A2

ACCROÎTRE (ah krwah truh)
to increase

Présent		Conditionnel	
j'accrois	ah krwah	j'accroîtrais	ah krwah treh
tu accrois	ah krwah	tu accroîtrais	ah krwah treh
elle/il accroît	ah krwah	elle/il accroîtrait	ah krwah treh
nous accroissons	ah krwah sohn	nous accroîtrions	ah krwah tree ohn
vous accroissez	ah krwah say	vous accroîtriez	ah krwah tree ay
elles/ils accroissent	ah krwahs	elles/ils accroîtraient	ah krwah treh

Passe composé		Subjonctif	
j'ai accrû	ah krew	j'accroisse	ah krwahs
tu as accrû	ah krew	tu accroisses	ah krwahs
elle/il a accrû	ah krew	elle/il accroisse	ah krwahs
nous avons accrû	ah krew	nous accroissions	ah krwah see ohn
vous avez accrû	ah krew	vous accroissiez	ah krwah see ay
elles/ils ont accrû	ah krew	elles/ils accroissent	ah krwahs

Futur		Imparfait	
j'accroîtrai	ah krwah tray	j'accroissais	ah krwah seh
tu accroîtras	ah krwah trah	tu accroissais	ah krwah seh
elle/il accroîtra	ah krwah trah	elle/il accroissait	ah krwah seh
nous accroîtrons	ah krwah trohn	nous accroissions	ah krwah see ohn
vous accroîtrez	ah krwah tray	vous accroissiez	ah krwah see ay
elles/ils accroîtront	ah krwah trohn	elles/ils accroissaient	ah krwah seh

Impératif		Participe présent	
accrois !	ah krwah	accroissant	ah krwah sawn
accroissons !	ah krwah sohn		
accroissez !	ah krwah say	Participe passé	
		accrû	ah krew

Here is a list of all the verbs in this book that follow the same conjugation pattern.

croître	(krwah truh)	to grow
décroître	(day krwah truh)	to drop / to subside

A3

ACCUEILLIR (ah kuh yeer)
to welcome

Présent		Conditionnel	
j'accueille	ah kuh yee	j'accueillerais	ah kuh yee uh reh
tu accueilles	ah kuh yee	tu accueillerais	ah kuh yee uh reh
il/elle accueille	ah kuh yee	il/elle accueillerait	ah kuh yee uh reh
nous accueillons	ah kuh yohn	nous accueillerions	ah kuh yee uh ree ohn
vous accueillez	ah kuh yay	vous accueilleriez	ah kuh yee uh ree ay
ils/elles accueillent	ah kuh yee	ils/elles accueilleraient	ah kuh yee uh reh

Passé composé		Subjonctif	
j'ai accueilli	ah kuh yee	j'accueille	ah kuh yee
tu as accueilli	ah kuh yee	tu accueilles	ah kuh yee
il/elle a accueilli	ah kuh yee	il/elle accueille	ah kuh yee
nous avons accueilli	ah kuh yee	nous accueillions	ah kuh yee ohn
vous avez accueilli	ah kuh yee	vous accueilliez	ah kuh yee ay
ils/elles ont accueilli	ah kuh yee	ils/elles accueillent	ah kuh yee

Futur		Imparfait	
j'accueillerai	ah kuh yee uh ray	j'accueillais	ah kuh yeh
tu accueilleras	ah kuh yee uh rah	tu accueillais	ah kuh yeh
il/elle accueillera	ah kuh yee uh rah	il/elle accueillait	ah kuh yeh
nous accueillerons	ah kuh yee uh rohn	nous accueillions	ah kuh yee ohn
vous accueillerez	ah kuh yee uh ray	vous accueilliez	ah kuh yee ay
ils/elles accueilleront	ah kuh yee uh rohn	ils/elles accueillaient	ah kuh yeh

Impératif		Participe présent	
accueille !	ah kuh yee	accueillant	ah kuh yawn
accueillons !	ah kuh yohn		
accueillez !	ah kuh yay	Participe passé	
		accueilli	ah kuh yee

Here is a list of all the verbs in this book that follow the same conjugation pattern.

cueillir	(kuh yeer)	to pick
recueillir	(ruh kuh yeer)	to collect

ACQUÉRIR (ah kay reer)
to acquire

Présent			Conditionnel	
j'acqu<u>iers</u>	ah kee ehr		j'acqu<u>errais</u>	ah kehr eh
tu acqu<u>iers</u>	ah kee ehr		tu acqu<u>errais</u>	ah kehr eh
elle/il acqu<u>iert</u>	ah kee ehr		elle/il acqu<u>errait</u>	ah kehr eh
nous acqué<u>rons</u>	ah kay rohn		nous acqu<u>errions</u>	ah kehr ee
vous acqué<u>rez</u>	ah kay ray		vous acqu<u>erriez</u>	ah kehr ee ay
elles/ils acqu<u>ièrent</u>	ah kee ehr		elles/ils acqu<u>erraient</u>	ah keh reh
Passe composé			Subjonctif	
j'ai acqu<u>is</u>	ah kwee		j'acqu<u>ière</u>	ah kee ehr
tu as acqu<u>is</u>	ah kwee		tu acqu<u>ières</u>	ah kee ehr
elle/il a acqu<u>is</u>	ah kwee		elle/ils acqu<u>ière</u>	ah kee ehr
nous avons acqu<u>is</u>	ah kwee		nous acqué<u>rions</u>	ah kay ree ohn
vous avez acqu<u>is</u>	ah kwee		vous acqué<u>riez</u>	ah kay ree ay
elles/ils ont acqu<u>is</u>	ah kwee		elles/ils acqu<u>ièrent</u>	ah kee ehr
Futur			Imparfait	
j'acqu<u>errai</u>	ah kehr ay		j'acqué<u>rais</u>	ah kay reh
tu acqu<u>erras</u>	ah kehr ah		tu acqué<u>rais</u>	ah kay reh
elle/il acqu<u>erra</u>	ah kehr ah		elle/il acqué<u>rait</u>	ah kay reh
nous acqu<u>errons</u>	ah kehr ohn		nous acqué<u>rions</u>	ah kay ree ohn
vous acqu<u>errez</u>	ah kehr ay		vous acqué<u>riez</u>	ah kay ree ay
elles/ils acqu<u>erront</u>	ah kehr ohn		elles/ils acqué<u>raient</u>	ah kay reh
Impératif			Participe présent	
acqu<u>iers</u> !	ah kee ehr		acqué<u>rant</u>	ah kayr awn
acqué<u>rons</u> !	ah kay rohn			
acqué<u>rez</u> !	ah kay ray		Participe passé	
			acqu<u>is</u>	ah kwee

Here is a list of all the verbs in this book that follow the same conjugation pattern.

conquérir	(kohn kay reer)	to conquer
enquérir (s')	(awn kay reer)	to inquire
reconquérir	(ruh kohn kay reer)	to reconquer
requérir	(ruh kay reer)	to request

A5

ALLÉCHER (ah lay shay)
to attempt

Présent		Conditionnel	
j'allèche	ah l<u>eh</u>sh	j'allécher<u>ais</u>	ah lay shuh r<u>eh</u>
tu allèch<u>es</u>	ah l<u>eh</u>sh	tu allécher<u>ais</u>	ah lay shuh r<u>eh</u>
il/elle allèche	ah l<u>eh</u>sh	il/elle allécher<u>ait</u>	ah lay shuh reh
nous alléch<u>ons</u>	ah lay sh<u>ohn</u>	nous allécher<u>ions</u>	ah lay shuh ree ohn
vous alléch<u>ez</u>	ah lay sh<u>ay</u>	vous allécher<u>iez</u>	ah lay shuh ree ay
ils/elles allèch<u>ent</u>	ah l<u>eh</u>sh	ils/elles allécher<u>aient</u>	ah lay shuh reh

Passe composé		Subjonctif	
j'ai alléch<u>é</u>	ah lay sh<u>ay</u>	j'allèche	ah l<u>eh</u>sh
tu as alléch<u>é</u>	ah lay sh<u>ay</u>	tu allèch<u>es</u>	ah l<u>eh</u>sh
il/elle a alléch<u>é</u>	ah lay sh<u>ay</u>	il/elle allèche	ah l<u>eh</u>sh
nous avons alléch<u>é</u>	ah lay sh<u>ay</u>	nous alléch<u>ions</u>	ah laysh ee ohn
vous avez alléch<u>é</u>	ah lay sh<u>ay</u>	vous alléch<u>iez</u>	ah laysh ee ay
ils/elles ont alléch<u>é</u>	ah lay sh<u>ay</u>	ils/elles allèch<u>ent</u>	ah l<u>eh</u>sh

Futur		Imparfait	
j'allécher<u>ai</u>	ah lay shuh r<u>ay</u>	j'alléch<u>ais</u>	ah lay sh<u>eh</u>
tu allécher<u>as</u>	ah lay shuh r<u>ah</u>	tu alléch<u>ais</u>	ah lay sh<u>eh</u>
il/elle allécher<u>a</u>	ah lay shuh r<u>ah</u>	il/elle alléch<u>ait</u>	ah lay sh<u>eh</u>
nous allécher<u>ons</u>	ah lay shuh r<u>ohn</u>	nous alléch<u>ions</u>	ah lay shee ohn
vous allécher<u>ez</u>	ah lay shuh r<u>ay</u>	vous alléch<u>iez</u>	ah lay shee ay
ils/elles allécher<u>ont</u>	ah lay shuh r<u>ohn</u>	ils/elles alléch<u>aient</u>	ah lay sh<u>eh</u>

Impératif		Participe présent	
allèche !	ah l<u>eh</u>sh	alléchant	ah lay sh<u>awn</u>
alléch<u>ons</u> !	ah lay sh<u>ohn</u>	Participe passé	
alléch<u>ez</u> !	ah lay sh<u>ay</u>	alléch<u>é</u>	ah lay sh<u>ay</u>

Here is a list of all the verbs in this book that follow the same conjugation pattern.

alléguer	(ah lay gay)	to allege / to invoke	reléguer	(ruh lay gay)	to relegate
déléguer	(day lay gay)	to delegate	sécher	(say shay)	to dry
dérégler	(day ray glay)	to affect/to upset	zébrer	(zay bray)	to streak
désintégrer	(day zahn tay gray)	to disintegrate			
dessécher	(day say shay)	to dry out			
exécrer	(eg zay kray)	to loathe			
intégrer	(ahn tay gray)	to integrate			
lécher	(lay shay)	to lick			
pécher	(pay shay)	to sin			
pénétrer	(pay nay tray)	to penetrate			
régler	(ray glay)	to adjust / to pay			
régner	(ray nyay)	to reign			
réintégrer	(ray ahn tay gray)	to return to / to reintegrate			

© 2010

A6

ALLER (ah lay)
to go

Présent			Conditionnel	
je vais	veh		j'irais	eer eh
tu vas	vah		tu irais	eer eh
elle/il va	vah		elle/il irait	eer eh
nous allons	ah lohn		nous irions	eer ee ohn
vous allez	ah lay		vous iriez	eer ee ay
elles/ils vont	vohn		elles/ils iraient	eer eh

Passe composé		Subjonctif	
je suis allé/-(e)	ah lay	j'aille	ah yee
tu es allé/-(e)	ah lay	tu ailles	ah yee
il/elle est allé/-(e)	ah lay	elle/il aille	ah yee
nous sommes allés/(es)	ah lay	nous allions	ah lee ohn
vous êtes allé/-(e)(s)(es)	ah lay	vous alliez	ah lee ay
ils/elles sont allés/-(es)	ah lay	elles/ils aillent	ah yee

Futur		Imparfait	
j'irai	eer ay	j'allais	ah leh
tu iras	eer ah	tu allais	ah leh
elle/il ira	eer ah	elle/il allait	ah leh
nous irons	eer ohn	nous allions	ah lee ohn
vous irez	eer ay	vous alliez	ah lee ay
elles/ils iront	eer ohn	elles/ils allaient	ah leh

Impératif		Participe présent	
va !	vah	allant	ah lawn
allons !	ah lohn		
allez !	ah lay	Participe passé	
		allé	ah lay

Aller is the only verb in this book that follows this conjugation pattern.

© 2010

A7

APERCEVOIR (ah pehr suh vwahr)
to perceive

Présent		Conditionnel	
j'aperçois	ah pehr swah	j'apercevrais	ah pehr suh vreh
tu aperçois	ah pehr swah	tu apercevrais	ah pehr suh vreh
il/elle aperçoit	ah pehr swah	il/elle apercevrait	ah pehr suh vreh
nous apercevons	ah pehr suh vohn	nous apercevrions	ah pehr suh vree ohn
vous apercevez	ah pehr suh vay	vous apercevriez	ah pehr suh vree ay
ils/elles aperçoivent	ah pehr swahv	ils/elles apercevraient	ah pehr suh vreh

Passe composé		Subjonctif	
j'ai aperçu	ah pehr sew	j'aperçoive	ah pehr swahv
tu as aperçu	ah pehr sew	tu aperçoives	ah pehr swahv
il/elle a aperçu	ah pehr sew	il/elle aperçoive	ah pehr swahv
nous avons aperçu	ah pehr sew	nous apercevions	ah pehr suh vee ohn
vous avez aperçu	ah pehr sew	vous aperceviez	ah pehr suh vee ay
ils/elles ont aperçu	ah pehr sew	ils/elles aperçoivent	ah pehr swahv

Futur		Imparfait	
j'apercevrai	ah pehr suh vray	j'apercevais	ah pehr suh veh
tu apercevras	ah pehr suh vrah	tu apercevais	ah pehr suh veh
il/elle apercevra	ah phr suh vrah	il/elle apercevait	ah pehr suh veh
nous apercevrons	ah pehr suh vrohn	nous apercevions	ah pehr suh vee ohn
vous apercevrez	ah pehr suh vray	vous aperceviez	ah pehr suh vee ay
ils/elles apercevront	ah pehr suh vrohn	ils/elles apercevaient	ah pehr suh veh

Impératif		Participe présent	
aperçois !	ah pehr swah	apercevant	ah pehr suh vawn
apercevons !	ah pehr suh vohn		
apercevez !	ah pehr suh vay	Participe passé	
		aperçu	ah pehr sew

Here is a list of all the verbs in this book that follow the same conjugation pattern.

concevoir	(kohn suh vwahr)	to conceive
décevoir	(day suh vwahr)	to disappoint
percevoir	(pehr suh vwahr)	to receive / to perceive
recevoir	(ruh svwahr)	to receive

A8

APPELER (ah play)
to call

Présent			Conditionnel	
j'appelle	ah pehll		j'appellerais	ah pehl luh reh
tu appelles	ah pehll		tu appellerais	ah pehl luh reh
elle/il appelle	ah pehll		elle/il appellerait	ah pehl luh reh
nous appelons	ah plohn		nous appellerions	ah pehl luh ree ohn
vous appelez	ah play		vous appelleriez	ah pehl luh ree ay
elles/ils appellent	ah pehll		elles/ils appelleraient	ah pehl luh reh

Passe composé			Subjonctif	
j'ai appelé	ah play		j'appelle	ah pehll
tu as appelé	ah play		tu appelles	ah pehll
elle/il a appelé	ah play		elle/il appelle	ah pehll
nous avons appelé	ah play		nous appelions	ah plee ohn
vous avez appelé	ah play		vous appeliez	ah plee ay
elles/ils ont appelé	ah play		elles/ils appellent	ah pehll

Futur			Imparfait	
j'appellerai	ah pehl luh ray		j'appelais	ah pleh
tu appelleras	ah pehl luh rah		tu appelais	ah pleh
elle/il appellera	ah pehl luh rah		elle/il appelait	ah pleh
nous appellerons	ah pehl luh rohn		nous appelions	ah plee ohn
vous appellerez	ah pehl luh ray		vous appeliez	ah plee ay
elles/ils appelleront	ah pehl luh rohn		elles/ils appelaient	ah pleh

Impératif				
appelle !	ah pehll			
appelons !	ah plohn			
appelez !	ah play			

Participe présent
appelant   ah plawn

Participe passé
appelé   ah play

Here is a list of all the verbs in this book that follow the same conjugation pattern.

amonceler	(ah mohn slay)	to accumulate
atteler	(aht lay)	to harness
chanceler	(shawn slay)	to stagger
déficeler	(day fee slay)	to untie
déniveler	(day nee vlay)	to make (sth) uneven
dételer	(dayt lay)	to unharness
épeler	(ay play)	to spell
ficeler	(fee slay)	to tie up
jumeler	(zhewm lay)	to double up / to combine
museler	(mew zuh lay)	to muzzle
niveler	(nev lay)	to level
rappeler	(rah play)	to recall / to remind
renouveler	(ruh noov lay)	to renew
ressemeler	(ruh suhm lay)	to resole

A9

APPRENDRE (ah prawn druh)
to learn / to teach

Présent		Conditionnel	
j'apprends	ah prawn	j'apprendrais	ah prawn dreh
tu apprends	ah prawn	tu apprendrais	ah prawn dreh
il/elle apprend	ah prawn	il/elle apprendrait	ah prawn dreh
nous apprenons	ah pruh nohn	nous apprendrions	ah prawn dree ohn
vous apprenez	ah pruh nay	vous apprendriez	ah prawn dree ay
ils/elles apprennent	ah prehnn	ils/elles apprendraient	ah prawn dreh

Passe composé		Subjonctif	
j'ai appris	ah pree	j'apprenne	ah prehnn
tu as appris	ah pree	tu apprennes	ah prehnn
il/elle a appris	ah pree	il/elle apprenne	ah prehnn
nous avons appris	ah pree	nous apprenions	ah pruh nee ohn
vous avez appris	ah pree	vous appreniez	ah pruh nee ay
ils/elles ont appris	ah pree	ils/elles apprennent	ah prehnn

Futur		Imparfait	
j'apprendrai	ah prawn dray	j'apprenais	ah pruh neh
tu apprendras	ah prawn drah	tu apprenais	ah pruh neh
il/elle apprendra	ah prawn drah	il/elle apprenait	ah pruh neh
nous apprendrons	ah prawn drohn	nous apprenions	ah pruh nee ohn
vous apprendrez	ah prawn dray	vous appreniez	ah pruh nee ay
ils/elles apprendront	ah prawn drohn	ils/elles apprenaient	ah pruh neh

Impératif		Participe présent	
apprends !	ah prawn	apprenant	ah pruh nawn
apprenons !	ah pruh nohn		
apprenez !	ah pruh nay	Participe passé	
		appris	ah pree

Here is a list of all the verbs in this book that follow the same conjugation pattern.

comprendre	(kohn prawn druh)	to understand
déprendre (se)	(day prawn druh)	to free oneself from
désapprendre	(day zah prawn druh)	to forget / to unlearn
entreprendre	(awn truh prawn druh)	to undertake
éprendre (s')	(ay prawn druh)	to fall in love with
méprendre (se)	(may prawn druh)	to be mistaken
prendre	(prawn druh)	to take
reprendre	(ruh prawn druh)	to take back
surprendre	(sewr prawn druh)	to surprise

A10

ASSAILLIR (ah sah yeer)
to assail

Présent			Conditionnel	
j'assaille	ah sah yee		j'assaillirais	ah sah yeer eh
tu assailles	ah sah yee		tu assaillirais	ah sah yeer eh
elle/il assaille	ah sah yee		elle/il assaillirait	ah sah yeer eh
nous assaillons	ah sah yohn		nous assaillirions	ah sah yeer ee ohn
vous assaillez	ah sah yay		vous assailliriez	ah sah yeer ee ay
elles/ils assaillent	ah sah yee		elles/ils assailliraient	ah sah yeer eh

Passe composé			Subjonctif	
j'ai assailli	ah sah yee		j'assaille	ah sah yee
tu as assailli	ah sah yee		tu assailles	ah sah yee
elle/il a assailli	ah sah yee		elle/il assaille	ah sah yee
nous avons assailli	ah sah yee		nous assaillions	ah sah yee ohn
vous avez assailli	ah sah yee		vous assailliez	ah sah yee ay
elles/ils ont assailli	ah sah yee		elles/ils assaillent	ah sah yee

Futur			Imparfait	
j'assaillirai	ah sah yeer ay		j'assaillais	ah sah yeh
tu assailliras	ah sah yeer ah		tu assaillais	ah sah yeh
elle/il assaillira	ah sah yeer ah		elle/il assaillait	ah sah yeh
nous assaillirons	ah sah yeer ohn		nous assaillions	ah sah yee ohn
vous assaillirez	ah sah yeer ay		vous assailliez	ah sah yee ay
elles/ils assailliront	ah sah yeer ohn		elles/ils assaillaient	ah sah yeh

Impératif			Participe présent	
assaille !	ah sah yee		assaillant	ah sah yawn
assaillons !	ah sah yohn			
assaillez !	ah sah yay		Participe passé	
			assailli	ah sah yee

Assaillir is the only verb in this book that follows this conjugation pattern.

A11

ASSEOIR (ah swahr)
to sit (s.o.)

Présent	
j'assieds	ah see eh
tu assieds	ah see eh
il/elle assied	ah see eh
nous asseyons	ah suh yohn
vous asseyez	ah suh yay
ils/elles asseyent	ah say

Conditionnel	
j'assiérais	ah see ayr eh
tu assiérais	ah see ayr eh
il/elle assiérait	ah see ayr eh
nous assiérions	ah see ayr ee ohn
vous assiériez	ah see ayr ee ay
ils/elles assiéraient	ah see ayr eh

Passe composé	
j'ai assis	ah see
tu as assis	ah see
il/elle a assis	ah see
nous avons assis	ah see
vous avez assis	ah see
ils/elles ont assis	ah see

Subjonctif	
j'asseye	ah seh yee
tu asseyes	ah seh yee
il/elle asseye	ah seh yee
nous asseyions	ah seh yee ohn
vous asseyiez	ah seh yee ay
ils/elles asseyent	ah seh yee

Futur	
j'assiérai	ah see ayr ay
tu assiéras	ah see ayr ah
il/elle assiéra	ah see ayr ah
nous assiérons	ah see ayr ohn
vous assiérez	ah see ayr ay
ils/elles assiéront	ah see ayr ohn

Imparfait	
j'asseyais	ah seh yeh
tu asseyais	ah seh yeh
il/elle asseyait	ah seh yeh
nous asseyions	ah seh yee ohn
vous asseyiez	ah seh yee ay
ils/elles asseyaient	ah seh yeh

Impératif	
assieds !	ah see eh
asseyons !	ah seh yohn
asseyez !	ah seh yay

Participe présent
asseyant   ah seh yawn

Participe passé
assis   ah see

Asseoir is the only verb in this book that follows this conjugation pattern.

A12

ATTEINDRE (ah tahn druh)
to attain

Présent		Conditionnel	
j'atteins	ah tahn	j'atteindrais	ah tahn dreh
tu atteins	ah tahn	tu atteindrais	ah tahn dreh
elle/il atteint	ah tahn	elle/il atteindrait	ah tahn dreh
nous atteignons	ah tahn yohn	nous atteindrions	ah tahn dree ohn
vous atteignez	ah tahn yay	vous atteindriez	ah tahn dree ay
elles/ils atteignent	ah tahn yuh	elles/ils atteindraient	ah tahn dreh

Passe composé		Subjonctif	
j'ai atteint	ah tahn	j'atteigne	ah tahn yuh
tu as atteint	ah tahn	tu atteignes	ah tahn yuh
elle/il a atteint	ah tahn	elle/il atteigne	ah tahn yuh
nous avons atteint	ah tahn	nous atteignions	ah tahn yee ohn
vous avez atteint	ah tahn	vous atteigniez	ah tahn yee ay
elles/ils ont atteint	ah tahn	elles/ils atteignent	ah tahn yuh

Futur		Imparfait	
j'atteindrai	ah tahn dray	j'atteignais	ah tahn yeh
tu atteindras	ah tahn drah	tu atteignais	ah tahn yeh
elle/il atteindra	ah tahn drah	elle/il atteignait	ah tahn yeh
nous atteindrons	ah tahn drohn	nous atteignions	ah tahn yee ohn
vous atteindrez	ah tahn dray	vous atteigniez	ah tahn yee ay
elles/ils atteindront	ah tahn drohn	elles/ils atteignaient	ah tahn yeh

Impératif		Participe présent	
atteins !	ah tahn	atteignant	ah tahn yawn
atteignons !	ah tahn yohn		
atteignez !	ah tahn yay	Participe passé	
		atteint	ah tahn

Here is a list of all the verbs in this book that follow the same conjugation pattern.

adjoindre	(ahd zhwahn druh)	to adjoin
astreindre	(ah strahn druh)	to compel
ceindre	(sahn druh)	to tie around
conjoindre	(kohn zhwahn druh)	to unite
contraindre	(kohn trahn druh)	to force
craindre	(krahn druh)	to fear
dépeindre	(deh pahn druh)	to depict
déteindre (se)	(day tahn druh)	to fade (colour)
disjoindre	(dees zhwahn druh)	to loosen / to separate
empreindre	(awn prahn druh)	to imprint

© 2010

A12

enfreindre	(awn frahn druh)	to infringe
enjoindre	(awn zhwan druh)	to enjoin
épreindre	(ay prahn druh)	to squeeze out
éteindre	(ay tahn druh)	to put out / to switch off
étreindre	(ay trahn druh)	to embrace
feindre	(fahn druh)	to feign
geindre	(zhahn druh)	to moan
joindre	(zhwahn druh)	to join / to enclose
peindre	(pahn druh)	to paint
plaindre	(plahn druh)	to pity
rejoindre	(ruh zhwahn druh)	to rejoin / to meet up with
repeindre	(ruh pahn druh)	to repaint
restreindre	(reh strahn druh)	to cut back
teindre	(tahn druh)	to dye

A13

AVANCER (ah vawn say)
to advance

Présent	
j'avance	ah vawns
tu avances	ah vawns
elle/il avance	ah vawns
nous avançons	ah vawn sohn
vous avancez	ah vawn say
elles/ils avancent	ah vawns

Conditionnel	
j'avancerais	ah vawns uh reh
tu avancerais	ah vawns uh reh
elle/il avancerait	ah vawns uh reh
nous avancerions	ah vawns uh ree ohn
vous avanceriez	ah vawns uh ree ay
elles/ils avanceraient	ah vawns uh reh

Passe composé	
j'ai avancé	ah vawn say
tu as avancé	ah vawn say
elle/il a avancé	ah vawn say
nous avons avancé	ah vawn say
vous avez avancé	ah vawn say
elles/ils ont avancé	ah vawn say

Subjonctif	
j'avance	ah vawns
tu avances	ah vawns
elle/il avance	ah vawns
nous avancions	ah vawn see ay
vous avanciez	ah vawn see ohn
elles/ils avancent	ah vawns

Futur	
j'avancerai	ah vawn suh ray
tu avanceras	ah vawn suh rah
elle/il avancera	ah vawn suh rah
nous avancerons	ah vawn suh rohn
vous avancerez	ah vawn suh ray
elle/ils avanceront	ah vawn suh rohn

Imparfait	
j'avançais	ah vawn seh
tu avançais	ah vawn seh
elle/il avançait	ah vawn seh
nous avancions	ah vawn see ohn
vous avanciez	ah vawn see ay
elles/ils avançaient	ah vawn seh

Impératif	
avance !	ah vawns
avançons !	ah vawn sohn
avancez !	ah vawn say

Participe présent	
avançant	ah vawn sawn

Participe passé	
avancé	ah vawn say

Here is a list of all the verbs in this book that follow the same conjugation pattern.

agacer	(ah gah say)	to annoy
amorcer	(ah mawr say)	to begin
annoncer	(ah nohn say)	to announce
balancer	(bah lawn say)	to swing / to balance
bercer	(behr say)	to rock
coincer	(kwahn say)	to wedge
commencer	(kaw mawn say)	to begin / to start

A13

concurrencer	(kohn kew rawn say)	to compete with
dédicacer	(day dee kah say)	to dedicate
défoncer	(day fohn say)	to smash
dénoncer	(day nohn say)	to denounce
dépecer	(day puh say)	to cut up
déplacer	(day plah say)	to move
désamorcer	(day zah mawr say)	to defuse / to drain
devancer	(duh vawn say)	to get ahead of
divorcer	(dee vawr say)	to divorce
effacer	(ay fah say)	to erase
efforcer (s')	(ay fawr say)	to strive
élancer (s')	(ay lawn say)	to dash forward
enfoncer	(awn fohn say)	to push in
enlacer	(awn lah say)	to embrace
énoncer	(ay nohn say)	to pronounce
entrelacer	(awn truh lah say)	to intertwine
épicer	(ay pee say)	to spice
exercer	(eg zehr say)	to exercise
fiancer	(fee awn say)	to get engaged
financer	(fee nawn say)	to finance
foncer	(fohn say)	to darken / to rush
forcer	(fawr say)	to force
froncer	(frohn say)	to gather / to frown
glacer	(glah say)	to freeze / to chill
grimacer	(gree mah say)	to grimace
grincer	(grahn say)	to creak
immiscer (s')	(ee mee say)	to interfere
influencer	(ahn flew awn say)	to influence
lacer	(lah say)	to lace up
lancer	(lawn say)	to throw
manigancer	(mah nee gawn say)	to scheme
menacer	(muh nah say)	to threaten
percer	(pehr say)	to pierce
pincer	(pahn say)	to pinch
placer	(plah say)	to place
prononcer	(praw nohn say)	to pronounce
recommencer	(ruh kaw mawn say)	to start again
relancer	(ruh lawn say)	to throw (sth) again
remplacer	(rawn plah say)	to replace
renforcer	(rawn fawr say)	to reinforce
renoncer	(ruh nawn say)	to give up / to abandon
sucer	(sew say)	to suck
tracer	(trah say)	to draw / to trace

A14

AVOIR (ah vwahr)
to have

Présent		Conditionnel	
j'ai	ay	j'aurais	oh reh
tu as	ah	tu aurais	oh reh
il/elle a	ah	il/elle aurait	oh reh
nous avons	ah vohn	nous aurions	oh ree ohn
vous avez	ah vay	vous auriez	oh ree ay
ils/elles ont	ohn	ils/elles auraient	oh reh

Passe composé		Subjonctif	
j'ai eu	ew	j'aie	eh
tu as eu	ew	tu aies	eh
elle/il a eu	ew	elle/il ait	eh
nous avons eu	ew	nous ayons	eh yohn
vous avez eu	ew	vous ayez	eh yay
elles/ils ont eu	ew	elles/ils aient	eh

Futur		Imparfait	
j'aurai	oh ray	j'avais	ah veh
tu auras	oh rah	tu avais	ah veh
il/elle aura	oh rah	il/elle avait	ah veh
nous aurons	oh rohn	nous avions	ah vee ohn
vous aurez	oh ray	vous aviez	ah vee ay
ils/elles auront	oh rohn	ils/elles avaient	ah veh

Impératif		Participe présent	
aie !	eh	ayant	eh yawn
ayons !	eh yohn		
ayez !	eh yay	Participe passé	
		eu	ew

Avoir is the only verb in this book that follows this conjugation pattern.

© 2010

A15

BOIRE (bwahr)
to drink

Présent		Conditionnel	
je bois	bwah	je boirais	bwahr eh
tu bois	bwah	tu boirais	bwahr eh
il/elle boit	bwah	il/elle boirait	bwahr eh
nous buvons	bew vohn	nous boirions	bwahr ee ohn
vous buvez	bew vay	vous boiriez	bwahr ee ay
ils/elles boivent	bwah	ils/elles boiraient	bwahr eh

Passe composé		Subjonctif	
j'ai bu	bew	je boive	bwahv
tu as bu	bew	tu boives	bwahv
il/elle a bu	bew	il/elle boive	bwahv
nous avons bu	bew	nous buvions	bew vee ohn
vous avez bu	bew	vous buviez	bew vee ay
ils/elles ont bu	bew	ils/elles boivent	bwahv

Futur		Imparfait	
je boirai	bwahr ay	je buvais	bew veh
tu boiras	bwahr ah	tu buvais	bew veh
il/elle boira	bwahr ah	il/elle buvait	bew veh
nous boirons	bwahr ohn	nous buvions	bew vee ohn
vous boirez	bwahr ay	vous buviez	bew vee ay
ils/elles boiront	bwahr ohn	ils/elles buvaient	bew veh

Impératif		Participe présent	
bois !	bwah	buvant	bew vawn
buvons !	bew vohn		
buvez !	bew vay	Participe passé	
		bu	bew

Boire is the only verb in this book that follows this conjugation pattern.

A16

BOUILLIR (boo yeer)
to boil

Présent	
je bous	boo
tu bous	boo
elle/il bout	boo
nous bouillons	boo yohn
vous bouillez	boo yay
elles/ils bouillent	boo yee

Passe composé	
j'ai bouilli	boo yee
tu as bouilli	boo yee
elle/il a bouilli	boo yee
nous avons bouilli	boo yee
vous avez bouilli	boo yee
elles/ils ont bouilli	boo yee

Futur	
je bouillirai	boo yeer ay
tu bouilliras	boo yeer ah
elle/il bouillira	boo yeer ah
nous bouillirons	boo yeer ohn
vous bouillirez	boo yeer ay
elles/ils bouilliront	boo yeer ohn

Impératif	
bous !	boo
bouillons !	boo yohn
bouillez !	boo yay

Conditionnel	
je bouillirais	boo yeer eh
tu bouillirais	boo yeer eh
elle/il bouillirait	boo yeer eh
nous bouillirions	boo yeer ee ohn
vous bouilliriez	boo yeer ee ay
elles/ils bouilliraient	boo yeer eh

Subjonctif	
je bouille	boo yee
tu bouilles	boo yee
elle/il bouille	boo yee
nous bouillions	boo yee ohn
vous bouilliez	boo yee ay
elles/ils bouillent	boo yee

Imparfait	
je bouillais	boo yeh
tu bouillais	boo yeh
elle/il bouillait	boo yeh
nous bouillions	boo yee ohn
vous bouilliez	boo yee ay
elles/ils bouillaient	boo yeh

Participe présent	
bouillant	boo yawn

Participe Passé	
bouilli	boo yee

Bouillir is the only verb in this book that follows this conjugation pattern.

© 2010

A17

CLORE (klawr)
to close

Présent		Conditionnel	
je clos	kloh	je clorais	klaw reh
tu clos	kloh	tu clorais	klaw reh
il/elle clôt	kloh	il/elle clorait	klaw reh
nous closons	klaw zohn	nous clorions	klaw ree ohn
vous closez	klaw zay	vous cloriez	klaw ree ay
ils/elles closent	klohz	ils/elles cloraient	klaw reh

Passe composé		Subjonctif	
j'ai clos	kloh	je close	klohz
tu as clos	kloh	tu closes	klohz
il/elle a clos	kloh	il/elle close	klohz
nous avons clos	kloh	nous closions	kloh zee ohn
vous avez clos	kloh	vous closiez	kloh zee ay
ils/elles ont clos	kloh	ils/elles closent	klohz

Futur		Imparfait	
je clorai	klaw ray	je closais	kloh zeh
tu cloras	klaw rah	tu closais	kloh zeh
il/elle clora	klaw rah	il/elle closait	kloh zeh
nous clorons	klaw rohn	nous closions	kloh zee ohn
vous clorez	klaw ray	vous closiez	kloh zee ay
ils/elles cloront	klaw rohn	ils/elles closaient	kloh zeh

Impératif		Participe présent	
clos !	kloh	closant	klaw zawn
closons !	klaw zohn		
closez !	klaw zay	Participe passé	
		clos	kloh

Here is the other verb in this book that follow the same conjugation pattern.

enclore   (awn klawr)   to enclose

A18

CONNAÎTRE (kaw neh truh)
to know

Présent		
je connais	kaw neh	
tu connais	kaw neh	
elle/il connaît	kaw neh	
nous connaissons	kaw neh sohn	
vous connaissez	kaw neh say	
elles/ils connaissent	kaw nehss	

Conditionnel	
je connaîtrais	kaw neh treh
tu connaîtrais	kaw neh treh
elle/il connaîtrait	kaw neh treh
nous connaîtrions	kaw neh tree ohn
vous connaîtriez	kaw neh tree ay
elles/ils connaîtraient	kaw neh treh

Passe composé	
j'ai connu	kaw new
tu as connu	kaw new
elle/il a connu	kaw new
nous avons connu	kaw new
vous avez connu	kaw new
elles/ils ont connu	kaw new

Subjonctif	
je connaisse	kaw ness
tu connaisses	kaw ness
elle/il connaisse	kaw ness
nous connaissions	kaw neh see ohn
vous connaissiez	kaw neh see ay
elles/ils connaissent	kaw ness

Futur	
je connaîtrai	kaw neh tray
tu connaîtras	kaw neh trah
elle/il connaîtra	kaw neh trah
nous connaîtrons	kaw neh trohn
vous connaîtrez	kaw neh tray
elles/ils connaîtront	kaw neh trohn

Imparfait	
je connaissais	kaw neh seh
tu connaissais	kaw neh seh
elle/il connaissait	kaw neh seh
nous connaissions	kaw neh see ohn
vous connaissiez	kaw neh see ay
elles/ils connaissaient	kaw neh seh

Impératif	
connais !	kaw nch
connaissons !	kaw neh sohn
connaissez !	kaw neh say

Participe présent	
connaissant	kaw neh sawn

Participe passé	
connu	kaw new

Here is a list of all the verbs in this book that follow the same conjugation pattern.

apparaître	(ah pah reh truh)	to appear / to seem
comparaître	(kohn pah reh truh)	to appear
disparaître	(dee spah reh truh)	to disappear / to vanish
méconnaître	(may kaw neh truh)	to misunderstand / to disregard
paraître	(pah reh truh)	to appear / to seem
reconnaître	(ruh kaw neh truh)	to recognize
reparaître	(ruh pah reh truh)	to reappear / to be back in print
transparaître	(trawn spah reh truh)	to show through

A19

CONVAINCRE (kohn vahn kruh)
to convince

Présent
je convaincs	kohn vahn
tu convaincs	kohn vahn
il/elle convainc	kohn vahn
nous convainquons	kohn vahn kohn
vous convainquez	kohn vahn kay
ils/elles convainquent	kohn vahnk

Conditionnel
je convaincrais	kohn vahn kreh
tu convaincrais	kohn vahn kreh
il/elle convaincrait	kohn vahn kreh
nous convaincrions	kohn vahn kree ohn
vous convaincriez	kohn vahn kree ay
ils/elles convaincraient	kohn vahn kreh

Passe composé
j'ai convaincu	kohn vahn kew
tu as convaincu	kohn vahn kew
il/elle a convaincu	kohn vahn kew
nous avons convaincu	kohn vahn kew
vous avez convaincu	kohn vahn kew
ils/elles ont convaincu	kohn vahn kew

Subjonctif
je convainque	kohn vahn kuh
tu convainques	kohn vahn kuh
il/elle convainque	kohn vahn kuh
nous convainquions	kohn vahn kee ohn
vous convainquiez	kohn vahn kee ay
ils/elles convainquent	kohn vahn kuh

Futur
je convaincrai	kohn vahn kray
tu convaincras	kohn vahn krah
il/elle convaincra	kohn vahn krah
nous convaincrons	kohn vahn krohn
vous convaincrez	kohn vahn kray
ils/elles convaincront	kohn vahn krohn

Imparfait
je convainquais	kohn vahn keh
tu convainquais	kohn vahn keh
il/elle convainquait	kohn vahn keh
nous convainquions	kohn vahn kee ohn
vous convainquiez	kohn vahn kee ay
ils/elles convainquaient	kohn vahn keh

Impératif
convaincs !	kohn vahn
convainquons !	kohn vahn kohn
convainquez !	kohn vahn kay

Participe présent
convainquant	kohn vahn kawn

Participe passé
convaincu	kohn vahn kew

Here is the other verb in this book that follows the same conjugation pattern.

vaincre   (vahn kruh)   to defeat / to overcome

A20

COUDRE (koo druh)
to sew

Présent		Conditionnel	
je couds	koo	je coudrais	koo dreh
tu couds	koo	tu coudrais	koo dreh
elle/il coud	koo	elle/il coudrait	koo dreh
nous cousons	koo zohn	nous coudrions	koo dree ohn
vous cousez	koo zay	vous coudriez	koo dree ay
elles/ils cousent	kooz	elles/ils coudraient	koo dreh

Passe composé		Subjonctif	
j'ai cousu	koo zew	je couse	kooz
tu as cousu	koo zew	tu couses	kooz
elle/il a cousu	koo zew	elle/il couse	kooz
nous avons cousu	koo zew	nous cousions	koo zee ohn
vous avez cousu	koo zew	vous cousiez	koo zee ay
elles/ils ont cousu	koo zew	elles/ils cousent	kooz

Futur		Imparfait	
je coudrai	koo dray	je cousais	koo zeh
tu coudras	koo drah	tu cousais	koo zeh
elle/il coudra	koo drah	elle/il cousait	koo zeh
nous coudrons	koo drohn	nous cousions	koo zee ohn
vous coudrez	koo dray	vous cousiez	koo zee ay
elles/ils coudront	koo drohn	elles/ils cousaient	koo zeh

Impératif		Participe présent	
couds !	koo	cousant	koo zawn
cousons !	koo zohn		
cousez !	koo zay	Participe passé	
		cousu	koo zew

Here is a list of all the verbs in this book that follow the same conjugation pattern.

| découdre | (day koo druh) | to unstitch |
| recoudre | (ruh koo druh) | to sew up |

A21

COURIR (koo reer)
to run

Présent		Conditionnel	
je cours	koor	je courrais	koor eh
tu cours	koor	tu courrais	koor eh
il/elle court	koor	il/elle courrait	koor eh
nous courons	koor ohn	nous courrions	koor ee ohn
vous courez	koor ay	vous courriez	koor ee ay
ils/elles courent	koor	elles/ils courraient	koor eh

Passe composé		Subjonctif	
j'ai couru	koor ew	je coure	koor
tu as couru	koor ew	tu coures	koor
il/elle a couru	koor ew	il/elle coure	koor
nous avons couru	koor ew	nous courions	koor ee ohn
vous avez couru	koor ew	vous couriez	koor ee ay
ils/elles ont couru	koor ew	ils/elles courent	koor

Futur		Imparfait	
je courrai	koor ay	je courais	koor eh
tu courras	koor ah	tu courais	koor eh
il/elle courra	koor ah	il/elle courait	koor eh
nous courrons	koor ohn	nous courions	koor ee ohn
vous courrez	koor ay	vous couriez	koor ee ay
ils/elles courront	koor ohn	ils/elles couraient	koor eh

Impératif		Participe présent	
cours !	koor	courant	koor awn
courons !	koor ohn		
courez !	koor ay	Participe passé	
		couru	koor ew

Here is a list of all the verbs in this book that follow the same conjugation pattern.

Accourir	(ah koo reer)	to rush
concourir	(kohn koo reer)	to compete
discourir	(dee skoo reer)	to hold forth
encourir	(awn koo reer)	to incure
parcourir	(pahr koo reer)	to travel all over
recourir	(ruh koo reer)	to resort to / to run again
secourir	(suh koo reer)	to help / to rescue

A22

CROIRE (krwahr)
to believe

Présent		Conditionnel	
je crois	krwah	je croirais	krwahr eh
tu crois	krwah	tu croirais	krwahr eh
elle/il croit	krwah	elle/il croirait	krwahr eh
nous croyons	krwah yohn	nous croirions	krwahr ee ohn
vous croyez	krwah yay	vous croiriez	krwahr ee ay
elles/ils croient	krwah	elles/ils croiraient	krwahr eh

Passe composé		Subjonctif	
j'ai cru	crew	je croie	krwah
tu as cru	crew	tu croies	krwah
elle/il a cru	crew	elle/il croie	krwah
nous avons cru	crew	nous croyions	krwah yee ohn
vous avez cru	crew	vous croyiez	krwah yee ay
elles/ils ont cru	crew	elles/ils croient	krwah

Futur		Imparfait	
je croirai	krwahr ay	je croyais	krwah yeh
tu croiras	krwahr ah	tu croyais	krwah yeh
elle/il croira	krwahr ah	elle/il croyait	krwah yeh
nous croirons	krwahr ohn	nous croyions	krwah yee ohn
vous croirez	krwahr ay	vous croyiez	krwah yee ay
elles/ils croiront	krwahr ohn	elles/ils croyaient	krwah yeh

Impératif		Participe présent	
crois !	krwah	croyant	krwah yawn
croyons !	krwah yohn		
croyez !	krwah yay	Participe passé	
		cru	crew

Croire is the only verb in this book that follows this conjugation pattern.

A23

DEVENIR (duh vneer)
to become

Présent		Conditionnel	
je deviens	duh vyahn	je deviendrais	duh vyahn dreh
tu deviens	duh vyahn	tu deviendrais	duh vyahn dreh
il/elle devient	duh vyahn	il/elle deviendrait	duh vyahn dreh
nous devenons	duh vuh nohn	nous deviendrions	duh vyahn dree ohn
vous devenez	duh vuh nay	vous deviendriez	duh vyahn dree ay
ils/elles deviennent	duh vyehn	ils/elles deviendraient	duh vyahn dreh

Passe composé		Subjonctif	
je suis devenu/-(e)	duh vuh new	je devienne	duh vyehn
tu es devenu/-(e)	duh vuh new	tu deviennes	duh vyehn
il/elle est devenu/-(e)	duh vuh new	il/elle devienne	duh vyehn
nous sommes devenus/-(es)	duh vuh new	nous devenions	duh vuhn ee ohn
vous êtes devenu/-(e)(es)(s)	duh vuh new	vous deveniez	duh vuhn ee ay
ils/elles sont devenus/-(es)	duh vuh new	ils/elles deviennent	duh vyehn

Futur		Imparfait	
je deviendrai	duh vyahn dray	je devenais	duh vuh neh
tu deviendras	duh vyahn drah	tu devenais	duh vuh neh
il/elle deviendra	duh vyahn drah	il/elle devenait	duh vuh neh
nous deviendrons	duh vyahn drohn	nous devenions	duh vuhn ee ohn
vous deviendrez	duh vyahn dray	vous deveniez	duh vuhn ee ay
ils/elles deviendront	duh vyahn drohn	ils/elles devenaient	duh vuh neh

Impératif		Participe présent	
deviens !	duh vyahn	devenant	duh vuh nawn
devenons !	duh vuh nohn		
devenez !	duh vuh nay	Participe passé	
		devenu	duh vuh new

Here is a list of all the verbs in this book that follow the same conjugation pattern.

abstenir	(ap stuh neer)	to abstain
advenir	(ahd vuh neer)	to happen
appartenir	(ah pahr tuh neer)	to belong to
circonvenir	(seer kohn vuh neer)	to circumvent
contenir	(kohn tuh neer)	to contain
contrevenir	(kohn truh vuh neer)	to contravene
convenir	(kohn vuh neer)	to admit / to be suitable

© 2010

A23

détenir	(day tuh neer)	to detain
disconvenir	(dee skohn vuh neer)	to deny
entretenir	(awn truh tuh neer)	to look after
intervenir	(ahn tehr vuh neer)	to intervene
maintenir	(mahn tuh neer)	to maintain
obtenir	(awp tuh neer)	to obtain
parvenir	(pahr vuh neer)	to reach
prévenir	(pray vuh neer)	to warn / to prevent
provenir	(praw vuh neer)	to come from
retenir	(ruh tuh neer)	to keep / to hold (so) up
revenir	(ruh vuh neer)	to come back
soutenir	(soo tuh neer)	to support
souvenir (se)	(soo vuh neer)	to remember
subvenir	(sewb vuh neer)	to provide for
survenir	(sewr vuh neer)	to occur
tenir	(tuh neer)	to hold
venir	(vuh neer)	to come

A24

DEVOIR (duh vwahr)
to have to (must) / to owe

Présent		Conditionnel	
je dois	dwah	je devrais	deh vreh
tu dois	dwah	tu devrais	deh vreh
elle/il doit	dwah	elle/il devrait	deh vreh
nous devons	duh vohn	nous devrions	deh vree ohn
vous devez	duh vay	vous devriez	deh vree ay
elles/ils doivent	dwahv	elles/ils devraient	deh vreh

Passe composé		Subjonctif	
j' ai dû	dew	je doive	dwahv
tu as dû	dew	tu doives	dwahv
elle/il a dû	dew	elle/il doive	dwahv
nous avons dû	dew	nous devions	duh vee ohn
vous avez dû	dew	vous deviez	duh vee ay
elles/ils ont dû	dew	elles/ils doivent	dwahv

Futur		Imparfait	
je devrai	deh vray	je devais	duh veh
tu devras	deh vrah	tu devais	duh veh
elle/il devra	deh vrah	elle/il devait	duh veh
nous devrons	deh vrohn	nous devions	duh vee ohn
vous devrez	deh vray	vous deviez	duh vee ay
elles/ils devront	deh vrohn	elles/ils devaient	duh veh

Impératif		Participe présent	
dois !	dwah	devant	duh vawn
devons !	duh vohn		
devez !	duh vay	Participe passé	
		dû	dew

Devoir is the only verb in this book that follows this conjugation pattern.

A25

DIRE (deer)
to say / to tell

Présent			Conditionnel	
je dis	dee		je dirais	dee reh
tu dis	dee		tu dirais	dee reh
il/elle dit	dee		il/elle dirait	dee reh
nous disons	dee zohn		nous dirions	dee ree ohn
vous dites	deet		vous diriez	dee ree ay
ils/elles disent	deez		ils/elles diraient	dee reh

Passe composé			Subjonctif	
j'ai dit	dee		je dise	deez
tu as dit	dee		tu dises	deez
il/elle a dit	dee		il/elle dise	deez
nous avons dit	dee		nous disions	dee zee ohn
vous avez dit	dee		vous disiez	dee zee ay
ils/elles ont dit	dee		ils/elles disent	deez

Futur			Imparfait	
je dirai	dee ray		je disais	dee zeh
tu diras	dee rah		tu disais	dee zeh
il/elle dira	dee rah		il/elle disait	dee zeh
nous dirons	dee rohn		nous disions	dee zee ohn
vous direz	dee ray		vous disiez	dee zee ay
ils/elles diront	dee rohn		ils/elles disaient	dee zeh

Impératif			Participe présent	
dis !	dee		disant	dee zawn
disons !	dee zohn			
dites !	deet		Participe passé	
			dit	dee

Here is a list of all the verbs in this book that follow the same conjugation pattern.

contredire	(kohn truh deer)	to contradict
dédire (se)	(day deer)	to retract one's statement
médire	(may deer)	to malign
prédire	(pray deer)	to predict
redire	(ruh deer)	to say again

A26

DISSOUDRE (dee soo druh)
to dissolve

Présent
je dissous	dee soo
tu dissous	dee soo
elle/il dissout	dee soo
nous dissolvons	dee sawl vohn
vous dissolvez	dee sawl vay
elles/ils dissolvent	dee sawlv

Conditionnel
je dissoudrais	dee soo dreh
tu dissoudrais	dee soo dreh
elle/il dissoudrait	dee soo dreh
nous dissoudrions	dee soo dree ohn
vous dissoudriez	dee soo dree ay
elles/ils dissoudraient	dee soo dreh

Passe composé
j'ai dissous	dee soo
tu as dissous	dee soo
elle/il a dissous	dee soo
nous avons dissous	dee soo
vous avez dissous	dee soo
elles/ils ont dissous	dee soo

Subjonctif
je dissolve	dee sawlv
tu dissolves	dee sawlv
elle/il dissolve	dee sawlv
nous dissolvions	dee sawl vee ohn
vous dissolviez	dee sawl vee ay
elles/ils dissolvent	dee sawlv

Futur
je dissoudrai	dee soo dray
tu dissoudras	dee soo drah
elle/il dissoudra	dee soo drah
nous dissoudrons	dee soo drohn
vous dissoudrez	dee soo dray
elles/ils dissoudront	dee soo drohn

Imparfait
je dissolvais	dee sawl veh
tu dissolvais	dee sawl veh
elle/il dissolvait	dee sawl veh
nous dissolvions	dee sawl vee ohn
vous dissolviez	dee sawl vee ay
elles/ils dissolvaient	dee sawl veh

Impératif
dissous !	dee soo
dissolvons !	dee sawl vohn
dissolvez !	dee sawl vay

Participe présent
dissolvant   dee sawl vawn

Participe passé
dissous   dee soo

Here is the other verb in this book that follows the same conjugation pattern.

résoudre   (ray zoo druh)   to solve / to resolve

A27

DORMIR (dohr meer)
to sleep

Présent		
je dors	dohr	
tu dors	dohr	
il/elle dort	dohr	
nous dormons	dohr mohn	
vous dormez	dorh may	
ils/elles dorment	dohrm	

Conditionnel		
je dormirais	dohr meer eh	
tu dormirais	dohr meer eh	
il/elle dormirait	dohr meer eh	
nous dormirions	dohr meer ee ohn	
vous dormiriez	dohr meer ee ay	
ils/elles dormiraient	dohr meer eh	

Passe composé		
j'ai dormi	dohr mee	
tu as dormi	dohr mee	
il/elle a dormi	dohr mee	
nous avons dormi	dohr mee	
vous avez dormi	dohr mee	
ils/elles ont dormi	dohr mee	

Subjonctif		
je dorme	dohrm	
tu dormes	dohrm	
il/elle dorme	dohrm	
nous dormions	dohr mee ohn	
vous dormiez	dohr mee ay	
ils/elles dorment	dohrm	

Futur		
je dormirai	dohr meer ay	
tu dormiras	dohr meer ah	
il/elle dormira	dohr meer ah	
nous dormirons	dohr meer ohn	
vous dormirez	dohr meer ay	
ils/elles dormiront	dohr meer ohn	

Imparfait		
je dormais	dohr meh	
tu dormais	dohr meh	
il/elle dormait	dohr meh	
nous dormions	dohr mee ohn	
vous dormiez	dohr mee ay	
ils/elles dormaient	dohr meh	

Impératif		
dors !	dohr	
dormons !	dohr mohn	
dormez !	dorh may	

Participe présent	
dormant	dohr mawn

Participe passé	
dormi	dohr mee

Here is a list of all the verbs in this book that follow the same conjugation pattern.

consentir	(kohn sawn teer)	to consent
démentir	(day mawn teer)	to deny
départir	(day pahr teer)	to allot
endormir	(awn dawr meer)	to send (so) to sleep
mentir	(mawn teer)	to lie
partir	(pahr teer)	to leave
pressentir	(pray sawn teer)	to have a premonition about
rendormir	(rawn dawr meer)	to put (so) back to sleep
repartir	(ruh pahr teer)	to leave again
repentir (se)	(ruh pawn teer)	to repent / to regret
ressentir	(ruh sawn teer)	to feel
ressortir	(ruh sawr teer)	to take/go/out again
sentir	(sawn teer)	to smell / to feel
servir	(sehr veer)	to serve
sortir	(sawr teer)	to go out / to bring out

© 2010

A28

ÉCRIRE (ay kreer)
to write

Présent			**Conditionnel**	
j'écris	ay kree		j'écrirais	ay kree reh
tu écris	ay kree		tu écrirais	ay kree reh
elle/il écrit	ay kree		elle/il écrirait	ay kree reh
nous écrivons	ay kree vohn		nous écririons	ay kree ree ohn
vous écrivez	ay kree vay		vous écririez	ay kree ree ay
elles/ils écrivent	ay kreev		elles/ils écriraient	ay kree reh
Passé composé			**Subjonctif**	
j'ai écrit	ay kree		j'écrive	ay kreev
tu as écrit	ay kree		tu écrives	ay kreev
elle/il a écrit	ay kree		elle/il écrive	ay kreev
nous avons écrit	ay kree		nous écrivions	ay kree vee ohn
vous avez écrit	ay kree		vous écriviez	ay kree vee ay
elles/ils ont écrit	ay kree		elles/ils écrivent	ay kreev
Futur			**Imparfait**	
j'écrirai	ay kree ray		j'écrivais	ay kree veh
tu écriras	ay kree rah		tu écrivais	ay kree veh
elle/il écrira	ay kree rah		elle/il écrivait	ay kree veh
nous écrirons	ay kree rohn		nous écrivions	ay kree vee ohn
vous écrirez	ay kree ray		vous écriviez	ay kree vee ay
elles/ils écriront	ay kree rohn		elles/ils écrivaient	ay kree veh
Impératif			**Participe présent**	
écris !	ay kree		écrivant	ay kree vawn
écrivons !	ay kree vohn			
écrivez !	ay kree vay		**Participe passé**	
			écrit	ay kree

Here is a list of all the verbs in this book that follow the same conjugation pattern.

circonscrire	(seer kohn skreer)	to circumscribe
décrire	(day kreer)	to describe
inscrire	(ahn skreer)	to enrol / to write down
prescrire	(preh skreer)	to prescribe
proscrire	(praw skreer)	to ban
récrire	(ray kreer)	to rewrite
souscrire	(soo skreer)	to subscribe to
transcrire	(trawn skreer)	to transcribe

A29

ÉMOUVOIR (ay moo vwahr)
to move deeply / to disturb

Présent		Conditionnel	
j'émeus	ay muh	j'émouvrais	ay moo vreh
tu émeus	ay muh	tu émouvrais	ay moo vreh
il/elle émeut	ay muh	il/elle émouvrait	ay moo vreh
nous émouvons	ay moo vohn	nous émouvrions	ay moo vree ohn
vous émouvez	ay moo vay	vous émouvriez	ay moo vree ay
ils/elles émeuvent	ay muhv	ils/elles émouvraient	ay moo vreh

Passé composé		Subjonctif	
j'ai ému	ay mew	j'émeuve	ay muhv
tu as ému	ay mew	tu émeuves	ay muhv
il/elle a ému	ay mew	il/elle émeuve	ay muhv
nous avons ému	ay mew	nous émouvions	ay moo vee ohn
vous avez ému	ay mew	vous émouviez	ay moo vee ay
ils/elles ont ému	ay mew	ils/elles émeuvent	ay muhv

Futur		Imparfait	
j'émouvrai	ay moo vray	j'émouvais	ay moo veh
tu émouvras	ay moo vrah	tu émouvais	ay moo veh
il/elle émouvra	ay moo vrah	il/elle émouvait	ay moo veh
nous émouvrons	ay moo vrohn	nous émouvions	ay moo vee ohn
vous émouvrez	ay moo vray	vous émouviez	ay moo vee ay
ils/elles émouvront	ay moo vrohn	ils/elles émouvaient	ay moo veh

Impératif		Participe présent	
émeus !	ay muh	émouvant	ay moo vawn
émouvons !	ay moo vohn		
émouvez !	ay moo vay	Participe passé	
		ému	ay mew

Here is a list of all the verbs in this book that follow the same conjugation pattern.

mouvoir   (moo vwahr)   to move
promouvoir   (praw moo vwahr) to promote

A30

ENNUYER (aw nwee yay)
to bore

Présent		Conditionnel	
j'ennuie	aw nwee	j'ennuierais	aw nwee uh reh
tu ennuies	aw nwee	tu ennuierais	aw nwee uh reh
elle/il ennuie	aw nwee	elle/il ennuierait	aw nwee uh reh
nous ennuyons	aw nwee yohn	nous ennuierions	aw nwee uh ree ohn
vous ennuyez	aw nwee yay	vous ennuieriez	aw nwee uh ree ay
elles/ils ennuient	aw nwee	elles/ils ennuieraient	aw nwee uh reh

Passé composé		Subjonctif	
j'ai ennuyé	aw nwee yay	j'ennuie	aw nwee
tu as ennuyé	aw nwee yay	tu ennuies	aw nwee
elle/il a ennuyé	aw nwee yay	elle/il ennuie	aw nwee
nous avons ennuyé	aw nwee yay	nous ennuyions	aw nwee yee ohn
vous avez ennuyé	aw nwee yay	vous ennuyiez	aw nwee yee ay
elles/ils ont ennuyé	aw nwee yay	elles/ils ennuient	aw nwee

Futur		Imparfait	
j'ennuierai	aw nwee uh ray	j'ennuyais	aw nwee yeh
tu ennuieras	aw nwee uh rah	tu ennuyais	aw nwee yeh
elle/il ennuiera	aw nwee uh rah	elle/il ennuyait	aw nwee yeh
nous ennuierons	aw nwee uh rohn	nous ennuyions	aw nwee yee ohn
vous ennuierez	aw nwee uh ray	vous ennuyiez	aw nwee yee ay
elles/ils ennuieront	aw nwee uh rohn	elles/ils ennuyaient	aw nwee yeh

Impératif		Participe présent	
ennuie !	aw nwee	ennuyant	aw nwe yawn
ennuyons !	aw nwee yohn		
ennuyez !	aw nwee yay	Participe passé	
		ennuyé	aw nwee yay

Here is a list of all the verbs in this book that follow the same conjugation pattern.

aboyer	(ah bwah yay)	to bark
apitoyer	(ah pee twah yay)	to move to pity
appuyer	(ah pwee yay)	to press / to lean
atermoyer	(ah tehr mwah yay)	to procrastinate
broyer	(brwah yay)	to grind
côtoyer	(koh twah yay)	to be next to
choyer	(shwah yay)	to pamper
déployer	(day plwah yay)	to display
désennuyer	(day zaw nwee yay)	to relieve boredom

A30

employer	(awn plwah yay)	to deploy/to employ
essuyer	(ay swee yay)	to dry / to wipe
foudroyer	(foo drwah yay)	to strike down
fourvoyer	(foor vwah yay)	to mislead
guerroyer	(gayr wah yay)	to wage war
larmoyer	(lahr mwah yay)	to water
louvoyer	(loo vwah yay)	to tack
nettoyer	(neh twah yay)	to clean
noyer	(nwah yay)	to drown
octroyer	(awk trwah yay)	to grant
tournoyer	(toor nwah yay)	to whirl
tutoyer	(tew twah yay)	to address (so) as "tu"
verdoyer	(vehr dwah yay)	to be green
vouvoyer	(voo vwah yay)	to address (so) as "vous"

A31

ENVOYER (awn vwah yay)
to send

Présent		Conditionnel	
j'envoie	awn vwah	j'enverrais	awn veh reh
tu envoies	awn vwah	tu enverrais	awn veh reh
il/elle envoie	awn vwah	il/elle enverrait	awn veh reh
nous envoyons	awn vwah yohn	nous enverrions	awn veh ree ohn
vous envoyez	awn vwah yay	vous enverriez	awn veh ree ay
ils/elles envoient	awn vwah	ils/elles enverraient	awn veh reh

Passe composé		Subjonctif	
j'ai envoyé	awn vwah yay	j'envoie	awn vwah
tu as envoyé	awn vwah yay	tu envoies	awn vwah
il/elle a envoyé	awn vwah yay	il/elle envoie	awn vwah
nous avons envoyé	awn vwah yay	nous envoyions	awn vwah yee ohn
vous avez envoyé	awn vwah yay	vous envoyiez	awn vwah yee ay
ils/elles ont envoyé	awn vwah yay	ils/elles envoient	awn vwah

Futur		Imparfait	
j'enverrai	awn veh ray	j'envoyais	awn vwah yeh
tu enverras	awn veh rah	tu envoyais	awn vwah yeh
il/elle enverra	awn veh rah	il/elle envoyait	awn vwah yeh
nous enverrons	awn veh rohn	nous envoyions	awn vwah yee ohn
vous enverrez	awn veh ray	vous envoyiez	awn vwah yee ay
ils/elles enverront	awn veh rohn	ils/elles envoyaient	awn vwah yeh

Impératif		Participe présent	
envoie !	awn vwah	envoyant	awn vwah yawn
envoyons !	awn vwah yohn		
envoyez !	awn vwah yay	Participe passé	
		envoyé	awn vwah yay

Here is the other verb in this book that follows the same conjugation pattern.

renvoyer   (rawn vwah yay)   to send back

ESPÉRER (eh spay ray)
to hope

Présent	
j'espère	eh sp<u>eh</u>r
tu espè<u>res</u>	eh sp<u>eh</u>r
elle/il espè<u>re</u>	eh sp<u>eh</u>r
nous espér<u>ons</u>	eh spay rohn
vous espér<u>ez</u>	eh spay r<u>ay</u>
elles/ils espè<u>rent</u>	eh sp<u>eh</u>r

Conditionnel	
j'espérer<u>ais</u>	eh spayr uh r<u>eh</u>
tu espérer<u>ais</u>	eh spayr uh r<u>eh</u>
elle/il espérer<u>ait</u>	eh spayr uh r<u>eh</u>
nous espérer<u>ions</u>	eh spayr uh r<u>ee ohn</u>
vous espérer<u>iez</u>	eh spayr uh r<u>ee ay</u>
elles/ils espérer<u>aient</u>	eh spayr uh r<u>eh</u>

Passe composé	
j'ai espér<u>é</u>	eh spayr <u>ay</u>
tu as espér<u>é</u>	eh spayr <u>ay</u>
elle/il a espér<u>é</u>	eh spayr <u>ay</u>
nous avons espér<u>é</u>	eh spayr ay
vous avez espér<u>é</u>	eh spayr ay
elles/ils ont espér<u>é</u>	eh spayr <u>ay</u>

Subjonctif	
j'espère	eh sp<u>eh</u>r
tu espè<u>res</u>	eh sp<u>eh</u>r
elle/il espè<u>re</u>	eh sp<u>eh</u>r
nous espér<u>ions</u>	eh spayr ee ohn
vous espér<u>iez</u>	eh spayr ee ay
elles/ils espè<u>rent</u>	eh sp<u>eh</u>r

Futur	
j'espérer<u>ai</u>	eh spayr uh r<u>ay</u>
tu espérer<u>as</u>	eh spayr uh r<u>ah</u>
elle/il espérer<u>a</u>	eh spayr uh r<u>ah</u>
nous espérer<u>ons</u>	eh spayr uh rohn
vous espérer<u>ez</u>	eh spayr uh r<u>ay</u>
elles/ils espérer<u>ont</u>	eh spayr uh rohn

Imparfait	
j'espér<u>ais</u>	eh spayr eh
tu espér<u>ais</u>	eh spayr eh
elle/il espér<u>ait</u>	eh spayr eh
nous espér<u>ions</u>	eh spayr ee ohn
vous espér<u>iez</u>	eh spayr ee ay
elles/ils espér<u>aient</u>	eh spayr eh

Impératif	
espè<u>re</u> !	eh sp<u>eh</u>r
espér<u>ons</u> !	eh spay rohn
espér<u>ez</u> !	eh spay r<u>ay</u>

Participe présent	
espér<u>ant</u>	eh spayr awn

Participe passé	
espér<u>é</u>	eh spayr ay

Here is a list of all the verbs in this book that follow the same conjugation pattern.

accéder	(ahk say day)	to reach
accélérer	(ahk say lay ray)	to accelerate
adhérer	(ah day ray)	to adhere to
aérer	(ayr ay)	to air
affréter	(ah fray tay)	to charter
altérer	(ahl tay ray)	to inpair
asséner	(ah say nay)	to strike (someone)

A32

céder	(say day)	to give up
compléter	(kohn play tay)	to complete
concéder	(kohn say day)	to concede
conférer	(kohn fay ray)	to confer
coopérer	(koh aw pay ray)	to cooperate
déblatérer	(day blah tay ray)	to rant on
décéder	(day say day)	to die
décélérer	(day say lay ray)	to slow down
décolérer	(day kaw lay ray)	to peel off
décréter	(day kray tay)	to decree
déférer	(day fay ray)	to refer
dégénérer	(day zhay nay ray)	to degenerate
délibérer	(day lee bay ray)	to deliberate
dépoussiérer	(day poo syay ray)	to dust
désaltérer	(day zahl tay ray)	to quench thirst
désespérer	(day zeh spay ray)	to fill (so) with despair
différer	(dee fay ray)	to postpone/to differ
digérer	(dee zhay ray)	to digest
écrémer	(ay kray may)	to skim (milk)
empiéter	(awn pyay tay)	to encroach upon
énumérer	(ay new may ray)	to enumerate
exagérer	(ehg zah zhay ray)	to exaggerate
exaspérer	(ehg zah spay ray)	to exasperate
excéder	(ek say day)	to exceed
exonérer	(eg zaw nay ray)	to exempt
gérer	(zhay ray)	to manage
hébéter	(ay bay tay)	to daze
inquiéter	(ahn kyay tay)	to worry
insérer	(ahn say ray)	to insert
intercéder	(ahn tehr say day)	to intercede
légiférer	(lay zhee fay ray)	to legislate
libérer	(lee bay ray)	to liberate
modérer	(maw day ray)	to moderate
oblitérer	(aw blee tay ray)	to obliterate
obséder	(awp say day)	to obsess/to hunt
opérer	(aw pay ray)	to operate (on)
persévérer	(pehr say vay ray)	to persevere
péter	(pay tay)	to break/to fart
posséder	(paw say day)	to possess
précéder	(pray say day)	to precede
préférer	(pray fay ray)	to prefer
procéder	(praw say day)	to proceed
rasséréner	(rah say ray nay)	to reassure
récupérer	(ray kew pay ray)	to recuperate/to retrieve
référer	(ray fay ray)	to refer
refléter	(ruh flay tay)	to reflect/to mirror
régénérer	(reh zhay nay ray)	to regenerate
répéter	(ray pay tay)	to repeat
révéler	(ray vay lay)	to reveal
révérer	(ray vay ray)	to revere
rouspéter	(roo spay tay)	to grumble
succéder	(sewk say day)	to succeed
suggérer	(sewg zhay ray)	to suggest
téter	(tay tay)	to suck at
tolérer	(taw lay ray)	to tolerate
transférer	(trawns fay ray)	to transfer
ulcérer	(ewl say ray)	to sicken/to ulcerate
végéter	(vay zhay tay)	to vegetate/to stagnate
vitupérer	(vee tew pay ray)	to rail against
vociférer	(vaw see fay ray)	to shout

A33

ESSAYER (ay say yay)
to try

Présent
j'essaie /essaye	ay say
tu essaies/essayes	ay say
il/elle essaie/essaye	ay say
nous essayons	ay say yohn
vous essayez	ay say yay
ils/elles essaient/essayent	ay say

Conditionnel
j'essaierais/essayerais	ay say uhr eh
tu essaierais/essayerais	ay say uhr eh
il/elle essaierait/essayerait	ay say uhr eh
nous essaierions/essayerions	ay say uhr ee ohn
vous essaieriez/essayeriez	ay say uhr ee ay
ils/elles essaieraient/essayeraient	ay say uhr eh

Passé composé
j'ai essayé	ay say yay
tu as essayé	ay say yay
il/elle a essayé	ay say yay
nous avons essayé	ay say yay
vous avez essayé	ay say yay
ils/elles ont essayé	ay say yay

Subjonctif
j'essaie/essaye	ay say
tu essaies/essayes	ay say
il/elle essaie/essaye	ay say
nous essayions	ay say ee ohn
vous essayiez	ay say ee ay
ils/elles essaient/essayent	ay say

Futur
j'essaierai/essayerai	ay seh uh ray
tu essaieras/essayeras	ay seh uh rah
il/elle essaiera/essayera	ay seh uh rah
nous essaierons/essayerons	ay seh uh rohn
vous essaierez/essayerez	ay seh uh ray
ils/elles essaieront/essayeront	ay seh uh rohn

Imparfait
j'essayais	ay say eh
tu essayais	ay say eh
il/elle essayait	ay say eh
nous essayions	ay say ee ohn
vous essayiez	ay say ee ay
ils/elles essayaient	ay say eh

Impératif
essaie! / essaye !	ay say yohn
essayons!	ay say yohn
essayez!	ay say yay

Participe présent
essayant	ay say yawn

Participe passé
essayé	ay say yay

Here is a list of all the verbs in this book that follow the same conjugation pattern.

bégayer	(bay gay yay)	to stutter
balayer	(bah lay yay)	to sweep up
débrayer	(day bray yay)	to declutch
délayer	(day lay yay)	to dilute
effrayer	(ay freh yay)	to scare
égayer	(ay gay yay)	to enliven
étayer	(ay tay yay)	to shore up/to prop up
frayer	(freh yay)	to clear a path
monnayer	(maw neh yay)	to convert into cash
payer	(pay yay)	to pay for
zézayer	(zay zay yay)	to lisp

A34

ÊTRE (eh truh)
to be

Présent
je suis	swee
tu es	eh
elle/il est	eh
nous sommes	sawm
vous êtes	eht
elles/ils sont	sohn

Passe composé
j'ai été	ay tay
tu as été	ay tay
elle/il a été	ay tay
nous avons été	ay tay
vous avez été	ay tay
elles/ils ont été	ay tay

Futur
je serai	suh ray
tu seras	suh rah
elle/il sera	suh rah
nous serons	suh rohn
vous serez	suh ray
elles/ils seront	suh rohn

Impératif
sois !	swah
soyons !	swah yohn
soyez !	swah yay

Conditionnel
je serais	suh reh
tu serais	suh reh
elle/il serait	suh reh
nous serions	suh ree ohn
vous seriez	suh ree ay
elles/ils seraient	suh reh

Subjonctif
je sois	swah
tu sois	swah
elle/il soit	swah
nous soyons	swah yohn
vous soyez	swah yay
elles/ils soient	swah

Imparfait
j'étais	ay teh
tu étais	ay teh
elle/il était	ay teh
nous étions	ay tee ohn
vous étiez	ay tee ay
elles/ils étaient	ay teh

Participe présent
étant	ay tawn

Participe passé
été	ay tay

Être is the only verb in this book that follows this conjugation pattern.

© 2010

EXTRAIRE (ek strehr)
to extract

Présent		Conditionnel	
j'extrais	ek streh	j'extrairais	ek strehr eh
tu extrais	ek streh	tu extrairais	ek strehr eh
il/elle extrait	ek streh	il/elle extrairait	ek strehr eh
nous extrayons	ek strah yohn	nous extrairions	ek strehr ee ohn
vous extrayez	ek strah yay	vous extrairiez	ek strehr ee ay
ils/elles extraient	ek streh	ils/elles extrairaient	ek strehr eh

Passe composé		Subjonctif	
j'ai extrait	ek streh	j'extraie	ek streh
tu as extrait	ek streh	tu extraies	ek streh
il/elle a extrait	ek streh	il/elle extraie	ek streh
nous avons extrait	ek streh	nous extrayions	ek strah yee ohn
vous avez extrait	ek streh	vous extrayiez	ek strah yee ay
ils/elles ont extrait	ek streh	ils/elles extraient	ek streh

Futur		Imparfait	
j'extrairai	ek strehr ay	j'extrayais	ek strah yeh
tu extrairas	ek strehr ah	tu extrayais	ek strah yeh
il/elle extraira	ek strehr ah	il/elle extrayait	ek strah yeh
nous extrairons	ek strehr ohn	nous extrayions	ek strah yee ohn
vous extrairez	ek strehr ay	vous extrayiez	ek strah yee ay
ils/elles extrairont	ek strehr ohn	ils/elles extrayaient	ek strah yeh

Impératif		Participe présent	
extrais !	ek streh	extrayant	ek strah yawn
extrayons !	ek strah yohn		
extrayez !	ek strah yay	Participe passé	
		extrait	ek streh

Here is a list of all the verbs in this book that follow the same conjugation pattern.

abstraire	(ap strehr)	to abstract
braire	(brehr)	to bray
distraire	(dee strehr)	to entertain / to distract
soustraire	(soo strehr)	to subtract
traire	(trehr)	to milk

A36

FAILLIR (fah yeer)
to almost do

Présent		Conditionnel	
je faux	foh	je faillirais	fah yeer eh
tu faux	foh	tu faillirais	fah yeer eh
elle/il faut	foh	elle/il faillirait	fah yeer eh
nous faillons	fah yohn	nous faillirions	fah yeer ee ohn
vous faillez	fah yay	vous failliriez	fah yeer ee ay
elles/ils faillent	fah yee	elles/ils failliraient	fah yeer eh

Passe composé		Subjonctif	
j'ai failli	fah yee	je faille	fah yee
tu as failli	fah yee	tu failles	fah yee
elle/il a failli	fah yee	elle/il faille	fah yee
nous avons failli	fah yee	nous faillions	fah yee ohn
vous avez failli	fah yee	vous failliez	fah yee ay
elles/ils ont failli	fah yee	elles/ils faillent	fah yee

Futur		Imparfait	
je faillirai	fah yeer ay	je faillais	fah yeh
tu failliras	fah yeer ah	tu faillais	fah yeh
elle/il faillira	fah yeer ah	elle/il faillait	fah ych
nous faillirons	fah yeer ohn	nous faillions	fah yee ohn
vous faillirez	fah yeer ay	vous failliez	fah yee ay
elles/ils failliront	fah yeer ohn	elles/ils faillaient	fah yeh

Impératif		Participe présent	
faux !	foh	faillant	fah yawn
faillons !	fah yohn		
faillez !	fah yay	Participe passé	
		failli	fah yee

Faillir is the only verb in this book that follows this conjugation pattern.

A37

FAIRE (fehr)
to make / to do

Présent			Conditionnel	
je fais	feh		je ferais	fuh reh
tu fais	feh		tu ferais	fuh reh
il/elle fait	feh		il/elle ferait	fuh reh
nous faisons	feh zohn		nous ferions	fuh ree ohn
vous faites	feht		vous feriez	fuh ree ay
ils/elles font	fohn		ils/elles feraient	fuh reh

Passe composé			Subjonctif	
j'ai fait	feh		je fasse	fahs
tu as fait	feh		tu fasses	fahs
il/elle a fait	feh		il/elle fasse	fahs
nous avons fait	feh		nous fassions	fah see ohn
vous avez fait	feh		vous fassiez	fah see ay
ils/elles ont fait	feh		ils/elles fassent	fahs

Futur			Imparfait	
je ferai	fuh ray		je faisais	feh zeh
tu feras	fuh rah		tu faisais	feh zeh
il/elle fera	fuh rah		il/elle faisait	feh zeh
nous ferons	fuh rohn		nous faisions	feh zee ohn
vous ferez	fuh ray		vous faisiez	feh zee ay
ils/elles feront	fuh rohn		ils/elles faisaient	feh zeh

Impératif			Participe présent	
fais !	feh		faisant	feh zawn
faisons !	feh zohn			
faites !	feht		Participe passé	
			fait	feh

Here is a list of all the verbs in this book that follow the same conjugation pattern.

contrefaire	(kohn truh fehr)	to counterfeit
défaire	(day fehr)	to undo
refaire	(ruh fehr)	to redo / to remake
satisfaire	(sah tees fehr)	to satisfy
surfaire	(sew fehr)	to overrate

A38

FALLOIR (fahl wahr)
to be necessary / to need

Présent		Conditionnel	
il faut	foh	il faudrait	foh dreh
Passe composé		Subjonctif	
il a fallu	fah lew	il faille	fah yee
Futur		Imparfait	
il faudra	foh drah	il fallait	fah leh

Falloir is the only verb in this book that follows this conjugation pattern.

A39

FUIR (fweer)
to flee

Présent		Conditionnel	
je fuis	fwee	je fuirais	fweer eh
tu fuis	fwee	tu fuirais	fweer eh
elle/il fuit	fwee	elle/il fuirait	fweer eh
nous fuyons	fwee yohn	nous fuirions	fweer ee ohn
vous fuyez	fwee yay	vous fuiriez	fweer ee ay
elles/ils fuient	fwee	elles/ils fuiraient	fweer eh

Passe composé		Subjonctif	
j'ai fui	fwee	je fuie	fwee
tu as fui	fwee	tu fuies	fwee
elle/il a fui	fwee	elle/il fuie	fwee
nous avons fui	fwee	nous fuyions	fwee yee ohn
vous avez fui	fwee	vous fuyiez	fwee yee ay
elles/ils ont fui	fwee	elles/ils fuient	fwee

Futur		Imparfait	
je fuirai	fweer ay	je fuyais	fwee yeh
tu fuiras	fweer ah	tu fuyais	fwee yeh
elle/il fuira	fweer ah	elle/il fuyait	fwee yeh
nous fuirons	fweer ohn	nous fuyions	fwee yee ohn
vous fuirez	fweer ay	vous fuyiez	fwee yee ay
elles/ils fuiront	fweer ohn	elles/ils fuyaient	fwee yeh

Impératif		Participe présent	
fuis !	fwee	fuyant	fwee yawn
fuyons !	fwee yohn		
fuyez !	fwee yay	Participe passé	
		fui	fwee

Here is the other verb in this book that follows the same conjugation pattern.

enfuir (s') (awn fwee eer) to run away

A40

HAïR (ah eer)
to hate

Présent	
je hais	eh
tu hais	eh
il/elle hait	eh
nous haïssons	ah ee sohn
vous haïssez	ah ee say
ils/elles haïssent	ah ees

Passe composé	
j'ai haï	ah ee
tu as haï	ah ee
il/elle a haï	ah ee
nous avons haï	ah ee
vous avez haï	ah ee
ils/elles ont haï	ah ee

Futur	
je haïrai	ah eer ay
tu haïras	ah eer ah
il/elle haïra	ah eer ah
nous haïrons	ah eer ohn
vous haïrez	ah eer ay
ils/elles haïront	ah eer ohn

Impératif	
hais !	eh
haïssons !	ah ee sohn
haïssez !	ah ee say

Conditionnel	
je haïrais	ah eer eh
tu haïrais	ah eer eh
il/elle haïrait	ah eer eh
nous haïrions	ah eer ee ohn
vous haïriez	ah eer ee ay
ils/elles haïraient	ah eer eh

Subjonctif	
je haïsse	ah ees
tu haïsses	ah ees
il/elle haïsse	ah ees
nous haïssions	ah ee see ohn
vous haïssiez	ah ee see ay
ils/elles haïssent	ah ees

Imparfait	
je haïssais	ah ee seh
tu haïssais	ah ee seh
il/elle haïssait	ah ee seh
nous haïssions	ah ee see ohn
vous haïssiez	ah ee see ay
ils/elles haïssaient	ah ee seh

Participe présent	
haïssant	ah ee sawn

Participe passé	
haï	ah ee

Haïr is the only verb in this book that follows this conjugation pattern.

A41

INCLURE (ahn klewr)
to include

Présent		Conditionnel	
j'inclus	ahn klew	j'inclurais	ahn klewr eh
tu inclus	ahn klew	tu inclurais	ahn klewr eh
elle/il inclut	ahn klew	elle/il inclurait	ahn klewr eh
nous incluons	ahn klew ohn	nous inclurions	ahn klewr ee ohn
vous incluez	ahn klew ay	vous incluriez	ahn klewr ee ay
elles/ils incluent	ahn klew	elles/ils incluraient	ahn klewr eh
Passe composé		Subjonctif	
j'ai inclus	ahn klew	j'inclue	ahn klew
tu as inclus	ahn klew	tu inclues	ahn klew
elle/il a inclus	ahn klew	elle/il inclue	ahn klew
nous avons inclus	ahn klew	nous incluions	ahn klew ee ohn
vous avez inclus	ahn klew	vous incluiez	ahn klew ee ay
elles/ils ont inclus	ahn klew	elles/ils incluent	ahn klew
Futur		Imparfait	
j'inclurai	ahn klewr ay	j'incluais	ahn klew eh
tu incluras	ahn klewr ah	tu incluais	ahn klew eh
elle/il inclura	ahn klewr ah	elle/il incluait	ahn klew eh
nous inclurons	ahn klewr ohn	nous incluions	ahn klew ee ohn
vous inclurez	ahn klewr ay	vous incluiez	ahn klew ee ay
elles/ils incluront	ahn klewr ohn	elles/ils incluaient	ahn klew eh
Impératif		Participe présent	
inclus !	ahn klew	incluant	ahn klew awn
incluons !	ahn klew ohn		
incluez !	ahn klew ay	Participe passé	
		inclus	ahn klew

Here is a list of all the verbs in this book that follow the same conjugation pattern.

conclure	(kohn klewr)	to conclude
exclure	(eks klewr)	to exclude

A42

INTERDIRE (ahn tehr deer)
to forbid

Présent
j'interdis	ahn tehr dee
tu interdis	ahn tehr dee
elle/il interdit	ahn tehr dee
nous interdisons	ahn tehr dee zohn
vous interdisez	ahn tehr dee zay
elles/ils interdisent	ahn tehr deez

Passe composé
j'ai interdit	ahn tehr dee
tu as interdit	ahn tehr dee
elle/il a interdit	ahn tehr dee
nous avons interdit	ahn tehr dee
vous avez interdit	ahn tehr dee
elles/ils ont interdit	ahn tehr dee

Futur
j'interdirai	ahn tehr deer ay
tu interdiras	ahn tehr deer ah
elle/il interdira	ahn tehr deer ah
nous interdirons	ahn tehr deer ohn
vous interdirez	ahn tehr deer ay
elles/ils interdiront	ahn tehr deer ohn

Impératif
interdis !	ahn tehr dee
interdisons !	ahn tehr dee zohn
interdisez !	ahn tehr dee zay

Conditionnel
j'interdirais	ahn tehr deer eh
tu interdirais	ahn tehr deer eh
elle/il interdirait	ahn tehr deer eh
nous interdirions	ahn tehr deer ee ohn
vous interdiriez	ahn tehr deer ee ay
elles/ils interdiraient	ahn tehr deer eh

Subjonctif
j'interdise	ahn tehr deez
tu interdises	ahn tehr deez
elle/il interdise	ahn tehr deez
nous interdisions	ahn tehr dee zee ohn
vous interdisiez	ahn tehr dee zee ay
elles/ils interdisent	ahn tehr deez

Imparfait
j'interdisais	ahn tehr dee zeh
tu interdisais	ahn tehr dee zeh
elle/il interdisait	ahn tehr dee zeh
nous interdisions	ahn tehr dee zee ohn
vous interdisiez	ahn tehr dee zee ay
elles/ils interdisaient	ahn tehr dee zeh

Participe présent
interdisant   ahn tehr dee zawn

Participe passé
interdit   ahn tehr dee

Interdire is the only verb in this book that follows this conjugation pattern.

A43

JETER (zhuh tay)
to throw

Présent		Conditionnel	
je jette	zhehtt	je jetterais	zheht tuh reh
tu jettes	zhehtt	tu jetterais	zheht tuh reh
elle/il jette	zhehtt	elle/il jetterait	zheht tuh reh
nous jetons	zhuh tohn	nous jetterions	zheht tuh ree ohn
vous jetez	zhuh tay	vous jetteriez	zheht tuh ree ay
elles/ils jettent	zhehtt	elles/ils jetteraient	zheht tuh reh

Passe composé		Subjonctif	
j'ai jeté	zhuh tay	je jette	zhehtt
tu as jeté	zhuh tay	tu jettes	zhehtt
elle/il a jeté	zhuh tay	elle/il jette	zhehtt
nous avons jeté	zhuh tay	nous jetions	zhuh tee ohn
vous avez jeté	zhuh tay	vous jetiez	zhuh tee ay
elles/ils ont jeté	zhuh tay	elles/ils jettent	zhehtt

Futur		Imparfait	
je jetterai	zheht tuh ray	je jetais	zhuh teh
tu jetteras	zheht tuh rah	tu jetais	zhuh teh
elle/il jettera	zheht tuh rah	elle/il jetait	zhuh teh
nous jetterons	zheht tuh rohn	nous jetions	zhuh tee ohn
vous jetterez	zheht tuh ray	vous jetiez	zhuh tee ay
elles/ils jetteront	zheht tuh rohn	elles/ils jetaient	zhuh teh

Impératif		Participe présent	
jette !	zhehtt	jetant	zhuh tawn
jetons !	zhuh tohn		
jetez !	zhuh tay	Participe passé	
		jeté	zhuh tay

Here is a list of all the verbs in this book that follow the same conjugation pattern.

becqueter	(behk tay)	to peck at / to eat
breveter	(bruh vtay)	to patent
déchiqueter	(day sheek tay)	to shred
déjeter	(day zhuh tay)	to warp
dépaqueter	(day pahk tay)	to unpack
étiqueter	(ay teek tay)	to label
feuilleter	(fuhy tay)	to leaf through
hoqueter	(awk tay)	to hiccup
projeter	(praw zhuh tay)	to plan / project
rejeter	(ruh htay)	to reject

© 2010

A44

LEVER (leh vay)
to lift

Présent		Conditionnel	
je lève	lehv	je lèverais	leh vuhr eh
tu lèves	lehv	tu lèverais	leh vuhr eh
il/elle lève	lehv	il/elle lèverait	leh vuhr eh
nous levons	luh vohn	nous lèverions	leh vuhr ee ohn
vous levez	luh vay	vous lèveriez	leh vuhr ee ay
ils/elles lèvent	lehv	ils/elles lèveraient	leh vuhr eh

Passe composé		Subjonctif	
j'ai levé	luh vay	je lève	lehv
tu as levé	luh vay	tu lèves	lehv
il/elle a levé	luh vay	il/elle lève	lehv
nous avons levé	luh vay	nous levions	luh vee ohn
vous avez levé	luh vay	vous leviez	luh vee ay
ils/elles ont levé	luh vay	ils/elles lèvent	lehv

Futur		Imparfait	
je lèverai	leh vuhr ay	je levais	luh veh
tu lèveras	leh vuhr ah	tu levais	luh veh
il/elle lèvera	leh vuhr ah	il/elle levait	luh veh
nous lèverons	leh vuhr ohn	nous levions	luh vee ohn
vous lèverez	leh vuhr ay	vous leviez	luh vee ay
ils/elles lèveront	leh vuhr ohn	ils/elles levaient	luh veh

Impératif		Participe présent	
lève !	lehv	levant	luh vawn
levons !	luh vohn		
levez !	luh vay	Participe passé	
		levé	luh vay

Here is a list of all the verbs in this book that follow the same conjugation pattern.

acheter	(ash tay)	to buy
achever	(ah shvay)	to complete
amener	(ahm nay)	to bring
celer	(suh lay)	to conceal
ciseler	(see zlay)	to chisel
congeler	(kohn zlay)	to freeze
crever	(kruh vay)	to burst

A44

crocheter	(krawsh tay)	to crochet
déceler	(day slay)	to detect
dégeler	(day zhlay)	to thaw
démanteler	(day mawn tlay)	to dismantle
démener (se)	(day muh nay)	to thrash about
élever	(ay lvay)	to raise
emmener	(awn mnay)	to take away
enlever	(awn lvay)	to remove
fileter	(fee l tay)	to thread
geler	(zhuh lay)	to freeze
haleter	(ahl tay)	to gasp for breath
harceler	(ahr suh lay)	to pester
malmener	(mahl muh nay)	to manhandle
marteler	(mahr tuh lay)	to hammer
mener	(muh nay)	to lead
modeler	(mawd lay)	to model
parachever	(pah rah shvay)	to perfect / to complete
peler	(puh lay)	to peel
peser	(puh zay)	to weigh / to consider
prélever	(pray lvay)	to take a sample of / to deduct
promener	(praw mnay)	to take for a walk
racheter	(rash tay)	to buy back
ramener	(rah mnay)	to bring back
receler	(ruh slay)	to conceal
relever	(ruh lvay)	to raise / to pick up
remmener	(rawn mnay)	to take (sth) back
semer	(suh may)	to sow
soulever	(soo lvay)	to lift
soupeser	(soo puh zay)	to weigh up
surgeler	(sewr zhuh lay)	to deep-freeze

A45

LIRE (leer)
to read

Présent		Conditionnel	
je lis	lee	je lirais	leer eh
tu lis	lee	tu lirais	leer eh
il/elle lit	lee	il/elle lirait	leer eh
nous lisons	lee zohn	nous lirions	leer ee ohn
vous lisez	lee zay	vous liriez	leer ee ay
ils/elles lisent	leez	ils/elles liraient	leer eh

Passe composé		Subjonctif	
j'ai lu	lew	je lise	leez
tu as lu	lew	tu lises	leez
il/elle a lu	lew	il/elle lise	leez
nous avons lu	lew	nous lisions	leez ee ohn
vous avez lu	lew	vous lisiez	leez ee ay
ils/elles ont lu	lew	ils/elles lisent	leez

Futur		Imparfait	
je lirai	leer ay	je lisais	lee zeh
tu liras	leer ah	tu lisais	lee zeh
il/elle lira	leer ah	il/elle lisait	lee zeh
nous lirons	leer ohn	nous lisions	lee zee ohn
vous lirez	leer ay	vous lisiez	lee zee ay
ils/elles liront	leer ohn	ils/elles lisaient	lee zeh

Impératif		Participe présent	
lis !	lee	lisant	lee zawn
lisons !	lee zohn		
lisez !	lee zay	Participe passé	
		lu	lew

Here is a list of all the verbs in this book that follow the same conjugation pattern.

| élire | (ay leer) | to elect |
| relire | (ruh leer) | to reread / to proofread |

A46

MANGER (mawn zhay)
to eat

Présent
je mange — mawnzh
tu manges — mawnzh
il/elle mange — mawnzh
nous mangeons — mawn zhohn
vous mangez — mawn zhay
ils/elles mangent — mawnzh

Conditionnel
je mangerais — mawn zhuh reh
tu mangerais — mawn zhuh reh
il/elle mangerait — mawn zhuh reh
nous mangerions — mawn zhuh ree ohn
vous mangeriez — mawn zhuh ree ay
ils/elles mangeraient — mawn zhuh reh

Passe composé
j'ai mangé — mawn zhay
tu as mangé — mawn zhay
il/elle a mangé — mawn zhay
nous avons mangé — mawn zhay
vous avez mangé — mawn zhay
ils/elles ont mangé — mawn zhay

Subjonctif
je mange — mawnzh
tu manges — mawnzh
il/elle mange — mawnzh
nous mangions — mawnzh ee ohn
vous mangiez — mawnzh ee ay
ils/elles mangent — mawnzh

Futur
je mangerai — mawn zhuh ray
tu mangeras — mawn zhuh rah
il/elle mangera — mawn zhuh rah
nous mangerons — mawn zhuh rohn
vous mangerez — mawn zhuh ray
ils/elles mangeront — mawn zhuh rohn

Imparfait
je mangeais — mawn zheh
tu mangeais — mawn zheh
il/elle mangeait — mawn zheh
nous mangions — mawn zhee ohn
vous mangiez — mawn zhee ay
ils/elles mangeaient — mawn zheh

Impératif
mange ! — mawnzh
mangeons ! — mawn zhohn
mangez ! — mawn zhay

Participe présent
mangeant — mawn zhawn

Participe passé
mangé — mawn zhay

Here is a list of all the verbs in this book that follow the same conjugation pattern.

abroger	(ah braw zhay)	to repeal
affliger	(ah flee zhay)	to afflict
allonger	(ah lohn zhay)	to lay down
aménager	(ah may nah zhay)	to organize
arranger	(ah rawn zhay)	to arrange
avantager	(ah vawn tah zhay)	to favour
bouger	(boo zhay)	to move
changer	(shawn zhay)	to change
charger	(shahr zhay)	to load

A46

corriger	(kaw ree zhay)	to correct
décharger	(day shahr zhay)	to unload
décourager	(day koo rah zhay)	to discourage
dédommager	(day daw mah zhay)	to compensate
dégager	(day gah zhay)	to free
déloger	(day law zhay)	to evict
déménager	(daymay nah zhay)	to relocate
départager	(day pahr tah zhay)	to decide between
déranger	(day rawn zhay)	to disturb
déroger	(day raw zhay)	to infringe
désavantager	(day zah vawn tah zhay)	to disadvantage
diriger	(dee ree zhay)	to direct/to manage
échanger	(ay shawn zhay)	to exchange
égorger	(ay gawr zhay)	to slit the throat of
émerger	(ay mehr zhay)	to emerge
emménager	(awn may nah zhay)	to move in
encourager	(awn koo rah zhay)	to encourage
endommager	(awn daw mah zhay)	to damage
engager	(awn gah zhay)	to hire/to engage
enneiger	(awn neh zhey)	to block with snow
enrager	(awn rah zhay)	to be furious
envisager	(awn vee zah zhay)	to envisage
éponger	(ay pohn zhay)	to mop up
exiger	(eg zee zhay)	to demand
figer	(fee zhay)	to congeal
forger	(fawr zhay)	to forge
héberger	(ay behr zhay)	to accommodate
infliger	(ahn flee zhay)	to inflict
insurger (s')	(ahn sewr zhay)	to rise up against
interroger	(ahn tehr raw zhay)	to interrogate
juger	(zhew zhay)	to judge
loger	(law zhay)	to house
mélanger	(may lawn zhay)	to blend
ménager	(may nah zhay)	to handle carefully
nager	(nah zhay)	to swim
négliger	(nay glee zhay)	to neglect
neiger	(neh zhay)	to snow
obliger	(aw blee zhay)	to force/to oblige
outrager	(oot rah zhay)	to offend/to outrage
partager	(pahr tah zhay)	to share
plonger	(plohn zhay)	to dive/to plunge
préjuger	(pray zhew zhay)	to prejudge
prolonger	(praw lohn zhay)	to prolong
rallonger	(rah lohn zhay)	to lengthen
rédiger	(ray dee zhay)	to write up/to draft
ronger	(rohn zhay)	to gnaw
saccager	(sah kah zhay)	to wreck
songer	(sohn zhay)	to think/to daydream
soulager	(soo lah zhay)	to relieve
submerger	(sewb mehr zhay)	to submerge
surcharger	(sewr shahr zhay)	to overload
vendanger	(vawn dawn zhay)	to harvest the grapes
venger	(vawn zhay)	to avenge
voyager	(vwah yah zhay)	to travel

A47

MAUDIRE (moh deer)
to curse

Présent	
je maudis	moh dee
tu maudis	moh dee
elle/il maudit	moh dee
nous maudissons	moh dee sohn
vous maudissez	moh dee say
elles/ils maudissent	moh dees

Passe composé	
j'ai maudit	moh dee
tu as maudit	moh dee
elle/il a maudit	moh dee
nous avons maudit	moh dee
vous avez maudit	moh dee
elles/ils ont maudit	moh dee

Futur	
je maudirai	moh deer ay
tu maudiras	moh deer ah
elle/il maudira	moh deer ah
nous maudirons	moh deer ohn
vous maudirez	moh deer ay
elles/ils maudiront	moh deer ohn

Impératif	
maudis !	moh dee
maudissons !	moh dee sohn
maudissez !	moh dee say

Conditionnel	
je maudirais	moh deer eh
tu maudirais	moh deer eh
elle/il maudirait	moh deer eh
nous maudirions	moh deer ee ohn
vous maudiriez	moh deer ee ay
elles/ils maudiraient	moh deer eh

Subjonctif	
je maudisse	moh dees
tu maudisses	moh dees
elle/il maudisse	moh dees
nous maudissions	moh dee see ohn
vous maudissiez	moh dee see ay
elles/ils maudissent	moh dees

Imparfait	
je maudissais	moh dee seh
tu maudissais	moh dee seh
elle/il maudissait	moh dee seh
nous maudissions	moh dee see ohn
vous maudissiez	moh dee see ay
elles/ils maudissaient	moh dee seh

Participe présent
maudissant   moh dee sawn

Participe passé
maudit   moh dee

Maudire is the only verb in this book that follows this conjugation pattern.

A48

METTRE (meh truh)
to put

Présent
je mets	meh
tu mets	meh
elle/il met	meh
nous mettons	meh tohn
vous mettez	meh tay
elles/ils mettent	meht

Passe composé
j'ai mis	mee
tu as mis	mee
elle/il a mis	mee
nous avons mis	mee
vous avez mis	mee
elles/ils ont mis	mee

Futur
je mettrai	meh tray
tu mettras	meh trah
elle/il mettra	meh trah
nous mettrons	meh trohn
vous mettrez	meh tray
elles/ils mettront	meh trohn

Impératif
mets !	meh
mettons !	meh tohn
mettez !	meh tay

Conditionnel
je mettrais	meh treh
tu mettrais	meh treh
elle/il mettrait	meh treh
nous mettrions	meh tree ohn
vous mettriez	meh tree ay
elles/ils mettraient	meh treh

Subjonctif
je mette	meht
tu mettes	meht
elle/il mette	meht
nous mettions	meh tee ohn
vous mettiez	meh tee ay
elles/ils mettent	meht

Imparfait
je mettais	meh teh
tu mettais	meh teh
elle/il mettait	meh teh
nous mettions	meh tee ohn
vous mettiez	meh tee ay
elles/ils mettaient	meh teh

Participe présent
mettant	meh tawn

Participe passé
mis	mee

Here is a list of all the verbs in this book that follow the same conjugation pattern.

admettre	(ahd meh truh)	to admit
commettre	(kaw meh truh)	to commit
compromettre	(kohn praw meh truh)	to compromise
démettre	(day meh truh)	to dislocate / to dismiss
émettre	(ay meh truh)	to emit
entremettre (s`)	(awn truh meh truh)	to mediate
omettre	(aw meh truh)	to omit
permettre	(pehr meh truh)	to permit
promettre	(praw meh truh)	to promise
remettre	(ruh meh truh)	to put back
retransmettre	(ruh trawns meh truh)	to broadcast
soumettre	(soo meh truh)	to subdue / to subject
transmettre	(trawns meh truh)	to convey / to transit

A49

MOUDRE (moo druh)
to grind

Présent			Conditionnel	
je mouds	moo		je moudrais	moo dreh
tu mouds	moo		tu moudrais	moo dreh
il/elle moud	moo		il/elle moudrait	moo dreh
nous moulons	moo lohn		nous moudrions	moo dree ohn
vous moulez	moo lay		vous moudriez	moo dree ay
ils/elles moulent	mool		ils/elles moudraient	moo dreh

Passé composé			Subjonctif	
j'ai moulu	moo lew		je moule	mool
tu as moulu	moo lew		tu moules	mool
il/elle a moulu	moo lew		il/elle moule	mool
nous avons moulu	moo lew		nous moulions	moo lee ohn
vous avez moulu	moo lew		vous mouliez	moo lee ay
ils/elles ont moulu	moo lew		ils/elles moulent	mool

Futur			Imparfait	
je moudrai	moo dray		je moulais	moo leh
tu moudras	moo drah		tu moulais	moo leh
il/elle moudra	moo drah		il/elle moulait	moo leh
nous moudrons	moo drohn		nous moulions	moo lee ohn
vous moudrez	moo dray		vous mouliez	moo lee ay
ils/elles moudront	moo drohn		ils/elles moulaient	moo leh

Impératif			Participe présent	
mouds !	moo		moulant	moo lawn
moulons !	moo lohn			
moulez !	moo lay		Participe passé	
			moulu	moo lew

Moudre is the only verb in this book that follows this conjugation pattern.

A50

MOURIR (moo reer)
to die

Présent
je meurs	muhr
tu meurs	muhr
elle/il meurt	muhr
nous mourons	moo rohn
vous mourez	moo ray
elles/ils meurent	muhr

Passe composé
je suis mort/-(e)	mawr(t)
tu es mort/-(e)	mawr(t)
il/elle est mort/-(e)	mawr(t)
nous sommes mort/-(s)(es)	mawr(t)
vous êtes morts/-(e)(es)	mawr(t)
ils/elles sont morts/-(es)	mawr(t)

Futur
je mourrai	moor ray
tu mourras	moor rah
elle/il mourra	moor rah
nous mourrons	moor rohn
vous mourrez	moor ray
elles/ils mourront	moor rohn

Impératif
meurs !	muhr
mourons !	moo rohn
mourez !	moo ray

Conditionnel
je mourrais	moor reh
tu mourrais	moor reh
elle/il mourrait	moor reh
nous mourrions	moor ree ohn
vous mourriez	moor ree ay
elles/ils mourraient	moor reh

Subjonctif
je meure	muhr
tu meures	muhr
elle/il meure	muhr
nous mourions	muhr ee ohn
vous mouriez	muhr ee ay
elles/ils meurent	muhr

Imparfait
je mourais	moo reh
tu mourais	moo reh
elle/il mourait	moo reh
nous mourions	moo ree ohn
vous mouriez	moo ree ay
elles/ils mouraient	moo reh

Participe présent
mourant	moo rawn

Participe passé
mort	mawr(t)

Mourir is the only verb in this book that follows this conjugation pattern.

A51

NAÎTRE (neh truh)
to be born

Présent	
je nais	neh
tu nais	neh
elle/il naît	neh
nous naissons	neh sohn
vous naissez	neh say
elles/ils naissent	nehs

Conditionnel	
je naîtrais	neht reh
tu naîtrais	neht reh
elle/il naîtrait	neht reh
nous naîtrions	neht ree ohn
vous naîtriez	neht ree ay
elles/ils naîtraient	neht reh

Passe composé	
je suis né/-(e)	nay
tu es né/-(e)	nay
il/elle est né/-(e)	nay
nous sommes nés/-(es)	nay
vous êtes né/-(e)(s) (es)	nay
ils/elles sont nés/-(es)	nay

Subjonctif	
je naisse	nehs
tu naisses	nehs
elle/il naisse	nehs
nous naissions	nehs ee ohn
vous naissiez	nehs ee ay
elles/ils naissent	nehs

Futur	
je naîtrai	neht ray
tu naîtras	neht rah
elle/il naîtra	neht rah
nous naîtrons	neht rohn
vous naîtrez	neht ray
elles/ils naîtront	neht rohn

Imparfait	
je naissais	nehs eh
tu naissais	nehs eh
elle/il naissait	nehs eh
nous naissions	nehs ee ohn
vous naissiez	nehs ee ay
elles/ils naissaient	nehs eh

Impératif	
nais !	neh
naissons !	neh sohn
naissez !	neh say

Participe présent	
naissant	neh sawn

Participe passé	
né	nay

Here is the other verb in this book that follows the same conjugation pattern.

renaître   (reh neh truh)   to come back to life

A52

OUVRIR (oov reer)
to open

Présent		Conditionnel	
j'ouvre	oo vruh	j'ouvrirais	oo vreer eh
tu ouvres	oo vruh	tu ouvrirais	oo vreer eh
il/elle ouvre	oo vruh	il/elle ouvrirait	oo vreer eh
nous ouvrons	oo vrohn	nous ouvririons	oo vreer ee ohn
vous ouvrez	oo vray	vous ouvririez	oo vreer ee ay
ils/elles ouvrent	oo vruh	ils/elles ouvriraient	oo vreer eh

Passe composé		Subjonctif	
j'ai ouvert	oo vehr	j'ouvre	oo vruh
tu as ouvert	oo vehr	tu ouvres	oo vruh
il/elle a ouvert	oo vehr	il/elle ouvre	oo vruh
nous avons ouvert	oo vehr	nous ouvrions	oo vree ohn
vous avez ouvert	oo vehr	vous ouvriez	oo vree ay
ils/elles ont ouvert	oo vehr	ils/elles ouvrent	oo vruh

Futur		Imparfait	
j'ouvrirai	oo vreer ay	j'ouvrais	oo vreh
tu ouvriras	oo vreer ah	tu ouvrais	oo vreh
il/elle ouvrira	oo vreer ah	il/elle ouvrait	oo vreh
nous ouvrirons	oo vreer ohn	nous ouvrions	oo vree ohn
vous ouvrirez	oo vreer ay	vous ouvriez	oo vree ay
ils/elles ouvriront	oo vreer ohn	ils/elles ouvraient	oo vreh

Impératif		Participe présent	
ouvre !	oo vruh	ouvrant	oo vrawn
ouvrons !	oo vrohn		
ouvrez !	oo vray	Participe passé	
		ouvert	oo vehr

Here is a list of all the verbs in this book that follow the same conjugation pattern.

couvrir	(koov reer)	to cover
découvrir	(day koov reer)	to discover
entrouvrir	(awn troo vreer)	to open a little
offrir	(aw freer)	to offer
recouvrir	(ruh koov reer)	to cover / to recover
rouvrir	(roo vreer)	to reopen
souffrir	(soo freer)	to suffer

A53

PLAIRE (plehr)
to please

Présent		Conditionnel	
je plais	pleh	je plairais	plehr eh
tu plais	pleh	tu plairais	plehr eh
elle/il plaît	pleh	elle/il plairait	plehr eh
nous plaisons	pleh zohn	nous plairions	plehr ee ohn
vous plaisez	pleh zay	vous plairiez	plehr ee ay
elles/ils plaisent	plehz	elles/ils plairaient	plehr eh

Passe composé		Subjonctif	
j'ai plu	plew	je plaise	plehz
tu as plu	plew	tu plaises	plehz
elle/il a plu	plew	elle/il plaise	plehz
nous avons plu	plew	nous plaisions	pleh zee ohn
vous avez plu	plew	vous plaisiez	pleh zee ay
elles/ils ont plu	plew	elles/ils plaisent	plehz

Futur		Imparfait	
je plairai	pleh ray	je plaisais	pleh zeh
tu plairas	pleh rah	tu plaisais	pleh zeh
elle/il plaira	pleh rah	elle/il plaisait	pleh zeh
nous plairons	pleh rohn	nous plaisions	pleh zee ohn
vous plairez	pleh ray	vous plaisiez	pleh zee ay
elles/ils plairont	pleh rohn	elles/ils plaisaient	pleh zeh

Impératif		Participe présent	
plais !	pleh	plaisant	pleh zawn
plaisons !	pleh zohn		
plaisez !	pleh zay	Participe passé	
		plu	plew

Here are the verbs in this book that follows the same conjugation pattern.

| déplaire | (day plehr) | to displease |
| complaire | (kohn plehr) | to delight in |

A54

PLEUVOIR (pluh vwahr)
to rain

Présent		Conditionnel	
il pleut	pluh	il pleuvrait	pluh vreh
Passé composé		Subjonctif	
il a plu	plew	il pleuvrait	pluh vreh
Futur		Imparfait	
il pleuvra	pluh vrah	il pleuvait	pluh veh
		Participe présent	
		pleuvant pluh vawn	
		Participe passé	
		plu plew	

Pleuvoir is the only verb in this book that follows this conjugation pattern.

A55

PUOVOIR (poo vwahr)
to be able to (can)

Présent	
je peux	puh
tu peux	puh
elle/il peut	puh
nous pouvons	poo vohn
vous pouvez	poo vay
elles/ils peuvent	puhv

Conditionnel	
je pourrais	poor eh
tu pourrais	poor eh
elle/il pourrait	poor eh
nous pourrions	poor ee ohn
vous pourriez	poor ee ay
elles/ils pourraient	poor eh

Passe composé	
j'ai pu	pew
tu as pu	pew
elle/il a pu	pew
nous avons pu	pew
vous avez pu	pew
elles/ils ont pu	pew

Subjonctif	
je puisse	pwees
tu puisses	pwees
elle/il puisse	pwees
nous puissions	pwee see ohn
vous puissiez	pwee see ay
elles/ils puissent	pwees

Futur	
je pourrai	poor ay
tu pourras	poor ah
elle/il pourra	poor ah
nous pourrons	poor ohn
vous pourrez	poor ay
elles/ils pourront	poor ohn

Imparfait	
je pouvais	poo veh
tu pouvais	poo veh
elle/il pouvait	poo veh
nous pouvions	poo vee ohn
vous pouviez	poo vee ay
elles/ils pouvaient	poo veh

Participe présent
pouvant   poo vawn

Participe passé
pu   pew

Pouvoir is the only verb in this book that follows this conjugation pattern.

© 2010

A56

PRÉVALOIR (pray vah lwahr)
to prevail

Présent		
je prévaux	pray voh	
tu prévaux	pray voh	
il/elle prévaut	pray voh	
nous prévalons	pray vah lohn	
vous prévalez	pray vah lay	
ils/elles prévalent	pray vahl	

Conditionnel	
je prévaudrais	pray voh dreh
tu prévaudrais	pray voh dreh
il/elle prévaudrait	pray voh dreh
nous prévaudrions	pray voh dree ohn
vous prévaudriez	pray voh dree ay
ils/elles prévaudraient	pray voh dreh

Passe composé	
j'ai prévalu	pray vah lew
tu as prévalu	pray vah lew
il/elle a prévalu	pray vah lew
nous avons prévalu	pray vah lew
vous avez prévalu	pray vah lew
ils/elles ont prévalu	pray vah lew

Subjonctif	
je prévaille	pray vah yee
tu prévailles	pray vah yee
il/elle prévaille	pray vah yee
nous prévalions	pray vah lee ohn
vous prévaliez	pray vah lee ay
ils/elles prévaillent	pray vah yee

Futur	
je prévaudrai	pray voh dray
tu prévaudras	pray voh drah
il/elle prévaudra	pray voh drah
nous prévaudrons	pray voh drohn
vous prévaudrez	pray voh dray
ils/elles prévaudront	pray voh drohn

Imparfait	
je prévalais	pray vah leh
tu prévalais	pray vah leh
il/elle prévalait	pray vah leh
nous prévalions	pray vah lee ohn
vous prévaliez	pray vah lee ay
ils/elles prévalaient	pray vah leh

Impératif	
prévaux !	pray voh
prévalons !	pray vah lohn
prévalez !	pray vah lay

Participe présent	
prévalant	pray vah lawn

Participe passé	
prévalu	pray vah lew

Here is a list of all the verbs in this book that follow the same conjugation pattern.

équivaloir	(ay kee vah lwahr)	to be equivalent to
revaloir	(ruh vah lwahr)	to pay back / to get even
valoir	(vah lwahr)	to be worth

A57

PROTÉGER (praw tay zhay)
to protect

Présent		Conditionnel	
je protège	praw tehzh	je protégerais	praw tay zhuh reh
tu protèges	praw tehzh	tu protégerais	praw tay zhuh reh
elle/il protège	praw tehzh	elle/il protégerait	praw tay zhuh reh
nous protégeons	praw tay zhohn	nous protégerions	praw tay zhuh ree ohn
vous protégez	praw tay zhay	vous protégeriez	praw tay zhuh ree ay
elles/ils protègent	praw tehzh	elles/ils protégeraient	praw tay zhuh reh

Passe composé		Subjonctif	
j'ai protégé	praw tay zhay	je protège	praw tehzh
tu as protégé	praw tay zhay	tu protèges	praw tehzh
elle/il a protégé	praw tay zhay	elle/il protège	praw tehzh
nous avons protégé	praw tay zhay	nous protégions	praw tay zhee ohn
vous avez protégé	praw tay zhay	vous protégiez	praw tay zhee ay
elles/ils ont protégé	praw tay zhay	elles/ils protègent	praw tehzh

Futur		Imparfait	
je protégerai	praw tay zhuh ray	je protégeais	praw tay zheh
tu protégeras	praw tay zhuh rah	tu protégeais	praw tay zheh
elle/il protégera	praw tay zhuh rah	elle/il protégeait	praw tay zheh
nous protégerons	praw tay zhuh rohn	nous protégions	praw tay zhee ohn
vous protégerez	praw tay zhuh ray	vous protégiez	praw tay zhee ay
elles/ils protégeront	praw tay zhuh rohn	elles/ils protégeaient	praw tay zheh

Impératif		Participe présent	
protège !	praw tehzh	protégeant	praw tay zhawn
protégeons !	praw tay zhohn		
protégez !	praw tay zhay	Participe passé	
		protégé	praw tay zhay

Here is a list of all the verbs in this book that follow the same conjugation pattern.

abréger	(ah bray zhay)	to shorten
alléger	(ah lay zhay)	to reduce
assiéger	(ah syay zhay)	to besiege
désagréger	(day zah gray zhay)	to disintegrate
piéger	(pyay zhay)	to trap
siéger	(syay zhay)	to sit

A58

RIRE (reer)
to laugh

Présent		Conditionnel	
je ris	ree	je rirais	reer eh
tu ris	ree	tu rirais	reer eh
elle/il rit	ree	elle/il rirait	reer eh
nous rions	ree ohn	nous ririons	reer ee ohn
vous riez	ree ay	vous ririez	reer ee ay
elles/ils rient	ree	elles/ils riraient	reer eh

Passe composé		Subjonctif	
j'ai ri	ree	je rie	ree
tu as ri	ree	tu ries	ree
elle/il a ri	ree	elle/il rie	ree
nous avons ri	ree	nous riions	ree ee ohn
vous avez ri	ree	vous riiez	ree ee ay
elles/ils ont ri	ree	elles/ils rient	ree

Futur		Imparfait	
je rirai	reer ay	je riais	ree eh
tu riras	reer ah	tu riais	ree eh
elle/il rira	reer ah	elle/il riait	ree eh
nous rirons	reer ohn	nous riions	ree ee ohn
vous rirez	reer ay	vous riiez	ree ee ay
elles/ils riront	reer ohn	elles/ils riaient	ree eh

Impératif		Participe présent	
ris !	ree	riant	ree awn
rions !	ree ohn		
riez !	ree ay	Participe passé	
		ri	ree

Here is the other verb in this book that follows the same conjugation pattern.

sourire   (soo reer)   to smile

A59

SAVOIR (sah vwahr)
to know

Présent			Conditionnel	
je sais	seh		je saurais	soh reh
tu sais	seh		tu saurais	soh reh
il/elle sait	seh		il/elle saurait	soh reh
nous savons	sah vohn		nous saurions	soh ree ohn
vous savez	sah vay		vous sauriez	soh ree ay
ils/elles savent	sahv		ils/elles sauraient	soh reh

Passe composé			Subjonctif	
j'ai su	sew		je sache	sahsh
tu as su	sew		tu saches	sahsh
il/elle a su	sew		il/elle sache	sahsh
nous avons su	sew		nous sachions	sah shee ohn
vous avez su	sew		vous sachiez	sah shee ay
ils/elles ont su	sew		ils/elles sachent	sahsh

Futur			Imparfait	
je saurai	soh ray		je savais	sah veh
tu sauras	soh rah		tu savais	sah veh
il/elle saura	soh rah		il/elle savait	sah veh
nous saurons	soh rohn		nous savions	sah vee ohn
vous saurez	soh ray		vous saviez	sah vee ay
ils/elles sauront	soh rohn		ils/elles savaient	sah veh

Impératif			Participe présent	
sache !	sahsh		sachant	sah shawn
sachons !	sah shohn			
sachez !	sah shay		Participe passé	
			su	sew

Savoir is the only verb in this book that follows this conjugation pattern.

A60

SUFFIRE (sew feer)
to be enough

Présent		Conditionnel	
je suffis	sew fee	je suffirais	sew feer eh
tu suffis	sew fee	tu suffirais	sew feer eh
elle/il suffit	sew fee	elle/il suffirait	sew feer eh
nous suffisons	sew fee zohn	nous suffirions	sew feer ee ohn
vous suffisez	sew fee zay	vous suffiriez	sew feer ee ay
elles/ils suffisent	sew feez	elles/ils suffiraient	sew feer eh

Passe composé		Subjonctif	
j'ai suffi	sew fee	je suffise	sew feez
tu as suffi	sew fee	tu suffises	sew feez
elle/il a suffi	sew fee	elle/il suffise	sew feez
nous avons suffi	sew fee	nous suffisions	sew fee zee ohn
vous avez suffi	sew fee	vous suffisiez	sew fee zee ay
elles/ils ont suffi	sew fee	elles/ils suffisent	sew feez

Futur		Imparfait	
je suffirai	sew feer ay	je suffisais	sew fee zeh
tu suffiras	sew feer ah	tu suffisais	sew fee zeh
elle/il suffira	sew feer ah	elle/il suffisait	sew fee zeh
nous suffirons	sew feer ohn	nous suffisions	sew fee zee ohn
vous suffirez	sew feer ay	vous suffisiez	sew fee zee ay
elles/ils suffiront	sew feer ohn	elles/ils suffisaient	sew fee zeh

Impératif		Participe présent	
suffis !	sew fee	suffisant	sew fee zawn
suffisons !	sew fee zohn		
suffisez !	sew fee zay	Participe passé	
		suffi	sew fee

Here is a list of all the verbs in this book that follow the same conjugation pattern.

circoncire	(seer kohn seer)	to circumcise
frire	(freer)	to fry

© 2010

A61

SUIVRE (sweev ruh)
to follow

Présent		Conditionnel	
je suis	swee	je suivrais	swee vreh
tu suis	swee	tu suivrais	swee vreh
il/elle suit	swee	il/elle suivrait	swee vreh
nous suivons	swee vohn	nous suivrions	swee vree ohn
vous suivez	swee vay	vous suivriez	swee vree ay
ils/elles suivent	sweev	ils/elles suivraient	swee vreh

Passe composé		Subjonctif	
j'ai suivi	swee vee	je suive	sweev
tu as suivi	swee vee	tu suives	sweev
il/elle a suivi	swee vee	il/elle suive	sweev
nous avons suivi	swee vee	nous suivion	swee vee ohn
vous avez suivi	swee vee	vous suiviez	swee vee ay
ils/elles ont suivi	swee vee	ils/elles suivent	sweev

Futur		Imparfait	
je suivrai	swee vray	je suivais	swee veh
tu suivras	swee vrah	tu suivais	swee veh
il/elle suivra	swee vrah	il/elle suivait	swee veh
nous suivrons	swee vrohn	nous suivions	swee vee ohn
vous suivrez	swee vray	vous suiviez	swee vee ay
ils/elles suivront	swee vrohn	ils/elles suivaient	swee veh

Impératif		Participe présent	
suis !	swee	suivant	swee vawn
suivons !	swee vohn		
suivez !	swee vay	Participe passé	
		suivi	swee vee

Here is a list of all the verbs in this book that follow the same conjugation pattern.

| ensuivre (s') | (awn swee vruh) | to follow |
| poursuivre | (poor swee vruh) | to pursue |

TAIRE (se) (tehr)
to hush up / to conceal

Présent			Conditionnel	
je tais	teh		je tairais	tehr eh
tu tais	teh		tu tairais	tehr eh
elle/il taît	teh		elle/il tairait	tehr eh
nous taisons	teh zohn		nous tairions	tehr ee ohn
vous taisez	teh zay		vous tairiez	tehr ee ay
elles/ils taisent	tehz		elles/ils tairaient	tehr eh

Passe composé			Subjonctif	
j'ai tu	tew		je taise	tehz
tu as tu	tew		tu taises	tehz
elle/il a tu	tew		elle/il taise	tehz
nous avons tu	tew		nous taisions	teh zee ohn
vous avez tu	tew		vous taisiez	teh zee ay
elles/ils ont tu	tew		elles/ils taisent	tehz

Futur			Imparfait	
je tairai	tehr ay		je taisais	teh zeh
tu tairas	tehr ah		tu taisais	teh zeh
elle/il taira	tehr ah		elle/il taisait	teh zeh
nous tairons	tehr ohn		nous taisions	teh zee ohn
vous tairez	tehr ay		vous taisiez	teh zee ay
elles/ils tairont	tehr ohn		elles/ils taisaient	teh zeh

Impératif			Participe présent	
tais !	teh		taisant	teh zawn
taisons !	teh zohn			
taisez !	teh zay		Participe passé	
			tu	tew

Taire is the only verb in this book that follows this conjugation pattern.

A63

TRADUIRE (trah dweer)
to translate

Présent			Conditionnel	
je tradui<u>s</u>	trah dwee		je traduir<u>ais</u>	trah dweer eh
tu tradui<u>s</u>	trah dwee		tu traduir<u>ais</u>	trah dweer eh
il/elle tradui<u>t</u>	trah dwee		il/elle traduir<u>ait</u>	trah dweer eh
nous tradui<u>sons</u>	trah dwee zohn		nous traduir<u>ions</u>	trah dweer ee rohn
vous tradui<u>sez</u>	trah dwee zay		vous traduir<u>iez</u>	trah dweer ee ay
ils/elles tradui<u>sent</u>	trah dweez		ils/elles traduir<u>aient</u>	trah dweer eh

Passe composé			Subjonctif	
j'ai tradui<u>t</u>	trah dwee		je tradui<u>se</u>	trah dweez
tu as tradui<u>t</u>	trah dwee		tu tradui<u>ses</u>	trah dweez
il/elle a tradui<u>t</u>	trah dwee		il/elle tradui<u>se</u>	trah dweez
nous avons tradui<u>t</u>	trah dwee		nous tradui<u>sions</u>	trah dwee zee ohn
vous avez tradui<u>t</u>	trah dwee		vous tradui<u>siez</u>	trah dwee zee ay
ils/elles ont tradui<u>t</u>	trah dwee		ils/elles tradui<u>sent</u>	trah dweez

Futur			Imparfait	
je traduir<u>ai</u>	trah dweer ay		je tradui<u>sais</u>	trah dwee zeh
tu traduir<u>as</u>	trah dweer ah		tu tradui<u>sais</u>	trah dwee zeh
il/elle traduir<u>a</u>	trah dweer ah		il/elle tradui<u>sait</u>	trah dwee zeh
nous traduir<u>ons</u>	trah dweer ohn		nous tradui<u>sions</u>	trah dwee zee ohn
vous traduir<u>ez</u>	trah dweer ay		vous tradui<u>siez</u>	trah dwee zee ay
ils/elles traduir<u>ont</u>	trah dweer ohn		ils/elles tradui<u>saient</u>	trah dwee zeh

Impératif			Participe présent	
tradui<u>s</u> !	trah dwee		tradui<u>sant</u>	trah dwee zawn
tradui<u>sons</u> !	trah dwee zohn			
tradui<u>sez</u> !	trah dwee zay		Participe passé	
			tradui<u>t</u>	trah dwee

Here is a list of all the verbs in this book that follow the same conjugation pattern.

conduire	(kohn dweer)	to drive
construire	(kohn strweer)	to build
cuire	(kweer)	to cook
déduire	(day dweer)	to deduce
détruire	(day trweer)	to destroy
éconduire	(ay kohn dweer)	to dismiss
enduire	(awn dweer)	to coat

© 2010

A63

induire	(ahn dweer)	to lead to / to infer
instruire	(ahn strweer)	to teach
introduire	(ahn traw dweer)	to insert / to introduce
nuire	(nweer)	to harm
produire	(praw dweer)	to produce
reconduire	(ruh kohn dweer)	to see (so) out
reconstruire	(ruh kohn strweer)	to reconstruct
recuire	(ruh kweer)	to reboil / to cook a bit more
réduire	(ray dweer)	to reduce
reluire	(ruh lweer)	to shine
reproduire	(ruh praw dweer)	to reproduce
séduire	(say dweer)	to captivate / to seduce

A64

VÊTIR (veh teer)
to dress

Présent
je vêt<u>s</u>	veh
tu vêt<u>s</u>	veh
elle/il vêt	veh
nous vêt<u>ons</u>	veh tohn
vous vêt<u>ez</u>	veh tay
elles/ils vêt<u>ent</u>	veht

Conditionnel
je vêtir<u>ais</u>	veh teer eh
tu vêtir<u>ais</u>	veh teer eh
elle/il vêtir<u>ait</u>	veh teer eh
nous vêtir<u>ions</u>	veh teer ee ohn
vous vêtir<u>iez</u>	veh teer ee ay
elles/ils vêtir<u>aient</u>	veh teer eh

Passe composé
j'ai vêt<u>u</u>	veh t<u>ew</u>
tu as vêt<u>u</u>	veh t<u>ew</u>
elle/il a vêt<u>u</u>	veh t<u>ew</u>
nous avons vêt<u>u</u>	veh t<u>ew</u>
vous avez vêt<u>u</u>	veh t<u>ew</u>
elles/ils ont vêt<u>u</u>	veh t<u>ew</u>

Subjonctif
je vête	veht
tu vêt<u>es</u>	veht
elle/il vête	veht
nous vêt<u>ions</u>	veh tee ohn
vous vêt<u>iez</u>	veh tee ay
elles/ils vêt<u>ent</u>	veht

Futur
je vêtir<u>ai</u>	veh teer ay
tu vêtir<u>as</u>	veh teer ah
elle/il vêtir<u>a</u>	veh teer ah
nous vêtir<u>ons</u>	veh teer ohn
vous vêtir<u>ez</u>	veh teer ay
elles/ils vêtir<u>ont</u>	veh teer ohn

Imparfait
je vêt<u>ais</u>	veh teh
tu vêt<u>ais</u>	veh teh
elle/il vêt<u>ait</u>	veh teh
nous vêt<u>ions</u>	veh tee ohn
vous vêt<u>iez</u>	veh tee ay
elles/ils vêt<u>aient</u>	veh teh

Impératif
vêt<u>s</u> !	veh
vêt<u>ons</u> !	veh tohn
vêt<u>ez</u> !	veh tay

Participe présent
vêt<u>ant</u>	veh tawn

Participe Passé
vêt<u>u</u>	veh t<u>ew</u>

Here is a list of all the verbs in this book that follow the same conjugation pattern.

dévêtir	(day veh teer)	to undress
revêtir	(ruh veh teer)	to put on / to assume (a role / appearance)

A65

VIVRE (vee vruh)
to live

Présent			Conditionnel	
je vis	vee		je vivrais	veev reh
tu vis	vee		tu vivrais	veev reh
il/elle vit	vee		il/elle vivrait	veev reh
nous vivons	vee vohn		nous vivrions	veev ree ohn
vous vivez	vee vay		vous vivriez	veev ree ay
ils/elles vivent	veev		ils/elles vivraient	veev reh

Passe composé			Subjonctif	
j'ai vécu	vay kew		je vive	veev
tu as vécu	vay kew		tu vives	veev
il/elle a vécu	vay kew		il/elle vive	veev
nous avons vécu	vay kew		nous vivions	veev ee ohn
vous avez vécu	vay kew		vous viviez	veev ee ay
ils/elles ont vécu	vay kew		ils/elles vivent	veev

Futur			Imparfait	
je vivrai	vee vray		je vivais	vee veh
tu vivras	vee vrah		tu vivais	vee veh
il/elle vivra	vee vrah		il/elle vivait	vee veh
nous vivrons	vee vrohn		nous vivions	vee vee ohn
vous vivrez	vee vray		vous viviez	vee vee ay
ils/elles vivront	vee vrohn		ils/elles vivaient	vee veh

Impératif			Participe présent	
vis !	vee		vivant	vee vawn
vivons !	vee vohn			
vivez !	vee vay		Participe passé	
			vécu	vay kew

Here is a list of all the verbs in this book that follow the same conjugation pattern.

revivre	(ruh vee vruh)	to relive / to revive
survivre	(sewr vee vruh)	to survive

VOIR (vwahr)
to see

Présent		
je vois	vwah	
tu vois	vwah	
elle/il voit	vwah	
nous voyons	vwah yohn	
vous voyez	vwah yay	
elles/ils voient	vwah	

Conditionnel	
je verrais	veh reh
tu verrais	veh reh
elle/il verrait	veh reh
nous verrions	veh ree ohn
vous verriez	veh ree ay
elles/ils verraient	veh reh

Passe composé	
j'ai vu	vew
tu as vu	vew
elle/il a vu	vew
nous avons vu	vew
vous avez vu	vew
elles/ils ont vu	vew

Subjonctif	
je voie	vwah
tu voies	vwah
elle/il voie	vwah
nous voyions	vwah yee ohn
vous voyiez	vwah yee ay
elles/ils voient	vwah

Futur	
je verrai	veh ray
tu verras	veh rah
elle/il verra	veh rah
nous verrons	veh rohn
vous verrez	veh ray
elles/ils verront	veh rohn

Imparfait	
je voyais	vwah yeh
tu voyais	vwah yeh
elle/il voyait	vwah yeh
nous voyions	vwah yee ohn
vous voyiez	vwah yee ay
elles/ils voyaient	vwah yeh

Impératif	
vois !	vwah
voyons !	vwah yohn
voyez !	vwah yay

Participe présent
voyant   vwah yawn

Participe passé
vu   vew

Here is a list of all the verbs in this book that follow the same conjugation pattern.

entrevoir	(awn truh vwahr)	to glimpse
prévoir	(pray vwahr)	to predict
revoir	(ruh vwahr)	to see again

A67

VOULOIR (voo lwahr)
to want

Présent	
je veux	vuh
tu veux	vuh
il/elle veut	vuh
nous voulons	voo lohn
vous voulez	voo lay
ils/elles veulent	vuhl

Conditionnel	
je voudrais	voo dreh
tu voudrais	voo dreh
il/elle voudrait	voo dreh
nous voudrions	voo dree ohn
vous voudriez	voo dree ay
ils/elles voudraient	voo dreh

Passe composé	
j'ai voulu	voo lew
tu as voulu	voo lew
il/elle a voulu	voo lew
nous avons voulu	voo lew
vous avez voulu	voo lew
ils/elles ont voulu	voo lew

Subjonctif	
je veuille	vuh yee
tu veuilles	vuh yee
il/elle veuille	vuh yee
nous voulions	voo lee ohn
vous vouliez	voo lee ay
ils/elles veuillent	vuh yee

Futur	
je voudrai	voo dray
tu voudras	voo drah
il/elle voudra	voo drah
nous voudrons	voo drohn
vous voudrez	voo dray
ils/elles voudront	voo drohn

Imparfait	
je voulais	voo leh
tu voulais	voo leh
il/elle voulait	voo leh
nous voulions	voo lee ohn
vous vouliez	voo lee ay
ils/elles voulaient	voo leh

Impératif	
veuille !	vuh yee
voulons !	voo lohn
veuillez !	voo lay

Participe présent	
voulant	voo lawn

Participe passé	
voulu	voo lew

Vouloir is the only verb in this book that follows this conjugation pattern.

FRENCH TO ENGLISH VERB INDEX

FRENCH VERB	PRONUNCIATION	ENGLISH MEANING	PAGE
abaisser R	(ah bay say)	to lower	R's
abandonner R	(ah bawn daw nay)	to abandon	R's
abasourdir *	(ah bah zoor deer)	to bewilder	*'s
abattre	(ah bah truh)	to destroy	A1
abêtir *	(ah bay teer)	to make stupid	*'s
abîmer R	(ah bee may)	to damage	R's
abolir *	(ah baw leer)	to abolish	*'s
abonder R	(ah bohn day)	to abound	R's
abonner R	(ah baw nay)	to subscribe	R's
aborder R	(ah bawr day)	to approach	R's
aboutir *	(ah boo teer)	to lead/to succeed	*'s
aboyer	(ah bwah yay)	to bark	A30
abréger	(ah bray zhay)	to shorten	A57
abreuver R	(ah bruh vay)	to water	R's
abriter R	(ah bree tay)	to shelter	R's
abroger	(ah braw zhay)	to repeal	A46
abrutir *	(ah brew teer)	to deafen	*'s
absenter (s') R	(ap sawn tay)	to leave	R's
absorber R	(ap sawr bay)	to absorb	R's
absoudre	(ap soo druh)	to absolve	A26
abstenir (s')	(ap stuh neer)	to abstain	A23
abstraire	(ap strehr)	to abstract	A35
abuser R	(ah bew zay)	to abuse	R's
accabler R	(ah kah blay)	to overwhelm	R's
accaparer R	(ah kah pah ray)	to monopolize	R's
accéder	(ahk say day)	to reach	A32
accélérer	(ahk say lay ray)	to accelerate	A32
accentuer R	(ahk sawn tway)	to accentuate	R's
accepter R	(ahk sep tay)	to accept	R's
acclamer R	(ah klah may)	to cheer	R's
accommoder R	(ah kaw maw day)	to prepare	R's
accompagner R	(ah kohn pah nyay)	to accompany	R's
accomplir *	(ah kohn pleer)	to accomplish	*'s
accorder R	(ah kawr day)	to grant	R's
accoter R	(ah kaw tay)	to lean	R's
accoucher R	(ah koo shay)	to give birth	R's
accouder (s') R	(ah koo day)	to lean on one's elbows	R's
accourir	(ah koo reer)	to rush	A21
accoutumer R	(ah koo tew may)	to accustom	R's
accrocher R	(ah kraw shay)	to hang up	R's
accroître	(ah krwah truh)	to increase	A2
accroupir (s') *	(ah kroo peer)	to squat	*'s
accueillir	(ah kuh yeer)	to welcome	A3
acculturer R	(ah kewl tew ray)	to acculturate	R's
accumuler R	(ah kew mew lay)	to accumulate	R's
accuser R	(ah kew zay)	to accuse	R's
acharner (s') R	(ah shar nay)	to persist	R's
acheminer R	(ah shuh mee nay)	to transport	R's
acheter	(ash tay)	to buy	A44

© 2010

FRENCH VERB	PRONUNCIATION	ENGLISH MEANING	PAGE
achever	(ah shvay)	to complete	A44
acquérir	(ah kay reer)	to acquire	A4
actionner R	(ahk syaw nay)	to activate	R's
actualiser R	(ak twa lee zay)	to update	R's
activer R	(ak tee vay)	to speed up	R's
adapter R	(ah dahp tay)	to adapt	R's
additionner R	(ah dee syaw nay)	to add	R's
adhérer	(ah day ray)	to adhere to	A32
adjoindre	(ahd zhwahn druh)	to adjoin	A12
admettre	(ahd meh truh)	to admit	A48
administrer R	(ahd mee nee stray)	to administer	R's
admirer R	(ahd mee ray)	to admire	R's
adopter R	(ah dawp tay)	to adopt	R's
adorer R	(ah daw ray)	to adore	R's
adosser R	(ah doh say)	to lean	R's
adoucir *	(ah doo seer)	to soften	*'s
adresser R	(ah dray say)	to address	R's
advenir	(ahd vuh neer)	to happen	A23
aérer	(ayr ay)	to air	A32
affaiblir *	(ah feh bleer)	to weaken	*'s
affairer (s') R	(ah fay ray)	to bustle about	R's
affaisser (s') R	(ah fay say)	to sag / to subside	R's
affamer R	(ah fah may)	to starve	R's
affecter R	(ah fehk tay)	to affect	R's
affermir *	(ah fehr meer)	to strengthen	*'s
afficher R	(ah fee shay)	to display	R's
affirmer R	(ah feer may)	to affirm	R's
affliger	(ah flee zhay)	to afflict	A46
affoler R	(ah faw lay)	to panic	R's
affranchir *	(ah frahn sheer)	to stamp	*'s
affréter	(ah fray tay)	to charter	A32
affronter R	(ah frohn tay)	to confront	R's
agacer	(ah gah say)	to annoy	A13
agenouiller (s') R	(ahzh noo yay)	to kneel	R's
aggraver R	(ah grah vay)	to aggravate	R's
agir *	(ah zheer)	to act	*'s
agiter R	(ah zhee tay)	to agitate	R's
agrandir *	(ah grawn deer)	to enlarge	*'s
agréer R	(ah gray ay)	to agree	R's
ahurir *	(ah ew reer)	to stun	*'s
aider R	(ay day)	to help	R's
aigrir *	(ay greer)	to embitter	*'s
aiguiser R	(ay gee zay)	to sharpen	R's
aimanter R	(eh mawn tay)	to magnetize	R's
aimer R	(ay may)	to love / to like	R's
ajouter R	(ah zhoo tay)	to add	R's
ajuster R	(ah zhew stay)	to adjust	R's
alarmer R	(ah lahr may)	to alarm	R's
alerter R	(ah lehr tay)	to alert	R's

© 2010

FRENCH VERB	PRONUNCIATION	ENGLISH MEANING	PAGE
alimenter R	(ah lee mawn tay)	to feed	R's
allécher	(ah lay shay)	to tempt	A5
alléger	(ah lay zhay)	to reduce	A57
alléguer	(ah lay gay)	to allege / to invoke	A5
aller	(ah lay)	to go	A6
allier R	(ah lyay)	to combine	R's
allonger	(ah lohn zhay)	to lay down	A46
allumer R	(ah lew may)	to light	R's
alourdir *	(ah loor deer)	to weigh down	*'s
alphabétiser R	(ahl fah bay tee zay)	to teach to read and write	R's
altérer	(ahl tay ray)	to impair	A32
alterner R	(ahl tehr nay)	to alternate	R's
alunir *	(ah lew neer)	to land on the moon	*'s
amaigrir *	(ah may greer)	to make thinner	*'s
ambitionner R	(awn bee syaw nay)	to aspire	R's
améliorer R	(ah may lyaw ray)	to improve	R's
aménager	(ah may nah zhay)	to organize	A46
amener	(ahm nay)	to bring	A44
ameuter R	(ah muh tay)	to rouse	R's
amincir *	(ah mahn seer)	to slim	*'s
amoindrir *	(ah mwahn dreer)	to weaken	*'s
amollir *	(ah maw leer)	to soften	*'s
amonceler	(ah mohn slay)	to accumulate	A8
amorcer	(ah mawr say)	to begin	A13
amplifier R	(awn plee fyay)	to amplify	R's
amputer R	(awn pew tay)	to amputate	R's
amuser R	(ah mew zay)	to amuse	R's
analyser R	(ah nah lee zay)	to analyze	R's
anéantir *	(ah nay awn teer)	to annihilate	*'s
angoisser R	(awn gwah say)	to worry	R's
animer R	(ah nee may)	to animate	R's
annexer R	(ah nehk say)	to annex	R's
annoncer	(ah nohn say)	to announce	A13
annoter R	(ah naw tay)	to annotate	R's
annuler R	(ah new lay)	to cancel	R's
anoblir *	(ah naw bleer)	to ennoble	*'s
anticiper R	(awn tee see pay)	to anticipate	R's
apaiser R	(ah pay zay)	to appease	R's
apercevoir	(ah pehr suh vwahr)	to perceive	A7
apitoyer	(ah pee twah yay)	to move to pity	A30
aplatir *	(ah plah teer)	to flatten	*'s
apparaître	(ah pah reh truh)	to appear/ to seem	A18
appareiller R	(ah pah ray yay)	to match up	R's
apparenter R	(ah pah rawn tay)	to resemble	R's
apparier R	(ah pah ryay)	to match	R's
appartenir	(ah pahr tuh neer)	to belong to	A23
appauvrir *	(ah poh vreer)	to impoverish	*'s
appeler	(ah play)	to call	A8
applaudir *	(ah ploh deer)	to applaud	*'s

FRENCH VERB	PRONUNCIATION	ENGLISH MEANING	PAGE
appliquer R	(ah plee kay)	to apply	R's
apporter R	(ah pawr tay)	to bring	R's
apprécier R	(ah pray syay)	to appreciate	R's
apprendre	(ah prawn druh)	to learn / to teach	A9
apprêter R	(ah preh tay)	to get ready	R's
apprivoiser R	(ah pree vwa zay)	to tame	R's
approcher R	(ah praw shay)	to approach	R's
approfondir *	(ah praw fohn deer)	to deepen	*'s
approprier (s) R	(ah praw pree yay)	to appropriate	R's
approuver R	(ah proo vay)	to approve of	R's
appuyer	(ah pwee yay)	to press / to lean	A30
argenter R	(ahr zhawn tay)	to silver	R's
arguer R	(ahr gay)	to argue	R's
armer R	(ahr may)	to arm	R's
arpenter R	(ahr pawn tay)	to pace up and down	R's
arracher R	(ah rah shay)	to pull out	R's
arranger	(ah rawn zhay)	to arrange	A46
arrêter R	(ah ray tay)	to stop	R's
arriver R	(ah ree vay)	to arrive	R's
arrondir *	(ah rohn deer)	to round off	*'s
arroser R	(ah roh zay)	to water	R's
asphyxier R	(ahs feek syay)	to suffocate	R's
aspirer R	(ah spee ray)	to inhale	R's
assagir *	(ah sah zheer)	to quiet down	*'s
assaillir	(ah sah yeer)	to assail	A10
assainir *	(ah say neer)	to clean up	*'s
assassiner R	(ah sah see nay)	to assassinate	R's
assembler R	(ah sawn blay)	to assemble	R's
asséner	(ah say nay)	to strike (someone)	A32
asseoir	(ah swahr)	to sit (so) down	A11
asservir *	(ah sehr veer)	to enslave	*'s
assiéger	(ah syay zhay)	to besiege	A57
assigner R	(ah see nyay)	to assign	R's
assimiler R	(ah see mee lay)	to assimilate	R's
assister R	(ah see stay)	to assist	R's
associer R	(ah saw syay)	to associate	R's
assombrir *	(ah sohn breer)	to darken	*'s
assommer R	(ah saw may)	to knock out	R's
assortir *	(ah sawr teer)	to match	*'s
assoupir *	(ah soo peer)	to make drowsy	*'s
assouplir *	(ah soo pleer)	to soften	*'s
assourdir *	(ah soor deer)	to deafen	*'s
assujettir *	(ah sew zheh teer)	to subject	*'s
assumer R	(ah sew may)	to assume	R's
assurer R	(ah sew ray)	to assure	R's
astiquer R	(ah stee kay)	to polish	R's
astreindre	(ah strahn druh)	to compel	A12
atermoyer	(ah tehr mwah yay)	to procrastinate	A30
attabler(s')R	(ah tah blay)	to sit at the table	R's

© 2010

FRENCH VERB	PRONUNCIATION	ENGLISH MEANING	PAGE
attacher R	(ah tah shay)	to attach	R's
attaquer R	(ah tah kay)	to attack	R's
attarder R	(ah tahr day)	to delay	R's
atteindre	(ah tahn druh)	to attain	A12
atteler	(aht lay)	to harness	A8
attendre #	(ah tawn druh)	to wait for	#'s
attendrir *	(ah tawn dreer)	to tenderize	*'s
atterrir *	(ah tay reer)	to land	*'s
attester R	(ah teh stay)	to attest / to testify	R's
attirer R	(ah tee ray)	to attract	R's
attraper R	(ah trah pay)	to catch	R's
attribuer R	(ah tree bway)	to attribute	R's
attrister R	(ah tree stay)	to sadden	R's
augmenter R	(ohg mawn tay)	to increase	R's
autoriser R	(oh taw ree zay)	to authorize	R's
avachir *	(ah vah sheer)	to wear out	*'s
avaler R	(ah vah lay)	to swallow	R's
avancer	(ah vawn say)	to advance	A13
avantager	(ah vawn tah zhay)	to favour	A46
aventurer R	(ah vawn tew ray)	to venture	R's
avertir *	(ah vehr teer)	to inform / to warn	*'s
aveugler R	(ah vuh glay)	to blind	R's
avili3r *	(ah vee leer)	to degrade	*'s
aviser R	(ah vee zay)	to inform	R's
aviver R	(ah vee vay)	to intensify	R's
avoir	(ah vwahr)	to have	A14
avorter R	(ah vawr tay)	to abort	R's
avouer R	(ah vway)	to confess	R's
bâcler R	(bah klay)	to botch	R's
bafouer R	(bah fway)	to scorn	R's
bagarrer R	(bah gah ray)	to fight / to argue	R's
baigner R	(bay nyay)	to bathe	R's
bâiller R	(bah yay)	to yawn	R's
baiser R	(bay zay)	to kiss	R's
baisser R	(bay say)	to lower	R's
balader R	(bah lah day)	to take for a walk	R's
balafrer R	(bah lah fray)	to slash	R's
balancer	(bah lawn say)	to swing / to balance	A13
balayer	(bah lay yay)	to sweep up	A33
balbutier R	(bahl bew syay)	to stammer	R's
baliser R	(bah lee zay)	to mark out	R's
bannir *	(bah neer)	to banish	*'s
baptiser R	(bah tee zay)	to baptize	R's
baratiner R	(bah rah tee nay)	to try to persuade	R's
barbouiller R	(bahr boo yay)	to smear	R's
barioler R	(bahr yaw lay)	to variegate	R's
barrer R	(bah ray)	to block	R's
barricader R	(bah ree kah day)	to barricade	R's
basculer R	(bah skew lay)	to topple over	R's

© 2010

FRENCH VERB	PRONUNCIATION	ENGLISH MEANING	PAGE
baser R	(bah zay)	to base	R's
batailler R	(bah tah yay)	to fight	R's
batifoler R	(bah tee faw lay)	to frolic	R's
bâtir *	(bah teer)	to build	*'s
battre	(bah truh)	to beat	A1
bavarder R	(bah vahr day)	to chat	R's
baver R	(bah vay)	to drool	R's
bêcher R	(bay shay)	to dig	R's
becqueter	(behk tay)	to peck at / to eat	A43
bégayer	(bay gay yay)	to stutter	A33
bêler R	(beh lay)	to bleat	R's
bénéficier R	(bay nay fee syay)	to benefit from	R's
bénir *	(bay neer)	to bless	*'s
bercer	(behr say)	to rock	A13
berner R	(behr nay)	to deceive	R's
beugler R	(buh glay)	to bellow	R's
beurrer R	(buh ray)	to butter	R's
biaiser R	(bee yeh zay)	to hedge	R's
bichonner R	(bee shaw nay)	to pamper	R's
biffer R	(bee fay)	to cross out	R's
blaguer R	(blah gay)	to joke	R's
blamer R	(blah may)	to criticize	R's
blanchir *	(blawn sheer)	to whiten	*'s
blaser R	(blah zay)	to make indifferent	R's
blêmir *	(blay meer)	to turn pale	*'s
blesser R	(blay say)	to injure	R's
bleuir *	(bluh eer)	to turn blue	*'s
bloquer R	(blaw kay)	to block	R's
blottir *	(blaw teer)	to nestle	*'s
boire	(bwahr)	to drink	A15
boiter R	(bwa tay)	to limp	R's
bombarder R	(bohn bahr day)	to bombard	R's
bondir *	(bohn deer)	to leap	*'s
bonifier R	(baw nee fyay)	to improve	R's
border R	(bawr day)	to border	R's
borner R	(bawr nay)	to limit	R's
boucher R	(boo shay)	to cork	R's
boucler R	(boo klay)	to fasten	R's
bouder R	(boo day)	to sulk	R's
bouffer R	(boo fay)	to eat	R's
bouffir *	(boo feer)	to make puffy	*'s
bouger	(boo zhay)	to move	A46
bouillir	(boo yeer)	to boil	A16
bouleverser R	(boo lvehr say)	to move deeply	R's
boulonner R	(boo law nay)	to bolt down	R's
bourdonner R	(boor daw nay)	to buzz	R's
bourrer R	(boo ray)	to cram	R's
boursoufler R	(boor soo flay)	to cause to swell	R's
bousculer R	(boo skew lay)	to bump into	R's

© 2010

FRENCH VERB	PRONUNCIATION	ENGLISH MEANING	PAGE
bousiller R	(boo zee yay)	to botch / to ruin	R's
boutonner R	(boo taw nay)	to button	R's
braconner R	(brah kaw nay)	to poach	R's
brailler R	(brah yay)	to yell out	R's
braire	(brehr)	to bray	A35
brancher R	(brawn shay)	to connect up	R's
brandir *	(brawn deer)	to brandish	*'s
branler R	(brawn lay)	to wobble	R's
braquer R	(brah kay)	to point	R's
braver R	(brah vay)	to brave	R's
bredouiller R	(bruh doo yay)	to mumble	R's
breveter	(bruh vtay)	to patent	A43
bricoler R	(bree kaw lay)	to do odd jobs	R's
brider R	(bree day)	to restrain	R's
briguer R	(bree gay)	to crave	R's
briller R	(bree yay)	to shine	R's
brimer R	(bree may)	to bully	R's
briser R	(bree zay)	to break	R's
broder R	(braw day)	to embroider	R's
broncher R	(brohn shay)	to stumble	R's
bronzer R	(brohn zay)	to tan	R's
brosser R	(braw say)	to brush	R's
brouiller R	(broo yay)	to mix up	R's
broyer	(brwah yay)	to grind	A3
bruiner R	(brwee nay)	to drizzle	R's
brûler R	(brew lay)	to burn	R's
brunir *	(brew neer)	to brown	*'s
buter R	(bew tay)	to trip	R's
cabrer R	(kah bray)	to rear up	R's
cacher R	(kah shay)	to hide	R's
cadrer R	(kah dray)	to centre / to tally	R's
cajoler R	(kah zhaw lay)	to coax	R's
calculer R	(kahl kew lay)	to calculate	R's
caler R	(kah lay)	to wedge	R's
câliner R	(kah lee nay)	to cuddle	R's
calmer R	(kahl may)	to calm	R's
calomnier R	(kah lawm nyay)	to slander	R's
calquer R	(kahl kay)	to copy	R's
camper R	(kawn pay)	to camp	R's
capituler R	(kah pee tew lay)	to capitulate	R's
capter R	(kahp tay)	to capture	R's
captiver R	(kahp tee vay)	to captivate	R's
capturer R	(kahp tew ray)	to capture	R's
caractériser R	(kah rahk tay ree zay)	to characterize	R's
caresser R	(kah ray say)	to caress	R's
caricaturer R	(kah ree kah tew ray)	to caricature	R's
caser R	(kah zay)	to place	R's
casser R	(kah say)	to break	R's
cataloguer R	(kah tah law gay)	to catalogue	R's

FRENCH VERB	PRONUNCIATION	ENGLISH MEANING	PAGE
catapulter R	(kah tah pewl tay)	to catapult	R's
causer R	(koh zay)	to cause	R's
céder	(say day)	to give up	A32
ceindre	(sahn druh)	to tie around	A12
celer	(suh lay)	to conceal	A44
censurer R	(sawn sew ray)	to censor	R's
centraliser R	(sawn trah lee zay)	to centralize	R's
cercler R	(sehr klay)	to circle	R's
cerner R	(sehr nay)	to surround	R's
certifier R	(sehr tee fyay)	to certify	R's
cesser R	(say say)	to stop	R's
chagriner R	(shah gree nay)	to grieve	R's
chahuter R	(shah ew tay)	to play up	R's
chamailler R	(shah mah yay)	to squabble	R's
chanceler	(shawn slay)	to stagger	A8
changer	(shawn zhay)	to change	A46
chanter R	(shawn tay)	to sing	R's
chantonner R	(shawn taw nay)	to hum	R's
charger	(shahr zhay)	to load	A46
charmer R	(shahr may)	to charm	R's
charrier R	(shah ryay)	to haul	R's
chasser R	(shah say)	to hunt	R's
châtier R	(shah tyay)	to punish	R's
chatouiller R	(shah too yay)	to tickle	R's
chauffer R	(shoh fay)	to heat	R's
chausser R	(shoh say)	to put (sth) on	R's
chercher R	(shehr shay)	to look for	R's
chérir *	(shay reer)	to cherish	*'s
chiffonner R	(shee faw nay)	to crumple	R's
chiffrer R	(shee fray)	to assess	R's
chiner R	(shee nay)	to bargain-hunt	R's
chipoter R	(shee paw tay)	to quibble	R's
choisir *	(schwa zeer)	to choose	*'s
chômer R	(shoh may)	to be idle	R's
choquer R	(shaw kay)	to shock	R's
choyer	(shwah yay)	to pamper	A30
chuchoter R	(shew shaw tay)	to whisper	R's
chuter R	(shew tay)	to fall	R's
cibler R	(see blay)	to target	R's
cicatriser R	(see kah tree zay)	to heal	R's
ciller R	(see yay)	to blink	R's
circoncire	(seer kohn seer)	to circumcise	A60
circonscrire	(seer kohn skreer)	to circumscribe	A28
circonvenir	(seer kohn vuh neer)	to circumvent	A23
circuler R	(seer kew lay)	to circulate	R's
cirer R	(see ray)	to polish	R's
ciseler	(see zlay)	to chisel	A44
citer R	(see tay)	to cite	R's
clarifier R	(klah ree fyay)	to clarify	R's

© 2010

FRENCH VERB	PRONUNCIATION	ENGLISH MEANING	PAGE
classer R	(klah say)	to file	R's
classifier R	(klah see fyay)	to classify	R's
cligner R	(klee nyay)	to blink	R's
clignoter R	(klee nyaw tay)	to twinkle	R's
clocher R	(klaw shay)	to be faulty	R's
cloîtrer R	(klwah tray)	to shut away	R's
clore	(klawr)	to close	A17
clouer R	(kloo ay)	to nail down	R's
cocher R	(kaw shay)	to tick	R's
cochonner R	(kaw shaw nay)	to mess up	R's
coder R	(kaw day)	to code	R's
codifier R	(kaw dee fyay)	to codify	R's
cogner R	(kaw nyay)	to hit / to knock	R's
cohabiter R	(koh ah bee tay)	to live together	R's
coiffer R	(kwa fay)	to do someone's hair	R's
coincer	(kwahn say)	to wedge	A13
coïncider R	(kaw ahn see day)	to coincide	R's
collaborer R	(kaw lah baw ray)	to collaborate with	R's
collectioner R	(kaw lehk syaw nay)	to collect	R's
coller R	(kaw lay)	to stick	R's
coloniser R	(kaw law nee zay)	to colonize	R's
colorer R	(kaw law ray)	to colour	R's
colorier R	(kaw law ryay)	to colour in	R's
combattre	(kohn bah truh)	to fight	A1
combler R	(kohn blay)	to fill in	R's
commander R	(kaw mawn day)	to order	R's
commémorer R	(kaw may maw ray)	to commemorate	R's
commencer	(kaw mawn say)	to begin / to start	A13
commenter R	(kaw mawn tay)	to comment	R's
commettre	(kaw meh truh)	to commit	A48
commuer R	(kaw mway)	to commute	R's
communier R	(kaw mew nyay)	to receive Communion	R's
communiquer R	(kaw mew nee kay)	to communicate	R's
comparaître	(kohn pah reh truh)	to appear	A18
comparer R	(kohn pah ray)	to compare	R's
compatir *	(kohn pah teer)	to sympathize	*'s
compenser R	(kohn pawn say)	to compensate	R's
compiler R	(kohn pee lay)	to compile	R's
complaire	(kohn plehr)	to delight in	A53
compléter	(kohn play tay)	to complete	A32
complimenter R	(kohn plee mawn tay)	to compliment	R's
compliquer R	(kohn plee kay)	to complicate	R's
comporter R	(kohn pawr tay)	to include	R's
composer R	(kohn poh zay)	to compose	R's
composter R	(kohn paw stay)	to date stamp	R's
comprendre	(kohn prawn druh)	to understand	A9
compromettre	(kohn praw meh truh)	to compromise	A48
compter R	(kohn tay)	to count	R's
concéder	(kohn say day)	to concede	A32

© 2010

FRENCH VERB	PRONUNCIATION	ENGLISH MEANING	PAGE
concentrer R	(kohn sawn tray)	to concentrate	R's
conceptualiser R	(kohn sep twah lee zay)	to conceptualize	R's
concerner R	(kohn sehr nay)	to concern	R's
concerter R	(kohn sehr tay)	to plan	R's
concevoir	(kohn suh vwahr)	to conceive	A7
concilier R	(kohn see lyay)	to reconcile	R's
conclure	(kohn klewr)	to conclude	A41
concourir	(kohn koo reer)	to compete	A21
concurrencer	(kohn kew rawn say)	to compete with	A13
condamner R	(kohn daw nay)	to condemn	R's
condenser R	(kohn dawn say)	to condense	R's
condescendre R	(kohn day sawn druh)	to condescend to	R's
conduire	(kohn dweer)	to drive	A63
conférer	(kohn fay ray)	to conferto confer	A32
confier R	(kohn fyay)	to confide / to trust	R's
confirmer R	(kohn feer may)	to confirm	R's
confisquer R	(kohn fee skay)	to confiscate	R's
confondre #	(kohn fohn druh)	to confuse	#'s
conforter R	(kohn fawr tay)	to consolidate	R's
congédier R	(kohn zhay dyay)	to dismiss	R's
congeler	(kohn zlay)	to freeze	A44
conjoindre	(kohn zhwahn druh)	to unite	A12
conjuguer R	(kohn zew gay)	to conjugate	R's
connaître	(kaw neh truh)	to know	A18
conquérir	(kohn kay reer)	to conquer	A4
consacrer R	(kohn sah kray)	to devote	R's
conseiller R	(kohn say yay)	to advise	R's
consentir	(kohn sawn teer)	to consent	A27
conserver R	(kohn sehr vay)	to conserve	R's
consigner R	(kohn see nyay)	to record	R's
consister R	(kohn see stay)	to consist of	R's
consoler R	(kohn saw lay)	to console	R's
consolider R	(kohn saw lee day)	to consolidate	R's
consommer R	(kohn saw may)	to consume	R's
conspirer R	(kohn spee ray)	to plot	R's
constater R	(kohn stah tay)	to note	R's
consterner R	(kohn stehr nay)	to dismay	R's
constituer R	(kohn stee tway)	to constitute	R's
construire	(kohn strweer)	to build	A63
consulter R	(kohn sewl tay)	to consult	R's
contacter R	(kohn tahk tay)	to contact	R's
contaminer R	(kohn tah mee nay)	to contaminate	R's
contempler R	(kohn tawn play)	to contemplate	R's
contenir	(kohn tuh neer)	to contain	A23
contenter R	(kohn tawn tay)	to satisfy	R's
conter R	(kohn tay)	to tell	R's
contester R	(kohn teh stay)	to question / to contest	R's
continuer R	(kohn tee nway)	to continue	R'S
contraindre	(kohn trahn druh)	to force	A12

© 2010

FRENCH VERB	PRONUNCIATION	ENGLISH MEANING	PAGE
contrarier R	(kohn trah ryay)	to annoy	R's
contraster R	(kohn trah stay)	to contrast	R's
contredire	(kohn truh deer)	to contradict	A25
contrefaire	(kohn truh fehr)	to counterfeit	A37
contrevenir	(kohn truh vuh neer)	to contravene	A23
contribuer R	(kohn tree bway)	to contribute	R's
contrôler R	(kohn troh lay)	to control	R's
contusionner R	(kohn tewz yaw nay)	to bruise	R's
convaincre	(kohn vahn kruh)	to convince	A19
convenir	(kohn vuh neer)	to be suitable/to admit	A23
converser R	(kohn vehr say)	to converse	R's
convertir *	(kohn vehr teer)	to convert	*'s
convier R	(kohn vyay)	to invite	R's
convoler R	(kohn vaw lay)	to marry	R's
convoquer R	(kohn vaw kay)	to convene	R's
coopérer	(koh aw pay ray)	to cooperate	A32
coordonner R	(koh awr daw nay)	to coordinate	R's
copier R	(kaw pyay)	to copy	R's
correspondre #	(kawr reh spohn druh)	to correspond	#'s
corriger	(kaw ree zhay)	to correct	A46
corrompre #	(kaw rohn pruh)	to corrupt	#'s
coter R	(kaw tay)	to rate	R's
côtoyer	(koh twah yay)	to be next to	A30
coucher R	(koo shay)	to put to bed	R's
coudre	(koo druh)	to sew	A20
couler R	(koo lay)	to flow	R's
couper R	(koo pay)	to cut	R's
courber R	(koor bay)	to bend	R's
courir	(koo reer)	to run	A21
couronner R	(koo raw nay)	to crown	R's
coûter R	(koo tay)	to cost	R's
couvrir	(koov reer)	to cover	A52
cracher R	(krah shay)	to spit out	R's
craindre	(krahn druh)	to fear	A12
cramer R	(krah may)	to burn	R's
cramponner R	(krawn paw nay)	to cling to	R's
craquer R	(krah kay)	to split	R's
créditer R	(kray dee tay)	to credit	R's
créer R	(kray ay)	to create	R's
crépir *	(kray peer)	to render	*'s
creuser R	(kruh zay)	to dig	R's
crever	(kruh vay)	to burst	A44
cribler R	(kree blay)	to riddle with	R's
crier R	(kree yay)	to shout	R's
crisper R	(kree spay)	to make tense	R's
critiquer R	(kree tee kay)	to criticize	R's
crocheter	(krawsh tay)	to crochet	A44
croire	(krwahr)	to believe	A22
croiser R	(krwah zay)	to cross	R's

FRENCH VERB	PRONUNCIATION	ENGLISH MEANING	PAGE
croître	(krwah truh)	to grow	A2
croquer R	(kraw kay)	to crunch	R's
crouler R	(kroo lay)	to collapse	R's
croupir *	(kroo peer)	to stagnate	*'s
crucifier R	(krew see fyay)	to crucify	R's
cueillir	(kuh yeer)	to pick	A3
cuire	(kweer)	to cook	A63
cuisiner R	(kwee zee nay)	to be cooking	R's
cuiter R	(kwee tay)	to get plastered	R's
culbuter R	(kewl bew tay)	to knock over	R's
culminer R	(kewl mee nay)	to peak	R's
cultiver R	(kewl tee vay)	to cultivate	R's
cumuler R	(kew mew lay)	to accumulate	R's
curer R	(kew ray)	to clean out	R's
daigner R	(day nyay)	to deign	R's
daller R	(dah lay)	to pave	R's
damner R	(dah nay)	to damn	R's
danser R	(dawn say)	to dance	R's
dater R	(dah tay)	to date	R's
déballer R	(day bah lay)	to unpack	R's
débarquer R	(day bahr kay)	to unload	R's
débarrasser R	(day bah rah say)	to clear out	R's
débattre	(day bah truh)	to discuss	A1
debaucher R	(day boh shay)	to lay off / to debauch	R's
débiliter R	(day bee lee tay)	to debilitate	R's
débiter R	(day bee tay)	to debit	R's
déblatérer	(day blah tay ray)	to rant on	A32
débloquer R	(day blaw kay)	to release	R's
déboîter R	(day bwah tay)	to dislocate	R's
déborder R	(day bawr day)	to overflow	R's
déboucher R	(day boo shay)	to unblock	R's
débourser R	(day boor say)	to pay out	R's
déboutonner R	(day boo taw nay)	to unbutton	R's
débrailler (se) R	(day brah yay)	to be untidy	R's
débrancher R	(day brawn shay)	to unplug	R's
débrayer	(day bray yay)	to declutch	A33
débrouiller R	(day broo yay)	to disentangle	R's
débuter R	(day bew tay)	to begin / to start	R's
décaler R	(day kah lay)	to shift	R's
décanter R	(day kawn tay)	to allow (sth) to settle	R's
décaper R	(day kah pay)	to clean	R's
décapsuler R	(day kahp sew lay)	to take the top off	R's
décarcasser (se) R	(day kahr kah say)	to put oneself to a lot of trouble	R's
décéder	(day say day)	to die	A32
déceler	(day slay)	to detect	A44
décélérer	(day say lay ray)	to slow down	A32
décentraliser R	(day sawn trah lee zay)	to decentralize	R's
décerner R	(day sehr nay)	to award	R's
décevoir	(day suh vwahr)	to disappoint	A7

© 2010

FRENCH VERB	PRONUNCIATION	ENGLISH MEANING	PAGE
déchaîner R	(day shay nay)	to unleash	R's
décharger	(day shahr zhay)	to unload	A46
déchiffrer R	(day shee fray)	to decipher	R's
déchiqueter	(day sheek tay)	to shred	A43
déchirer R	(day shee ray)	to rip	R's
décider R	(day see day)	to decide	R's
décimer R	(day see may)	to decimate	R's
déclamer R	(day klah may)	to declaim	R's
déclarer R	(day klah ray)	to declare	R's
déclasser R	(day klah say)	to downgrade	R's
déclencher R	(day klawn shay)	to set off	R's
décliner R	(day klee nay)	to decline	R's
décoder R	(day kaw day)	to decode	R's
décolérer	(day kaw lay ray)	to let up	A32
décoller R	(day kaw lay)	to peel off	R's
décommander R	(day kaw mawn day)	to call off	R's
déconcerter R	(day kohn sehr tay)	to disconcert	R's
déconseiller R	(day kohn say yay)	to advise against	R's
décontracter R	(day kohn trahk tay)	to relax	R's
décorer R	(day kaw ray)	to decorate	R's
découdre	(day koo druh)	to unstitch	A20
découler R	(day koo lay)	to follow	R's
découper R	(day koo pay)	to cut up / to carve	R's
décourager	(day koo rah zhay)	to discourage	A46
découvrir	(day koov reer)	to discover	A52
décréter	(day kray tay)	to decree	A32
décrier R	(day kree yay)	to disparage	R's
décrire	(day kreer)	to describe	A28
décrocher R	(day kraw shay)	to take down	R's
décroître	(day krwa truh)	to drop / to subside	A2
dédaigner R	(day day nyay)	to despise	R's
dédicacer	(day dee kah say)	to dedicate	A13
dédier R	(day dyay)	to devote / to dedicate	R's
dédire (se)	(day deer)	to retract one's statement	A25
dédommager	(day daw mah zhay)	to compensate	A46
dédouaner R	(day dwah nay)	to clear (sth) through customs	R's
dédoubler R	(day doo blay)	to split in two	R's
déduire	(day dweer)	to deduce	A63
défaire	(day fehr)	to undo	A37
défalquer R	(day fahl kay)	to deduct	R's
défavoriser R	(day fah vaw ree zay)	to be unfair to	R's
défendre #	(day fawn druh)	to defend	#'s
déférer	(day fay ray)	to refer	A32
déficeler	(day fee slay)	to untie	A8
défier R	(day fyay)	to challenge	R's
défigurer R	(day fee gew ray)	to disfigure	R's
défiler R	(day fee lay)	to march / to parade	R's
définir *	(day fee neer)	to define	*'s
défoncer	(day fohn say)	to smash	A13

© 2010

FRENCH VERB	PRONUNCIATION	ENGLISH MEANING	PAGE
déformer R	(day fawr may)	to distort / to bend	R's
défraîchir *	(day fray sheer)	to fade	*'s
dégager	(day gah zhay)	to free	A46
dégainer R	(day geh nay)	to draw	R's
dégauchir *	(day goh sheer)	to surface / to straighten	*'s
dégeler	(day zhlay)	to thaw	A44
dégénérer	(day zhay nay ray)	to degenerate	A32
dégonfler R	(day gohn flay)	to deflate	R's
dégourdir *	(day goor deer)	to warm (sth) up	*'s
dégoûter R	(day goo tay)	to disgust	R's
dégrader R	(day grah day)	to damage	R's
dégringoler R	(day grahn gaw lay)	to tumble	R's
dégriser R	(day gree zay)	to sober (so) up	R's
déguerpir *	(day gehr peer)	to clear off	*'s
dégueuler R	(day guh lay)	to vomit	R's
déguiser R	(day gee zay)	to disguise	R's
déguster R	(day gew stay)	to savour	R's
déjeter	(day zhuh tay)	to warp	A43
déjeuner R	(day zhuh nay)	to have lunch	R's
déjouer R	(day zhway)	to foil	R's
délaisser R	(day lay say)	to abandon	R's
délasser R	(day lah say)	to relax	R's
délayer	(day lay yay)	to dilute	A33
déléguer	(day lay gay)	to delegate	A5
délibérer	(day lee bay ray)	to deliberate	A32
délier R	(day lyay)	to unbind	R's
délirer R	(day lee ray)	to be delirious	R's
délivrer R	(day lee vray)	to liberate	R's
déloger	(day law zhay)	to evict	A46
demander R	(duh mawn day)	to ask for	R's
démanteler	(day mawn tlay)	to dismantle	A44
démarquer R	(day mahr kay)	to mark down	R's
démarrer R	(day mah ray)	to start up	R's
démêler R	(day may lay)	to disentangle	R's
déménager	(day may nah zhay)	to relocate	A46
démener (se)	(day muh nay)	to thrash about	A44
démentir	(day mawn teer)	to deny	A27
démettre	(day meh truh)	to dislocate / to dismiss	A48
demeurer R	(duh muh ray)	to reside	R's
démissionner R	(day mee syaw nay)	to resign	R's
démolir *	(day maw leer)	to demolish	*'s
démonter R	(day mohn tay)	to take down	R's
démontrer R	(day mohn tray)	to demonstrate	R's
démultiplier R	(day mewl tee plee yay)	to reduce	R's
démunir *	(day mew neer)	to divest	*'s
dénaturer R	(day nah tew ray)	to denature	R's
dénier R	(day nyay)	to deny	R's
dénigrer R	(day nee gray)	to denigrate	R's
déniveler	(day nee vlay)	to make (sth) uneven	A8

© 2010

FRENCH VERB	PRONUNCIATION	ENGLISH MEANING	PAGE
dénoncer	(day nohn say)	to denounce	A13
dénouer R	(day nway)	to unravel / to undo	R's
dépanner R	(day pah nay)	to fix	R's
dépaqueter	(day pahk tay)	to unpack	A43
départager	(day pahr tah zhay)	to decide between	A46
départir	(day pahr teer)	to allot	A27
dépasser R	(day pah say)	to overtake	R's
dépayser R	(day peh zay)	to change surroundings	R's
dépecer	(day puh say)	to cut up	A13
dépêcher R	(day pay shay)	to dispatch	R's
dépeindre	(deh pahn druh)	to depict	A12
dépendre #	(day pawn druh)	to depend on	#'s
dépenser R	(day pawn say)	to spend	R's
dépérir *	(day pay reer)	to waste away	*'s
dépister R	(day pee stay)	to track down	R's
déplacer	(day plah say)	to move	A13
déplaire	(day plehr)	to displease	A53
déplier R	(day plee yay)	to unfold	R's
déployer	(day plwah yay)	to display	A30
dépolir *	(day paw leer)	to frost	*'s
déposer R	(day poh zay)	to put down / to dump	R's
dépouiller R	(day poo yay)	to skin / to strip	R's
dépoussiérer	(day poo syay ray)	to dust	A32
déprécier R	(day pray syay)	to depreciate	R's
déprendre (se)	(day prawn druh)	to free oneself from	A9
déprimer R	(day pree may)	to depress	R's
déraciner R	(day rah see nay)	to uproot	R's
déranger	(day rawn zhay)	to disturb	A46
déraper R	(day rah pay)	to skid /to get out of control	R's
dérégler	(day ray glay)	to affect /to upset	A5
dérober R	(day raw bay)	to steal /to hide	R's
déroger	(day raw zhay)	to infringe	A46
dérouler R	(day roo lay)	to unroll	R's
dérouter R	(day roo tay)	to reroute	R's
désaccoutumer R	(day zah koo tew may)	to cure (so's) addiction	R's
désagréger	(day zah gray zhay)	to disintegrate	A57
désaltérer	(day zahl tay ray)	to quench thirst	A32
désamorcer	(day zah mawr say)	to defuse / to drain	A13
désapprendre	(day zah prawn druh)	to forget / to unlearn	A9
désapprouver R	(day zah proo vay)	to disapprove of	R's
désavantager	(day zah vawn tah zhay)	to disadvantage	A46
désavouer R	(day zah vway)	to disown / deny	R's
descendre #	(deh sawn druh)	to descend / to take (sth) down	#'s
désemparer R	(day zawn pah ray)	to throw into confusion	R's
désennuyer	(day zaw nwee yay)	to relieve boredom	A30
désensibiliser R	(day sawn see bee lee zay)	to desensitize	R's
désentraver R	(day zawn trah vay)	to unshackle	R's
déséquilibrer R	(day zay kee lee bray)	to make unstable	R's
déserter R	(day zehr tay)	to desert	R's

FRENCH VERB	PRONUNCIATION	ENGLISH MEANING	PAGE
désespérer	(day zeh spay ray)	to fill (so) with despair	A32
déshabiller R	(day zah bee yay)	to undress	R's
déshabituer	(day zah bee tway)	to get out of the habit	R's
déshériter R	(day zay ree tay)	to disinherit	R's
désigner R	(day zee nyay)	to designate	R's
désinfecter R	(day zahn fehk tay)	to disinfect	R's
désintégrer	(day zahn tay gray)	to disintegrate	A5
désintéresser	(day zahn tay ray say)	to make (so) lose interest	R's
désintoxiquer R	(day zahn tawks ee kay)	to detoxify	R's
désirer R	(day zee ray)	to desire	R's
désister (se) R	(day zee stay)	to withdraw	R's
désobéir *	(day zaw bay eer)	to disobey	*'s
désoler R	(day zaw lay)	to distresss	R's
désorganiser R	(day zawr gah nee zay)	to disorganize	R's
désorienter R	(day zaw ryahn tay)	to disorientate	R's
dessaisir *	(day seh zeer)	to remove	*'s
dessécher	(day say shay)	to dry out	A5
desserrer R	(day say ray)	to loosen	R's
dessiner R	(day see nay)	to draw	R's
destiner R	(deh stee nay)	to destine	R's
destituer R	(deh stee tway)	to discharge	R's
désunir *	(day zew neer)	to divide	*'s
détacher R	(day tah shay)	to detach	R's
détailler R	(day tah yay)	to detail	R's
détecter R	(day tehk tay)	to detect	R's
déteindre	(day tahn druh)	to fade (colour)	A12
dételer	(dayt lay)	to unharness	A8
détendre #	(day tawn druh)	to release/to lossen	#'s
détenir	(day tuh neer)	to detain	A23
détériorer R	(day tay ryaw ray)	to damage	R's
déterminer R	(day tehr mee nay)	to determine	R's
détester R	(day teh stay)	to detest	R's
détonner R	(day taw nay)	to be out of place	R's
détordre #	(day tawr druh)	to unwind	#'s
détourner	(day toor nay)	to divert	R's
détraquer R	(day trah kay)	to wreck	R's
détromper R	(day trohn pay)	to disabuse	R's
détruire	(day trweer)	to destroy	A63
dévaler R	(day vah lay)	to hurtle down	R's
devancer	(duh vawn say)	to get ahead of	A13
développer R	(day vlaw pay)	to develop	R's
devenir	(duh vneer)	to become	A23
déverser R	(day vehr say)	to pour out	R's
dévêtir	(day veh teer)	to undress	A64
dévier R	(day vyay)	to divert	R's
deviner R	(duh vee nay)	to guess	R's
dévisser R	(day vee say)	to unscrew	R's
dévoiler R	(day vwah lay)	to unveil	R's
devoir	(duh vwahr)	to have to (must) / to owe	A24

© 2010

FRENCH VERB	PRONUNCIATION	ENGLISH MEANING	PAGE
dévorer R	(day vaw ray)	to devour	R's
dévouer R	(day vway)	to devote oneself to	R's
dicter R	(deek tay)	to dictate	R's
différer	(dee fay ray)	to postpone / to differ	A32
diffuser R	(dee few zay)	to broadcast / to spread	R's
digérer	(dee zhay ray)	to digest	A32
diluer R	(dee lway)	to dilute	R's
diminuer R	(dee mee nway)	to reduce	R's
dîner R	(dee nay)	to dine	R's
dire	(deer)	to say / to tell	A25
diriger	(dee ree zhay)	to direct/to manage	A46
disconvenir	(dee skohn vuh neer)	to deny	A23
discourir	(dee skoo reer)	to hold forth	A21
discriminer R	(dee scree mee nay)	to categorize	R's
discuter R	(dee skoo tay)	to discuss	R's
disjoindre	(dees zhwahn druh)	to loosen / to separate	A12
disparaître	(dee spah reh truh)	to disappear / to vanish	A18
dispenser R	(dee spawn say)	to hand out	R's
disperser R	(dee spehr say)	to scatter	R's
disposer R	(dee spoh zay)	to arrange	R's
disputer R	(dee spew tay)	to compete	R's
disséminer R	(dee say mee nay)	to disseminate	R's
dissiper R	(dee see pay)	to dispel	R's
dissocier R	(dee saw syay)	to dissociate	R's
dissoudre	(dee soo druh)	to dissolve	A26
dissuader R	(dee swah day)	to dissaude	R's
distendre #	(dee stawn druh)	to distend / to strain	#'s
distinguer R	(dee stahn gay)	to distinguish	R's
distordre #	(dec stawr druh)	to distort	#'s
distraire	(dee strehr)	to entertain / to distract	A35
distribuer R	(dee stree bway)	to distribute	R's
diversifier R	(dee vehr see fyay)	to vary	R's
diviser R	(dee vee zay)	to divide	R's
divorcer	(dee vawr say)	to divorce	A13
dominer R	(daw mee nay)	to dominate	R's
dompter R	(dohn tay)	to tame	R's
donner R	(daw nay)	to give	R's
dorer R	(daw ray)	to gild	R's
dormir	(dohr meer)	to sleep	A27
doubler R	(doo blay)	to double	R's
doucher R	(doo shay)	to shower someone / to dampen	R's
douer R	(dway)	to endow	R's
douter R	(doo tay)	to doubt	R's
draguer R	(drah gay)	to chat up	R's
dresser R	(dray say)	to train / to put up	R's
duper R	(dew pay)	to fool	R's
durcir *	(dewr seer)	to set / to harden	*'s
durer R	(dew ray)	to last	R's
ébahir *	(ay bah eer)	to astound	*'s

FRENCH VERB	PRONUNCIATION	ENGLISH MEANING	PAGE
ébattre (s')	(ay bah truh)	to frolic	A1
ébaucher R	(ay boh shay)	to sketch out	R's
éblouir *	(ay bloo eer)	to dazzle	*'s
ébranler R	(ay brawn lay)	to shake	R's
écarter R	(ay kahr tay)	to move apart	R's
échanger	(ay shawn zhay)	to exchange	A46
échapper R	(ay shah pay)	to escape	R's
échauder R	(ay shoh day)	to put (so) off / to scald	R's
échauffer R	(ay shoh fay)	to warm up	R's
échelonner R	(aysh law nay)	to space (sth) out	R's
échouer R	(ay shway)	to fail	R's
éclabousser R	(ay klah boo say)	to splash	R's
éclaircir *	(ay klehr seer)	to lighten	*'s
éclairer R	(ay klay ray)	to illuminate	R's
éclater R	(ay klah tay)	to explode	R's
éclipser R	(ay kleep say)	to eclipse / to overshadow	R's
écœurer R	(ay kuh ray)	to sicken	R's
éconduire	(ay kohn dweer)	to dismiss	A63
économiser R	(ay kaw naw mee zay)	to economize	R's
écorcher R	(ay kawr shay)	to skin / to chafe	R's
écouler R	(ay koo lay)	to sell / to pass	R's
écouter R	(ay koo tay)	to listen to	R's
écraser R	(ay krah zay)	to crush	R's
écrémer	(ay kray may)	to skim (milk)	A32
écrier (s')R	(ay kree yay)	to exclaim	R's
écrire	(ay kreer)	to write	A28
écrouler (s') R	(ay kroo lay)	to collapse	R's
édifier R	(ay dee fyay)	to construct	R's
éditer R	(ay dee tay)	to edit	R's
éduquer R	(ay dew kay)	to educate	R's
effacer	(ay fah say)	to erase	A13
effarer R	(ay fah ray)	to alarm	R's
effaroucher R	(ay fah roo shay)	to frighten away	R's
effectuer R	(ay fehk tway)	to carry out	R's
effeuiller R	(ay fuh yay)	to thin out leaves	R's
effondrer R	(ay fohn dray)	to collapse	R's
efforcer (s')	(ay fawr say)	to strive	A13
effrayer	(ay freh yay)	to scare	A33
égaler R	(ay gah lay)	to equal	R's
égarer R	(ay gah ray)	to lead astray	R's
égayer	(ay gay yay)	to enliven	A33
égorger	(ay gawr zhay)	to slit the throat of	A46
élaborer R	(ay lah baw ray)	to develop	R's
élancer (s')	(ay lawn say)	to dash forward	A13
élargir *	(ay lahr zheer)	to widen	*'s
électrifier R	(ay lehk tree fyay)	to electrify	R's
élever	(ay lvay)	to raise	A44
élider R	(ay lee day)	to elide	R's
éliminer R	(ay lee mee nay)	to eliminate	R's

© 2010

FRENCH VERB	PRONUNCIATION	ENGLISH MEANING	PAGE
élire	(ay leer)	to elect	A45
éloigner R	(ay lwah nyay)	to move away	R's
élucider R	(ay lew see day)	to solve	R's
éluder R	(ay lew day)	to evade	R's
émanciper R	(ay mawn see pay)	to emancipate	R's
émaner R	(ay mah nay)	to emanate	R's
embarquer R	(awn bahr kay)	to embark /to load	R's
embarrasser R	(awn bah rah say)	to embarrass	R's
embaucher R	(awn boh shay)	to hire	R's
embellir *	(awn beh leer)	to embellish	*'s
emboîter R	(awn bwah tay)	to fit together	R's
embourgeoiser (s') R	(awn boorzh wah zay)	to become middle- class	R's
embrasser R	(awn brah say)	to kiss	R's
émerger	(ay mehr zhay)	to emerge	A46
émettre	(ay meh truh)	to emit	A48
émigrer R	(ay mee gray)	to emigrate	R's
emménager	(awn may nah zhay)	to move in	A46
emmener	(awn mnay)	to take away	A44
émouvoir	(ay moo vwahr)	to move deeply / to disturb	A29
emparer (s') R	(awn pah ray)	to take over	R's
empêcher R	(awn pay shay)	to prevent	R's
empiéter	(awn pyay tay)	to encroach upon	A32
empirer R	(awn pee ray)	to get worse	R's
emplir *	(awn pleer)	to fill	*'s
employer	(awn plwah yay)	to employ	A30
empoisonner R	(awn pwah zaw nay)	to poison	R's
emporter R	(awn pawr tay)	to take away	R's
empreindre	(awn prahn druh)	to imprint	A12
empresser (s') R	(awn pray say)	to hasten	R's
emprisonner R	(awn pree zaw nay)	to imprison	R's
emprunter R	(awn pruhn tay)	to borrow	R's
encadrer R	(awn kah dray)	to supervise	R's
encaisser R	(awn kay say)	to cash	R's
enchaîner R	(awn sheh nay)	to chain up	R's
enchanter R	(awn shawn tay)	to delight	R's
enclore	(awn klawr)	to enclose	A17
encombrer R	(awn kohn bray)	to clutter up	R's
encourager	(awn koo rah zhay)	to encourage	A46
encourir	(awn koo reer)	to incur	A21
endetter R	(awn day tay)	to put (so) into debt	R's
endoctriner R	(awn dawk tree nay)	to indoctrinate	R's
endommager	(awn daw mah zhay)	to damage	A46
endormir	(awn dawr meer)	to send (so) to sleep	A27
enduire	(awn dweer)	to coat	A63
endurcir *	(awn dewr seer)	to strengthen	*'s
énerver R	(ay nehr vay)	to irritate	R's
enfanter R	(awn fawn tay)	to give birth	R's
enfermer R	(awn fehr may)	to shut in	R's
enfiler R	(awn fee lay)	to slip on	R's

© 2010

FRENCH VERB	PRONUNCIATION	ENGLISH MEANING	PAGE
enflammer R	(awn flah may)	to set fire to	R's
enfler R	(awn flay)	to inflate	R's
enfoncer	(awn fohn say)	to push in	A13
enfouir *	(awn fweer)	to bury	*'s
enfreindre	(awn frahn druh)	to infringe	A12
enfuir (s')	(awn fwee eer)	to run away	A39
engager	(awn gah zhay)	to hire / to engage	A46
engloutir *	(awn gloo teer)	to engulf	*'s
engourdir *	(awn goor deer)	to numb	*'s
engraisser R	(awn gray say)	to fatten	R's
engueuler R	(awn guh lay)	to tell off	R's
enivrer R	(awn nee vray)	to intoxicate	R's
enjoindre	(awn zhwan druh)	to enjoin	A12
enjoliver R	(awn zhaw lee vay)	to embellish	R's
enlacer	(awn lah say)	to embrace	A13
enlever	(awn lvay)	to remove	A44
enneiger	(awn neh zhay)	to block with snow	A46
ennuyer	(aw nwee yay)	to bore	A30
énoncer	(ay nohn say)	to pronounce	A13
enquérir (s')	(awn kay reer)	to inquire	A4
enquêter R	(awn kay tay)	to investigate	R's
enraciner R	(awn rah see nay)	to root	R's
enrager	(awn rah zhay)	to be furious	A46
enregistrer R	(awn ruh zhee stray)	to record / to register	R's
enrichir *	(awn ree sheer)	to make rich	*'s
enrouler R	(awn roo lay)	to wind	R's
enseigner R	(awn say nyay)	to teach	R's
ensevelir *	(awn suh vuh leer)	to bury / to hide	*'s
ensuivre (s')	(awn swee vruh)	to follow	A61
entamer R	(awn tah may)	to initiate	R's
entasser R	(awn tah say)	to pile up	R's
entendre #	(awn tawn druh)	to hear	#'s
enterrer R	(awn tay ray)	to bury	R's
enthousiasmer R	(awn too zy ahs may)	to enthuse	R's
enticher (s') R	(awn tee shay)	to become infatuated	R's
entourer R	(awn too ray)	to surround	R's
entraîner R	(awn tray nay)	to train / to lead to	R's
entraver R	(awn trah vay)	to hinder	R's
entrelacer	(awn truh lah say)	to intertwine	A13
entremettre (s')	(awn truh meh truh)	to mediate	A48
entreprendre	(awn truh prawn druh)	to undertake	A9
entrer R	(awn tray)	to enter	R's
entretenir	(awn truh tuh neer)	to look after	A23
entrevoir	(awn truh vwahr)	to glimpse	A66
entrouvrir	(awn troo vreer)	to open a little	A52
énumérer	(ay new may ray)	to enumerate	A32
envahir *	(awn vah eer)	to invade	*'s
envelopper R	(awn vlaw pay)	to wrap up	R's
envier R	(awn vyay)	to envy	R's

© 2010

FRENCH VERB	PRONUNCIATION	ENGLISH MEANING	PAGE
envisager	(awn vee zah zhay)	to envisage	A46
envoyer	(awn vwah yay)	to send	A31
épandre #	(ay pawn druh)	to spread	#'s
épanouir *	(ay pahn weer)	to open out / to lighten up	*'s
épargner R	(ay pahr nyay)	to save	R's
éparpiller R	(ay pahr pee yay)	to scatter	R's
épater R	(ay pah tay)	to impress	R's
épeler	(ay play)	to spell	A8
épicer	(ay pee say)	to spice	A13
épier R	(ay pyay)	to spy on	R's
éplucher R	(ay plew shay)	to peel	R's
éponger	(ay pohn zhay)	to mop up	A46
épouser R	(ay poo zay)	to marry	R's
épouvanter R	(ay poo vawn tay)	to terrify	R's
épreindre	(ay prahn druh)	to squeeze out	A12
éprendre (s')	(ay prawn druh)	to fall in love with	A9
éprouver R	(ay proo vay)	to feel	R's
épuiser R	(ay pwee zay)	to exhaust	R's
équilibrer R	(ay kee lee bray)	to balance	R's
équiper R	(ay kee pay)	to provide	R's
équivaloir	(ay kee vah lwahr)	to be equivalent to	A56
errer R	(eh ray)	to wander	R'S
esclaffer (s') R	(eh sklah fay)	to burst out laughing	R's
escorter R	(eh skawr tay)	to escort	R's
espérer	(eh spay ray)	to hope	A32
espionner R	(eh spyaw nay)	to spy on	R's
esquisser R	(eh skee say)	to sketech	R's
esquiver R	(eh skee vay)	to duck	R's
essayer	(ay say yay)	to try	A33
essorer R	(ay sawr ray)	to wring	R's
essouffler R	(ay soo flay)	to leave (so) breathless	R's
essuyer	(ay swee yay)	to dry / to wipe	A30
estimer R	(eh stee may)	to feel / to estimate	R's
estropier R	(eh straw pyay)	to maim	R's
établir *	(ay tah bleer)	to set up	*'s
étaler R	(ay tah lay)	to spread out	R's
étayer	(ay tay yay)	to shore up/to to prop up	A33
éteindre	(ay tahn druh)	to put out / to switch off	A12
étendre #	(ay tawn druh)	to stretch	#'s
éternuer R	(ay tehr nway)	to sneeze	R's
étiqueter	(ay teek tay)	to label	A43
étirer R	(ay tee ray)	to draw	R's
étoffer R	(ay taw fay)	to expand	R's
étonner R	(ay taw nay)	to surprise	R's
étouffer R	(ay too fay)	to stifle	R's
étourdir *	(ay toor deer)	to stun	*'s
étrangler R	(ay trawn glay)	to strangle	R's
être	(eh truh)	to be	A34
étreindre	(ay trahn druh)	to embrace	A12

FRENCH VERB	PRONUNCIATION	ENGLISH MEANING	PAGE
étudier R	(ay tew dyay)	to study	R's
évader (s') R	(ay vah day)	to escape	R's
évaluer R	(ay vah lway)	to estimate	R's
évanouir (s') *	(ay vah nweer)	to faint	*'s
évaporer R	(ay vah paw ray)	to evaporate	R's
éveiller R	(ay vay yay)	to arouse	R's
éventer R	(ay vawn tay)	to discover	R's
évertuer (s') R	(ay vehr tway)	to try one's best	R's
éviter R	(ay vee tay)	to avoid	R's
évoluer R	(ay vaw lway)	to evolve	R's
évoquer R	(ay vaw kay)	to recall	R's
exagérer	(ehg zah zhay ray)	to exaggerate	A32
exalter R	(ehg zahl tay)	to elate / to exalt	R's
examiner R	(ehg zah mee nay)	to examine	R's
exaspérer	(ehg zah spay ray)	to exasperate	A32
excéder	(ek say day)	to exceed	A32
exciter R	(ek see tay)	to excite	R's
exclamer (s') R	(eks klah may)	to exclaim	R's
exclure	(eks klewr)	to exclude	A41
excommunier R	(eks kaw mew nyay)	to excommunicate	R's
excuser R	(eks kew zay)	to excuse	R's
exécrer	(eg zay kray)	to loathe	A5
exécuter R	(eg zay kew tay)	to carry out	R's
exempter R	(eg zawn tay)	to exempt from	R's
exercer	(eg zehr say)	to exercise	A13
exhiber R	(eg zee bay)	to flaunt	R's
exhorter R	(eg zawr tay)	to motivate	R's
exiger	(eg zee zhay)	to demand	A46
exiler R	(eg zee lay)	to exile	R's
exister R	(eg zee stay)	to exist	R's
exonérer	(eg zaw nay ray)	to exempt	A32
expédier R	(ek spay dyay)	to dispatch / to expedite	R's
expérimenter R	(ek spay ree mawn tay)	to test	R's
expirer R	(ek spee ray)	to exhale / to expire	R's
expliquer R	(ek splee kay)	to explain	R's
exploiter R	(ek splwa tay)	to exploit	R's
exploser R	(ek sploh zay)	to explode	R's
exporter R	(ek spawr tay)	to export	R's
exposer R	(ek spoh zay)	to exhibit	R's
exprimer R	(ek spree may)	to express	R's
expulser R	(ek spewl say)	to evict	R's
exterminer R	(ek stehr mee nay)	to exterminate	R's
extraire	(ek strehr)	to extract	A35
exulter R	(eg zewl tay)	to exult	R's
fabriquer R	(fah bree kay)	to make	R's
fabuler R	(fah bew lay)	to make things up	R's
fâcher R	(fah shay)	to anger	R's
faciliter R	(fah see lee tay)	to facilitate	R's
façonner R	(fah saw nay)	to manufacture	R's

© 2010

FRENCH VERB	PRONUNCIATION	ENGLISH MEANING	PAGE
facturer R	(fahk tew ray)	to invoice	R's
faillir	(fah yeer)	to almost do	A36
fainéanter R	(fay nay awn tay)	to laze about	R's
faire	(fehr)	to make / to do	A37
falloir	(fahl wahr)	to be necessary / to need	A38
falsifier R	(fahl see fyay)	to falsify	R's
familiariser R	(fah meel yah ree zay)	to familiarize	R's
farcir *	(fahr seer)	to stuff	*'s
farder R	(fahr day)	to disguise	R's
fasciner R	(fah see nay)	to fascinate	R's
fatiguer R	(fah tee gay)	to make tired	R's
faucher R	(foh shay)	to mow / to flatten	R's
faufiler R	(foh fee lay)	to baste	R's
fausser R	(foh say)	to distort	R's
favoriser R	(fah vaw ree zay)	to favour	R's
feindre	(fahn druh)	to feign	A12
feinter R	(fahn tay)	to make a feint	R's
fêler R	(feh lay)	to crack	R's
féliciter R	(fay lee see tay)	to congratulate	R's
fendre #	(fawn druh)	to chop / to split	#'s
ferler R	(fehr lay)	to furl	R's
fermenter R	(fehr mawn tay)	to ferment	R's
fermer R	(fehr may)	to close	R's
fessser R	(fay say)	to spank	R's
fêter R	(fay tay)	to celebrate	R's
feuilleter	(fuhy tay)	to leaf through	A43
fiancer	(fee awn say)	to get engaged	A13
ficeler	(fee slay)	to tie up	A8
ficher R	(fee shay)	to file	R's
fier (se) R	(fyay)	to trust	R's
figer	(fee zhay)	to congeal	A46
figurer R	(fee gew ray)	to represent	R's
filer R	(fee lay)	to spin	R's
fileter	(fee l tay)	to thread	A44
filtrer R	(feel tray)	to filter	R's
financer	(fee nawn say)	to finance	A13
finir *	(fee neer)	to finish	*'s
fixer R	(feek say)	to fix	R's
flairer R	(flay ray)	to sniff	R's
flamber R	(flawn bay)	to singe	R's
flancher R	(flawn shay)	to crack up	R's
flâner R	(flah nay)	to stroll	R's
flanquer R	(flawn kay)	to flank	R's
flatter R	(flah tay)	to flatter	R's
fléchir *	(flay sheer)	to bend	*'s
flemmarder R	(fleh mahr day)	to loaf around	R's
flétrir *	(flay treer)	to fade	*'s
fleurir *	(fluh reer)	to decorate with flowers	*'s
flirter R	(fluhr tay)	to flirt	R's

FRENCH VERB	PRONUNCIATION	ENGLISH MEANING	PAGE
flotter R	(flaw tay)	to float	R's
foirer R	(fwah ray)	to be a complete disaster	R's
foisonner R	(fwah zaw nay)	to abound	R's
fomenter R	(faw mawn tay)	to foment	R's
foncer	(fohn say)	to darken	A13
fonctionner R	(fohnk syaw nay)	to work	R's
fonder R	(fohn day)	to found	R's
fondre #	(fohn druh)	to melt	#'s
forcer	(fawr say)	to force	A13
forger	(fawr zhay)	to forge	A46
formaliser R	(fawr mah lee zay)	to formalize	R's
former R	(fawr may)	to form	R's
formuler R	(fawr mew lay)	to express	R's
fortifier R	(fawr tee fyay)	to strengthen	R's
foudroyer	(foo drwah yay)	to strike down	A30
fouetter R	(fweh tay)	to flog	R's
fouiller R	(foo yay)	to search	R's
fouiner R	(fwee nay)	to forage about	R's
fourmiller R	(foor mee yay)	to abound	R's
fournir *	(foor neer)	to supply	*'s
fourrer R	(foo ray)	to stuff / to line	R's
fourvoyer	(foor vwah yay)	to mislead	A30
fracasser R	(frah kah say)	to smash	R's
franchir *	(frawn sheer)	to cross / to get over	*'s
frapper R	(frah pay)	to hit	R's
frayer	(freh yay)	to clear a path	A33
freiner R	(freh nay)	to slow down	R's
frémir *	(fray meer)	to quiver	*'s
fréquenter R	(fray kawn tay)	to associate with	R's
frimer R	(free may)	to show off	R's
frire	(freer)	to fry	A60
friser R	(free zay)	to curl	R's
frissonner R	(free saw nay)	to shiver	R's
froisser R	(frwah say)	to crease / to hurt	R's
frôler R	(froh lay)	to brush	R's
froncer	(frohn say)	to gather / to frown	A13
frotter R	(fraw tay)	to rub	R's
fructifier R	(frewk tee fyay)	to flourish / to yield a profit	R's
frustrer R	(frew stray)	to frustrate	R's
fuir	(fweer)	to flee	A39
fumer R	(few may)	to smoke	R's
fuser R	(few zay)	to ring out / to rocket	R's
fusiller R	(few zee yay)	to shoot	R's
gâcher R	(gah shay)	to waste	R's
gagner R	(gah nyay)	to win / to earn	R's
galoper R	(gah law pay)	to gallop	R's
garantir *	(gah rawn teer)	to guarantee	*'s
garder R	(gahr day)	to keep	R's
garer R	(gah ray)	to park	R's

© 2010

FRENCH VERB	PRONUNCIATION	ENGLISH MEANING	PAGE
garnir *	(gahr neer)	to fill	*'s
gaspiller R	(gah spee yay)	to squander	R's
gâter R	(gah tay)	to spoil	R's
gauchir *	(goh sheer)	to warp	*'s
gaufrer R	(goh fray)	to emboss	R's
gausser (s)R	(goh say)	to mock	R's
geindre	(zhahn druh)	to moan	A12
geler	(zhuh lay)	to freeze	A44
gémir *	(zhay meer)	to groan	*'s
gêner R	(zheh nay)	to disturb	R's
généraliser R	(zhay nay rah lee zay)	to generalize	R's
gérer	(zhay ray)	to manage	A32
gifler R	(zhee flay)	to slap	R's
givrer R	(zhee vray)	to frost over	R's
glacer	(glah say)	to freeze / to chill	A13
glisser R	(glee say)	to slip	R's
glorifier R	(glaw ree fyay)	to glorify	R's
gommer R	(gaw may)	to erase	R's
gonfler R	(gohn flay)	to inflate	R's
goûter R	(goo tay)	to taste	R's
gouverner R	(goo vehr nay)	to govern	R's
gracier R	(grah syay)	to pardon	R's
grandir *	(grawn deer)	to grow	*'s
gratifier R	(grah tee fyay)	to gratify	R's
gratter R	(grah tay)	to scratch	R's
graver R	(grah vay)	to engrave	R's
gravir *	(grah veer)	to climb up	*'s
greffer R	(gray fay)	to graft	R's
grêler R	(grch lay)	to hail	R's
grelotter R	(gruh law tay)	to shiver	R's
griffer R	(gree fay)	to scratch	R's
griffoner R	(gree faw nay)	to scrawl	R's
grignoter R	(gree nyaw tay)	to nibble	R's
griller R	(gree yay)	to grill	R's
grimacer	(gree mah say)	to grimace	A13
grimper R	(grahn pay)	to climb	R's
grincer	(grahn say)	to creak	A13
griser R	(gree zay)	to exhilarate	R's
grogner R	(graw nyay)	to mutter	R's
grommeler	(grawm lay)	to mutter	A8
gronder R	(grohn day)	to tell off	R's
grossir *	(groh seer)	to enlarge / to put on weight	*'s
grouiller R	(groo yay)	to swarm about	R's
grouper R	(groo pay)	to put together	R's
guérir *	(gay reer)	to cure / to recover	*'s
guerroyer	(gayr wah yay)	to wage war	A30
guetter R	(gay tay)	to watch out for	R's
guider R	(gee day)	to guide	R's
guinder R	(gahn day)	to make awkward	R's

© 2010

FRENCH VERB	PRONUNCIATION	ENGLISH MEANING	PAGE
habiller R	(ah bee yay)	to dress	R's
habiter R	(ah bee tay)	to live in	R's
habituer R	(ah bee tway)	to get used to	R's
hacher R	(ah shay)	to mince	R's
haïr	(ah eer)	to hate	A40
haleter	(ahl tay)	to gasp for breath	A40
halluciner R	(ah lew see nay)	to hallucinate	R's
handicaper R	(awn dee kah pay)	to handicap	R's
hanter R	(awn tay)	to haunt	R's
harceler	(ahr suh lay)	to pester	A44
harmoniser R	(ahr maw nee zay)	to harmonize	R's
hasarder R	(ah zahr day)	to venture / to risk	R's
hâter R	(ah tay)	to hasten	R's
hausser R	(oh say)	to shrug	R's
héberger	(ay behr zhay)	to accomodate	A46
hébéter	(ay bay tay)	to daze	A32
hennir *	(ay neer)	to neigh	*'s
hérisser R	(ay ree say)	to ruffle up	R's
hériter R	(ay ree tay)	to inherit	R's
hésiter R	(ay see tay)	to hesitate	R's
heurter R	(uhr tay)	to hit	R's
hocher R	(aw shay)	to nod	R's
honorer R	(aw naw ray)	to honour	R's
hoqueter	(awk tay)	to hiccup	A43
horrifier R	(aw ree fyay)	to horrify	R's
huer R	(wee ay)	to boo	R's
humaniser R	(ew mah nee zay)	to humanize	R's
humidifier R	(ew mee dee fyay)	to humidify	R's
humilier R	(ew mee lyay)	to humiliate	R's
hurler R	(ewr lay)	to yell	R's
hypnotiser R	(eep naw tee zay)	to hypnotize	R's
idéaliser R	(ee day ah lee zay)	to idealize	R's
identifier R	(ee dawn tee fyay)	to identify	R's
ignorer R	(ee nyaw ray)	to ignore / not to know	R's
illuminer R	(ee lew mee nay)	to illuminate	R's
illustrer R	(ee lew stray)	to illustrate	R's
imaginer R	(ee mah zhee nay)	to imagine	R's
imiter R	(ee mee tay)	to imitate	R's
immigrer R	(ee mee gray)	to immigrate	R's
immiscer (s')	(ee mee say)	to interfere	A13
immobiliser R	(ee maw bee lee zay)	to immobilize	R's
immoler R	(ee maw lay)	to sacrifice	R's
impatienter R	(ahn pah syawn tay)	to irritate	R's
impliquer R	(ahn plee kay)	to implicate	R's
implorer R	(ahn plaw ray)	to implore	R's
importer R	(ahn pawr tay)	to import	R's
impressionner R	(ahn preh syaw nay)	to impress	R's
imprimer R	(ahn pree may)	to print	R's
improviser R	(ahn praw vee zay)	to improvise	R's

© 2010

FRENCH VERB	PRONUNCIATION	ENGLISH MEANING	PAGE
inaugurer R	(ee noh gew ray)	to inaugurate / to unveil	R's
inciter R	(ahn see tay)	to incite / to encourage	R's
incliner R	(ahn klee nay)	to tilt	R's
inclure	(ahn klewr)	to include	A41
incommoder R	(ahn kaw maw day)	to bother	R's
incorporer R	(ahn kawr paw ray)	to blend in / to incorporate	R's
incriminer R	(ahn kree mee nay)	to accuse / to incriminate	R's
inculper R	(ahn kewl pay)	to charge	R's
indiquer R	(ahn dee kay)	to point out / to indicate	R's
induire	(ahn dweer)	to lead to / to infer	A63
infecter R	(ahn fehk tay)	to infect	R's
infirmer R	(ahn feer may)	to invalidate	R's
infliger	(ahn flee zhay)	to inflict	A46
influencer	(ahn flew awn say)	to influence	A13
informer R	(ahn fawr may)	to inform	R's
ingénier (s') R	(ahn zhayn yay)	to do one's utmost / to engineer	R's
inhaler R	(ee nah lay)	to inhale	R's
initier R	(ee nee syay)	to initiate	R's
injurier R	(ahn zhewr yay)	to swear at / to insult	R's
innover R	(ee naw vay)	to innovate	R's
inoculer R	(ee naw kew lay)	to inoculate	R's
inonder R	(ee nohn day)	to flood / to inundate	R's
inquiéter	(ahn kyay tay)	to worry	A32
inscrire	(ahn skreer)	to enrol / to write down	A28
insensibiliser R	(ahn sawn see bee lee zay)	to anaesthetize	R's
insérer	(ahn say ray)	to insert	A32
insinuer R	(ahn see nway)	to insinuate	R's
insister R	(ahn see stay)	to insist	R's
inspecter R	(ahn spchk tay)	to inspect	R's
inspirer R	(ahn spee ray)	to inspire	R's
installer R	(ahn stah lay)	to install	R's
instituer R	(ahn stee tway)	to institute	R's
instruire	(ahn strweer)	to teach	A63
insulter R	(ahn sewl tay)	to insult	R's
insurger (s')	(ahn sewr zhay)	to rise up against	A46
intégrer	(ahn tay gray)	to integrate	A5
intensifier R	(ahn tawn see fyay)	to intensify	R's
intercéder	(ahn tehr say day)	to intercede	A32
interdire	(ahn tehr deer)	to forbid	A42
intéresser R	(ahn tay ray say)	to interest	R's
interloquer R	(ahn tehr law kay)	to take (so) aback	R's
interroger	(ahn tehr raw zhay)	to interrogate	A46
interrompre #	(ahn tay rohn pruh)	to interrupt / to stop	#'s
intervenir	(ahn tehr vuh neer)	to intervene	A23
intituler R	(ahn tee tew lay)	to call / to entitle	R's
intriguer R	(ahn tree gay)	to intrigue	R's
introduire	(ahn traw dweer)	to insert / to introduce	A63
inventer R	(ahn vawn tay)	to invent	R's
inverser R	(ahn vehr say)	to reverse	R's

FRENCH VERB	PRONUNCIATION	ENGLISH MEANING	PAGE
invertir *	(ahn vehr teer)	to invert	*'s
investir *	(ahn veh steer)	to invest	*'s
inviter R	(ahn vee tay)	to invite	R's
invoquer R	(ahn vaw kay)	to invoke	R's
irriter R	(ee ree tay)	to irritate	R's
isoler R	(ee zaw lay)	to isolate	R's
jaillir *	(zhah yeer)	to gush out	*'s
jaser R	(zhah zay)	to gossip	R's
jaunir *	(zhoh neer)	to turn yellow	*'s
jeter	(zhuh tay)	to throw	A43
jeûner R	(zhuh nay)	to fast	R's
joindre	(zhwahn druh)	to join / to enclose	A12
jouer R	(zhway)	to play	R's
jouir *	(zhweer)	to enjoy	*'s
juger	(zhew zhay)	to judge	A46
jumeler	(zhewm lay)	to double / to combine	A8
jurer R	(zhew ray)	to pledge	R's
justifier R	(zhew stee fyay)	to justify	R's
kidnapper R	(keed nah pay)	to kidnap	R's
klaxonner R	(klahk saw nay)	to honk	R's
labourer R	(lah boo ray)	to plough	R's
lacer	(lah say)	to lace up	A13
lâcher R	(lah shay)	to release	R's
laisser R	(lay say)	to leave	R's
lamenter (se) R	(lah mawn tay)	to moan	R's
lancer	(lawn say)	to throw	A13
languir *	(lawn geer)	to languish	*'s
larmoyer	(lahr mwah yay)	to water	A30
laver R	(lah vay)	to wash	R's
lécher	(lay shay)	to lick	A5
légaliser R	(lay gah lee zay)	to legalize	R's
légiférer	(lay zhee fay ray)	to legislate	A32
lésiner R	(lay zee nay)	to skimp on	R's
lever	(leh vay)	to lift	A44
libérer	(lee bay ray)	to liberate	A32
licencier R	(lee sawn syay)	to make (so) redundant	R's
lier R	(lyay)	to tie up	R's
ligoter R	(lee gaw tay)	to truss up	R's
limer R	(lee may)	to file down	R's
limiter R	(lee mee tay)	to limit	R's
liquéfier R	(lee kay fyay)	to liquefy	R's
liquider R	(lee kee day)	to liquidate	R's
lire	(leer)	to read	A45
livrer R	(lee vray)	to deliver	R's
loger	(law zhay)	to house	A46
lorgner R	(lawr nyay)	to eye up	R's
lotir *	(law teer)	to allot	*'s
loucher R	(loo shay)	to squint	R's
louer R	(loo ay)	to let / to rent / to hire	R's

© 2010

FRENCH VERB	PRONUNCIATION	ENGLISH MEANING	PAGE
louper R	(loo pay)	to miss / to screw up	R's
louvoyer	(loo vwah yay)	to tack	A30
lubrifier R	(lew bree fyay)	to lubricate	R's
lutter R	(lew tay)	to struggle	R's
mâcher R	(mah shay)	to chew	R's
machiner R	(mah shee nay)	to plot	R's
magnifier R	(mah nyee fyay)	to idealize	R's
maigrir *	(meh greer)	to lose weight	*'s
maintenir	(mahn tuh neer)	to maintain	A23
maîtriser R	(meh tree zay)	to control	R's
majorer R	(mah zhaw ray)	to increase	R's
malmener	(mahl muh nay)	to manhandle	A44
maltraiter R	(mahl treh tay)	to mistreat	R's
manger	(mawn zhay)	to eat	A46
manier R	(mah nyay)	to handle	R's
manifester R	(mah nee feh stay)	to show	R's
manigancer	(mah nee gawn say)	to scheme	A13
manipuler R	(mah nee pew lay)	to manipulate / to handle	R's
manœuvrer R	(mah nuh vray)	to manoeuvre	R's
manquer R	(mawn kay)	to miss	R's
manufacturer R	(mah new fahk tew ray)	to manufacture	R's
manutentionner R	(mah new tawn syaw nay)	to handle	R's
marcher R	(mahr shay)	to walk	R's
marier R	(mah ryay)	to marry	R's
marquer R	(mahr kay)	to mark	R's
marteler	(mahr tuh lay)	to hammer	A44
masquer R	(mah skay)	to conceal	R's
massacrer R	(mah sah kray)	to massacre	R's
matérialiser R	(mah tay ryah lee zay)	to materialize	R's
maudire	(moh deer)	to curse	A47
maugréer R	(moh gray ay)	to grumble	R's
mécaniser R	(may kah nee zay)	to mechanize	R's
méconnaître	(may kaw neh truh)	to misunderstand / to disregard	A18
mécontenter R	(may kohn tawn tay)	to annoy	R's
médire	(may deer)	to malign	A25
méditer R	(may dee tay)	to contemplate / to meditate	R's
méfier R	(may fyay)	to mistrust	R's
mélanger	(may lawn zhay)	to blend	A46
mêler R	(may lay)	to mix	R's
menacer	(muh nah say)	to threaten	A13
ménager	(may nah zhay)	to handle carefully	A46
mendier R	(mawn dyay)	to beg	R's
mener	(muh nay)	to lead	A44
mentionner R	(mawn syaw nay)	to mention	R's
mentir	(mawn teer)	to lie	A27
méprendre (se)	(may prawn druh)	to be mistaken	A9
mépriser R	(may pree zay)	to despise	R's
mériter R	(may ree tay)	to deserve	R's
mesurer R	(muh zew ray)	to measure	R's

© 2010

FRENCH VERB	PRONUNCIATION	ENGLISH MEANING	PAGE
mettre	(meh truh)	to put	A48
meubler R	(muh blay)	to furnish	R's
meugler R	(muh glay)	to moo	R's
meurtrir *	(muhr treer)	to hurt	*'s
miauler R	(myoh lay)	to meow	R's
mijoter R	(mee zhaw tay)	to prepare	R's
mimer R	(mee may)	to mimic	R's
miner R	(mee nay)	to mine / to undermine	R's
minimiser R	(mee nee mee zay)	to minimize	R's
mobiliser R	(maw bee lee zay)	to mobilize	R's
modeler	(mawd lay)	to model	A44
modérer	(maw day ray)	to moderate	A32
moderniser R	(maw dehr nee zay)	to modernize	R's
modifier R	(maw dee fyay)	to modify	R's
moisir *	(mwa zeer)	to go mouldy	*'s
moissonner R	(mwah saw nay)	to harvest	R's
mollir *	(maw leer)	to fail / to diminish	*'s
monnayer	(maw neh yay)	to convert into cash	A33
monopoliser R	(maw naw paw lee zay)	to monopolize	R's
monter R	(mohn tay)	to take (so/sth) up / to go up	R's
montrer R	(mohn tray)	to show	R's
moquer R	(maw kay)	to mock	R's
mordre #	(mawr druh)	to bite	#'s
morfondre (se) #	(mawr fohn druh)	to hang around	#'s
mortifier R	(mawr tee fyay)	to mortify	R's
motiver R	(maw tee vay)	to motivate	R's
moucher (se) R	(moo shay)	to blow one's nose	R's
moudre	(moo druh)	to grind	A49
mouiller R	(moo yay)	to wet	R's
mourir	(moo reer)	to die	A50
mouvoir	(moo vwahr)	to move	A29
muer R	(moo ay)	to transform	R's
multiplier R	(mewl tee plee yay)	to multiply	R's
munir *	(mew neer)	to provide	*'s
mûrir *	(mew reer)	to ripen	*'s
murmurer R	(mewr mew ray)	to murmur	R's
museler	(mew zuh lay)	to muzzle	A8
muter R	(mew tay)	to mutate	R's
mutiler R	(mew tee lay)	to mutilate	R's
mystifier R	(mee stee fyay)	to deceive / to mystify	R's
nager	(nah zhay)	to swim	A46
naître	(neh truh)	to be born	A51
nantir *	(nawn teer)	to provide	*'s
narrer R	(nah ray)	to narrate	R's
naviguer R	(nah vee gay)	to sail	R's
navrer R	(nah vray)	to upset	R's
nécessiter R	(nay say see tay)	to require	R's
négliger	(nay glee zhay)	to neglect	A46
négocier R	(nay gaw syay)	to negotiate	R's

© 2010

FRENCH VERB	PRONUNCIATION	ENGLISH MEANING	PAGE
neiger	(neh zhay)	to snow	A46
nettoyer	(neh twah yay)	to clean	A30
nier R	(nyay)	to deny	R's
niveler	(neev lay)	to level	A8
noircir *	(nwahr seer)	to blacken	*'s
nommer R	(naw may)	to appoint / to name	R's
normaliser R	(nawr mah lee zay)	to normalize	R's
noter R	(naw tay)	to note down	R's
nouer R	(nway)	to tie	R's
nourrir *	(noo reer)	to nourish	*'s
noyer	(nwah yay)	to drown	A30
nuire	(nweer)	to harm	A63
numéroter R	(new may raw tay)	to mumber	R's
obéir *	(aw bay eer)	to obey	*'s
objecter R	(awb zhehk tay)	to object	R's
obliger	(aw blee zhay)	to force / to oblige	A46
oblitérer	(aw blee tay ray)	to obliterate	A32
obscurcir *	(awp skewr seer)	to obscure	*'s
obséder	(awp say day)	to obsess / to haunt	A32
observer R	(awp sehr vay)	to observe	R's
obstiner (s)	(awp stee nay)	to persist	R's
obtenir	(awp tuh neer)	to obtain	A23
occuper R	(aw kew pay)	to occupy	R's
octroyer	(awk trwah yay)	to grant	A30
offenser R	(aw fawn say)	to offend	R's
offrir	(aw freer)	to offer	A52
omettre	(aw meh truh)	to omit	A48
opérer	(aw pay ray)	to operate (on)	A32
opposer R	(aw poh zay)	to oppose	R's
opprimer R	(aw pree may)	to oppress	R's
ordonner R	(awr daw nay)	to order / to prescribe	R's
organiser R	(awr gah nee zay)	to organize	R's
orner R	(awr nay)	to decorate	R's
orthographier R	(awr taw grah fyay)	to spell	R's
osciller R	(aw see lay)	to swing / to oscillate	R's
oser R	(oh zay)	to dare	R's
ôter R	(oh tay)	to remove	R's
oublier R	(oo blee yay)	to forget	R's
outrager	(oot rah zhay)	to offend / to outrage	A46
ouvrir	(oov reer)	to open	A52
oxyder R	(awk see day)	to oxidize	R's
pacifier R	(pah see fyay)	to pacify	R's
pâlir *	(pah leer)	to grow pale	*'s
palper R	(pahl pay)	to palpate	R's
palpiter R	(pahl pee tay)	to pulse / to palpitate	R's
paniquer R	(pah nee kay)	to panic	R's
panser R	(pawn say)	to bandage	R's
parachever	(pah rah shvay)	to perfect / to complete	A44
parachuter R	(pah rah shew tay)	to parachute	R's

FRENCH VERB	PRONUNCIATION	ENGLISH MEANING	PAGE
paraître	(pah reh truh)	to appear / to seem	A18
paralyser R	(pah rah lee zay)	to paralyse	R's
parcourir	(pahr koo reer)	to travel all over	A21
pardonner R	(pahr daw nay)	to forgive	R's
parer R	(pah ray)	to ward off	R's
parfumer R	(pahr few may)	to scent / to flavour	R's
parier R	(pah ryay)	to bet	R's
parler R	(pahr lay)	to speak	R's
parquer R	(pahr kay)	to coop up / to park	R's
partager	(pahr tah zhay)	to share	A46
participer R	(pahr tee see pay)	to participate	R's
partir	(pahr teer)	to leave	A27
parvenir	(pahr vuh neer)	to reach	A23
passer R	(pah say)	to pass	R's
passionner R	(pah syaw nay)	to fascinate	R's
patienter R	(pah syawn tay)	to wait for	R's
pâtir *	(pah teer)	to suffer	*'s
paver R	(pah vay)	to pave	R's
pavoiser R	(pah vwa zay)	to put out flags / to be jubilant	R's
payer	(pay yay)	to pay for	A33
pécher	(pay shay)	to sin	A5
pêcher R	(peh shay)	to fish	R's
peigner R	(pay nyay)	to comb	R's
peindre	(pahn druh)	to paint	A12
peler	(puh lay)	to peel	A44
pencher R	(pawn shay)	to tilt	R's
pendre #	(pawn druh)	to hang	#'s
pénétrer	(pay nay tray)	to penetrate	A5
penser R	(pawn say)	to think	R's
percer	(pehr say)	to pierce	A13
percevoir	(pehr suh vwahr)	to receive / to perceive	A7
perdre #	(pehr druh)	to lose	#'s
perfectionner R	(pehr fehk syaw nay)	to perfect	R's
perforer R	(pehr faw ray)	to perforate	R's
périr *	(pay reer)	to die / to perish	*'s
permettre	(pehr meh truh)	to permit	A48
persécuter R	(pehr say kew tay)	to persecute	R's
persévérer	(pehr say vay ray)	to persevere	A32
persister R	(pehr see stay)	to persist	R's
persuader R	(pehr swah day)	to persuade	R's
pervertir *	(pehr vehr teer)	to pervert	*'s
peser	(puh zay)	to weigh / to consider	A44
péter	(pay tay)	to break / to fart	A32
pétrifier R	(pay tree fyay)	to petrify	R's
pétrir *	(pay treer)	to knead	*'s
peupler R	(puh play)	to populate	R's
photographier R	(faw toh grah fyay)	to photograph	R's
picoter R	(pee kaw tay)	to sting	R's
piéger	(pyay zhay)	to trap	A57

© 2010

FRENCH VERB	PRONUNCIATION	ENGLISH MEANING	PAGE
piétiner R	(pyay tee nay)	to trample	R's
pincer	(pahn say)	to pinch	A13
placer	(plah say)	to place	A13
plaider R	(play day)	to plead	R's
plaindre	(plahn druh)	to pity	A12
plaire	(plehr)	to please	A53
planifier R	(plah nee fyay)	to plan	R's
pleurer R	(pluh ray)	to mourn	R's
pleuvoir	(pluh vwahr)	to rain	A54
plier R	(plee yay)	to fold	R's
plonger	(plohn zhay)	to dive / to plunge	A46
polir *	(paw leer)	to polish	*'s
polluer R	(pawl lway)	to pollute	R's
pomper R	(pohn pay)	to pump	R's
ponctuer R	(pohnk tway)	to punctuate	R's
pondre #	(pohn druh)	to lay / to produce	#'s
porter R	(pawr tay)	to carry	R's
poser R	(poh zay)	to put down	R's
posséder	(paw say day)	to possess	A32
poster R	(paw stay)	to post	R's
pourfendre #	(poor fawn druh)	to lambast	#'s
pourrir *	(poo reer)	to rot	*'s
poursuivre	(poor swee vruh)	to pursue	A61
pousser R	(poo say)	to push / to grow	R's
pouvoir	(poo vwahr)	to be able to (can)	A55
pratiquer R	(prah tee kay)	to practise	R's
précéder	(pray say day)	to precede	A32
prêcher R	(pray shay)	to preach	R's
préciser R	(pray see zay)	to specify	R's
prédire	(pray deer)	to predict	A25
préférer	(pray fay ray)	to prefer	A32
préjuger	(pray zhew zhay)	to prejudge	A46
prélever	(pray lvay)	to take a sample of / to deduct	A44
préméditer R	(pray may dee tay)	to premeditate	R's
prendre	(prawn druh)	to take	A9
préparer R	(pray pah ray)	to prepare	R's
prescrire	(preh skreer)	to prescribe	A28
présenter R	(pray zawn tay)	to present / to introduce	R's
préserver R	(pray zehr vay)	to preserve / to protect	R's
présider R	(pray zee day)	to preside over	R's
pressentir	(pray sawn teer)	to have a premonition about	A27
présumer R	(pray zew may)	to presume	R's
prétendre #	(pray tawn druh)	to claim	#'s
prêter R	(preh tay)	to lend	R's
prévaloir	(pray vah lwahr)	to prevail	A56
prévenir	(pray vneer)	to warn / to prevent	A23
prévoir	(pray vwahr)	to predict	A66
prier R	(pree yay)	to pray	R's
priver R	(pree vay)	to deprive	R's

© 2010

FRENCH VERB	PRONUNCIATION	ENGLISH MEANING	PAGE
privilégier R	(pree vee layzh yay)	to favour	R's
procéder	(praw say day)	to proceed	A32
proclamer R	(praw klah may)	to proclaim	R's
procréer R	(praw kray ay)	to procreate	R's
produire	(praw dweer)	to produce	A63
profiter R	(praw fee tay)	to profit from/to take advantage	R's
progresser R	(praw gray say)	to make progress	R's
projeter	(praw zhuh tay)	to plan / to project	A43
prolonger	(praw lohn zhay)	to prolong	A46
promener	(praw mnay)	to take for a walk	A44
promettre	(praw meh truh)	to promise	A48
promouvoir	(praw moo vwahr)	to promote	A29
prononcer	(praw nohn say)	to pronounce	A13
proposer R	(praw poh zay)	to suggest / to offer	R's
proscrire	(praw skreer)	to ban	A28
protéger	(praw tay zhay)	to protect	A57
protester R	(praw teh stay)	to protest	R's
prouver R	(proo vay)	to prove	R's
provenir	(praw vneer)	to come from	A23
publier R	(pew blee yay)	to publish	R's
punir *	(pew neer)	to punish	*'s
purifier R	(pew ree fyay)	to purify	R's
qualifier R	(kah lee fyay)	to describe / to qualify	R's
quereller (se) R	(kuh reh lay)	to quarrel	R's
questionner R	(keh styaw nay)	to question	R's
quêter R	(kay tay)	to look for	R's
quitter R	(kee tay)	to leave	R's
rabattre	(rah bah truh)	to shut / to pull down	A1
raccommoder R	(rah kaw maw day)	to mend	R's
raccompagner R	(rah kohn pah nyay)	to walk (so) back home	R's
raccorder R	(rah kawr day)	to connect	R's
raccourcir *	(rah koor seer)	to shorten	*'s
raccrocher R	(rah kraw shay)	to hang (sth) back up	R's
racheter	(rash tay)	to buy back	A44
racler R	(rah klay)	to scrape (sth) clean	R's
racoler R	(rah kaw lay)	to solicit	R's
raconter R	(rah kohn tay)	to tell	R's
raffermir *	(rah fehr meer)	to tone / to strengthen	*'s
raffiner R	(rah fee nay)	to refine	R's
raffoler R	(rah faw lay)	to be crazy about	R's
rafler R	(rah flay)	to swipe	R's
rafraîchir *	(rah freh sheer)	to cool / to refresh	*'s
ragaillardir *	(rah gah yahr deer)	to cheer (so) up	*'s
raidir *	(reh deer)	to tighten	*'s
railler R	(rah yay)	to make fun of	R's
raisonner R	(reh zaw nay)	to reason	R's
rajeunir *	(rah zhuh neer)	to rejuvenate	*'s
rajouter R	(rah zhoo tay)	to add more	R's
rajuster R	(rah zhew stay)	to readjust	R's

© 2010

FRENCH VERB	PRONUNCIATION	ENGLISH MEANING	PAGE
ralentir *	(rah lawn teer)	to slow down	*'s
rallier R	(rah lyay)	to rally / to win over	R's
rallonger	(rah lohn zhay)	to lengthen	A46
rallumer R	(rah lew may)	to relight	R's
ramasser R	(rah mah say)	to collect	R's
ramener	(rah mnay)	to bring back	A44
ramollir *	(rah maw leer)	to soften	*'s
ranimer R	(rah nee may)	to revive	R's
rappeler	(rah play)	to recall / to remind	A8
rapporter R	(rah pawr tay)	to bring back	R's
rapprocher R	(rah praw shay)	to bring nearer	R's
raser R	(rah zay)	to shave	R's
rassembler R	(rah sawn blay)	to gather	R's
rasséréner	(rah say ray nay)	to reassure	A32
rassurer R	(rah sew ray)	to reassure	R's
rater R	(rah tay)	to fail	R's
rationaliser R	(rah syaw nah lee zay)	to rationalise	R's
rattraper R	(rah trah pay)	to catch up with	R's
ravir *	(rah veer)	to delight	*'s
ravitailler R	(rah vee tah yay)	to refuel	R's
réagir *	(ray ah zheer)	to react	*'s
réaliser R	(ray ah lee zay)	to fulfil / to realize	R's
rebattre	(ruh bah truh)	to reshuffle	A1
rebondir *	(ruh bohn deer)	to bounce / to rebound	*'s
rebuter R	(ruh bew tay)	to repel / to disgust	R's
receler	(ruh slay)	to conceal	A44
recenser R	(ruh sawn say)	to take a census of	R's
recevoir	(ruh svwahr)	to receive	A7
réchapper R	(ray shah pay)	to come through (sth)	R's
réchauffer R	(ray shoh fay)	to reheat / to heat up	R's
rechercher R	(ruh shehr shay)	to look for	R's
réciter R	(ray see tay)	to recite	R's
réclamer R	(ray klah may)	to ask for / to claim	R's
récolter R	(ray kawl tay)	to harvest	R's
recommander R	(ruh kaw mawn day)	to advise	R's
recommencer	(ruh kaw mawn say)	to start again	A13
récompenser R	(ray kohn pawn say)	to reward	R's
réconcilier R	(ray kohn see lyay)	to reconcile	R's
reconduire	(ruh kohn dweer)	to see (so) out	A63
réconforter R	(ray kohn fawr tay)	to comfort	R's
reconnaître	(ruh kaw neh truh)	to recognize	A18
reconquérir	(ruh kohn kay reer)	to reconquer	A4
reconstruire	(ruh kohn strweer)	to reconstruct	A63
reconvertir *	(ruh kohn vehr teer)	to restructure	*'s
recopier R	(ruh kaw pyay)	to recopy	R's
recoudre	(ruh koo druh)	to sew up	A20
recourir	(ruh koo reer)	to resort to / to run again	A21
recouvrir	(ruh koov reer)	to cover / to recover	A52
recréer R	(ruh kree ay)	to recreate	R's

FRENCH VERB	PRONUNCIATION	ENGLISH MEANING	PAGE
récrier (se) R	(ray kree yay)	to exclaim	R's
récrire	(ray kreer)	to rewrite	A28
rectifier R	(rehk tee fyay)	to rectify	R's
recueillir	(ruh kuh yeer)	to collect	A3
recuire	(ruh kweer)	to reboil/to cook a bit more	A63
reculer R	(ruh kew lay)	to move back	R's
récupérer	(ray kew pay ray)	to recuperate / to retrieve	A32
recycler R	(ruh see klay)	to recycle	R's
redescendre #	(ruh deh sawn druh)	to take (so/sth) back down	#'s
rédiger	(ray dee zhay)	to write up / to draft	A46
redire	(ruh deer)	to say again	A25
redoubler R	(ruh doo blay)	to repeat a year / to reduplicate	R's
redouter R	(ruh doo tay)	to dread	R's
redresser R	(ruh dray say)	to put right	R's
réduire	(ray dweer)	to reduce	A63
refaire	(ruh fehr)	to redo / to remake	A37
référer	(ray fay ray)	to refer	A32
refermer R	(ruh fehr may)	to close (again)	R's
réfléchir *	(ray flay sheer)	to think / to reflect	*'s
refléter	(ruh flay tay)	to reflect / to mirror	A32
refondre #	(ruh fohn druh)	to recast / to rework	#'s
réformer R	(ray fawr may)	to reform	R's
refroidir *	(ruh frwah deer)	to cool down	*'s
réfugier (se) R	(ray few zhee ay)	to take refuge	R's
refuser R	(ruh few zay)	to refuse	R's
réfuter R	(ray few tay)	to refute	R's
regagner R	(ruh gah nyay)	to get bact to / to regain	R's
regarder R	(ruh gahr day)	to look at	R's
régénérer	(reh zhay nay ray)	to regenerate	A32
régir *	(ray zheer)	to govern	*'s
régler	(ray glay)	to pay	A5
régner	(ray nyay)	to reign	A5
regretter R	(ruh gray tay)	to regret	R's
regrouper R	(ruh groo pay)	to group together	R's
réhabiliter R	(ray ah bee lee tay)	to rehabilitate	R's
réhabituer R	(ray ah bee tway)	to reaccustom	R's
rehausser R	(ruh oh say)	to raise / to enhance	R's
réimprimer R	(ray ahn pree may)	to reprint	R's
réintégrer	(ray ahn tay gray)	to return to / to reintegrate	A32
rejaillir *	(ruh zhah yeer)	to splash back	*'s
rejeter	(ruh zhtay)	to reject	A43
rejoindre	(ruh zhwahn druh)	to rejoin / to meet up with	A12
réjouir *	(ray zhweer)	to delight	*'s
relâcher R	(ruh lah shay)	to loosen	R's
relancer	(ruh lawn say)	to throw again	A13
reléguer	(ruh lay gay)	to relegate	A5
relever	(ruh lvay)	to raise / to pick up	A44
relier R	(ruh lyay)	to link up	R's
relire	(ruh leer)	to reread / to proofread	A45

© 2010

FRENCH VERB	PRONUNCIATION	ENGLISH MEANING	PAGE
reluire	(ruh lweer)	to shine	A63
remanier R	(ruh mahn yay)	to modify	R's
remarier R	(ruh mahr yay)	to remarry	R's
remarquer R	(ruh mahr kay)	to point out	R's
rembourser R	(rawn boor say)	to pay off / to reimbourse	R's
remédier R	(ruh may dyay)	to remedy	R's
remercier R	(ruh mehr syay)	to thank	R's
remettre	(ruh meh truh)	to put back	A48
remmener	(rawn mnay)	to take (sth) back	A44
remonter R	(ruh mohn tay)	to take (so/sth) back up	R's
remontrer R	(ruh mohn tray)	to show again	R's
remorquer R	(ruh mawr kay)	to tow	R's
remplacer	(rawn plah say)	to replace	A13
remplir *	(rawn pleer)	to fill	*'s
remporter R	(rawn pawr tay)	to win / to take away	R's
remuer R	(ruh mway)	to move	R's
renaître	(reh neh truh)	to come back to life	A51
renchérir *	(rawn shay reer)	to increase	*'s
rencontrer R	(rawn kohn tray)	to meet	R's
rendormir	(rawn dawr meer)	to put (so) back to sleep	A27
rendre #	(rawn druh)	to give back	#'s
renfermer R	(rawn fehr may)	to contain	R's
renfler R	(rawn flay)	to puff out	R's
renforcer	(rawn fawr say)	to reinforce	A13
renier R	(ruhn yay)	to renounce	R's
renifler R	(ruh nee flay)	to sniff	R's
renommer R	(ruh naw may)	to reappoint	R's
renoncer	(ruh nawn say)	to give up	A13
renouer R	(ruh nway)	to retie / to renew	R's
renouveler	(ruh noov lay)	to renew	A8
rénover R	(ray naw vay)	to renovate	R's
renseigner R	(rawn say nyay)	to give information	R's
rentrer R	(rawn tray)	to re-enter / to return home	R's
renverser R	(rawn vehr say)	to knock over	R's
renvoyer	(rawn vwah yay)	to send back	A31
réorganiser R	(ray awr gah nee zay)	to reorganize	R's
répandre #	(ray pawn druh)	to spread / to pour	#'s
reparaître	(ruh pah reh truh)	to reappear / to be back in print	A18
réparer R	(ray pah ray)	to repair	R's
repartir	(ruh pahr teer)	to leave again	A27
répartir *	(ray pahr teer)	to share out	*'S
repeindre	(ruh pahn druh)	to repaint	A12
repentir (se)	(ruh pawn teer)	to repent / to regret	A27
reperdre #	(ruh pehr druh)	to lose (sth) again	#'s
répéter	(ray pay tay)	to repeat	A32
répondre #	(ray pohn druh)	to answer	#'s
repousser R	(ruh poo say)	to push back	R's
reprendre	(ruh prawn druh)	to take back	A9
représenter R	(ruh pray zawn tay)	to represent	R's

© 2010

FRENCH VERB	PRONUNCIATION	ENGLISH MEANING	PAGE
reproduire	(ruh praw dweer)	to reproduce	A63
répudier R	(ray pew dyay)	to repudiate	R's
requérir	(ruh kay reer)	to request	A4
réserver R	(ray zehr vay)	to reserve	R's
résider R	(ray zee day)	to reside	R's
résigner R	(ray zee nyay)	to relinquish	R's
résilier R	(ray zee lyay)	to terminate	R's
résister R	(ray zee stay)	to resist	R's
résonner R	(ray zaw nay)	to ring out	R's
résoudre	(ray zoo druh)	to solve / to resolve	A26
respirer R	(reh spee ray)	to breathe in	R's
resplendir *	(reh splawn deer)	to shine brightly	*'s
ressaisir *	(ruh seh zeer)	to recapture	*'s
ressembler R	(ruh sawn blay)	to resemble	R's
ressemeler	(ruh suhm lay)	to resole	A8
ressentir	(ruh sawn teer)	to feel	A27
ressortir	(ruh sawr teer)	to take/go out again	A27
rester R	(reh stay)	to stay	R's
restreindre	(reh strahn druh)	to cut back	A12
résulter R	(ray zewl tay)	to result from	R's
résumer R	(ray zew may)	to summarize	R's
resurgir *	(ruh sewr zheer)	to re-emerge	*'s
rétablir *	(ray tah bleer)	to restore	*'s
retaper R	(ruh tah pay)	to do up	R's
retarder R	(ruh tahr day)	to make (so) late	R's
retenir	(ruh tneer)	to keep / to hold (so) up	A23
retirer R	(ruh tee ray)	to withdraw / to remove	R's
retomber R	(ruh tohn bay)	to fall again	R's
retourner R	(ruh toor nay)	to return / to turn over	R's
retrancher R	(ruh trawn shay)	to subtract	R's
retransmettre	(ruh trawns meh truh)	to broadcast	A48
rétrécir *	(ray tray seer)	to shrink	*'s
retrousser R	(ruh troo say)	to roll up	R's
retrouver R	(ruh troo vay)	to rediscover	R's
réunir *	(ray ew neer)	to bring together	*'s
réussir *	(ray ew seer)	to succeed	*'s
revaloir	(ruh vah lwahr)	to pay back / to get even	A56
réveiller R	(ray vay yay)	to wake (so) up	R's
révéler	(ray vay lay)	to reveal	A32
revendiquer R	(ruh vawn dee kay)	to claim / to demand	R's
revendre #	(ruh vawn druh)	to sell / to retail	#'s
revenir	(ruh vneer)	to come back	A23
rêver R	(ray vay)	to dream	R's
révérer	(ray vay ray)	to revere	A32
revêtir	(ruh veh teer)	to put on / to assume *(a role)*	A64
réviser R	(ray vee zay)	to revise	R's
revivre	(ruh vee vruh)	to relive / to revive	A65
revoir	(ruh vwahr)	to see again	A66
révolter R	(ray vawl tay)	to appal	R's

FRENCH VERB	PRONUNCIATION	ENGLISH MEANING	PAGE
rhabiller R	(rah bee yay)	to dress (so) again	R's
ridiculiser R	(ree dee kew lee zay)	to ridicule	R's
rigoler R	(ree gaw lay)	to laugh	R's
rire	(reer)	to laugh	A58
risquer R	(ree skay)	to risk	R's
rivaliser R	(ree vah lee zay)	to rival	R's
rogner R	(raw nyay)	to trim	R's
rompre #	(rohn pruh)	to break	#'s
ronfler R	(rohn flay)	to snore	R's
ronger	(rohn zhay)	to gnaw	A46
rôtir *	(raw teer)	to roast	*'s
rougir *	(roo zheer)	to redden	*'s
rouler R	(roo lay)	to roll	R's
rouspéter	(roo spay tay)	to grumble	A32
rouvrir	(roo vreer)	to reopen	A52
ruiner R	(rwee nay)	to ruin	R's
saccager	(sah kah zhay)	to wreck	A46
saisir *	(say zeer)	to seize	*'s
salir *	(sah leer)	to dirty	*'s
saluer R	(sah lway)	to greet	R's
sanctifier R	(sahnk tee fyay)	to sanctify	R's
sangloter R	(sawn glaw tay)	to sob	R's
satisfaire	(sah tees fehr)	to satisfy	A37
sauter R	(soh tay)	to jump	R's
sauvegarder R	(sohv gahr day)	to safeguard	R's
sauver R	(soh vay)	to save	R's
savoir	(sah vwahr)	to know	A59
scier R	(syay)	to saw	R's
scinder R	(sahn day)	to split	R's
scintiller R	(sahn tee yay)	to sparkle	R's
sécher	(say shay)	to dry	A5
secouer R	(suh kway)	to shake	R's
secourir	(suh koo reer)	to help / to rescue	A21
séduire	(say dweer)	to captivate / to seduce	A63
sembler R	(sawn blay)	to seem	R's
semer	(suh may)	to sow	A44
sentir	(sawn teer)	to smell / to feel	A27
séparer R	(say pah ray)	to separate	R's
serrer R	(say ray)	to grip	R's
sertir *	(sehr teer)	to set	*'s
servir	(sehr veer)	to serve	A27
sévir *	(say veer)	to clamp down on	*'s
sevrer R	(suh vray)	to wean	R's
siéger	(syay zhay)	to sit	A57
siffler R	(see flay)	to whistle	R's
signaler R	(see nyah lay)	to point out / to signal	R's
signer R	(see nyay)	to sign	R's
signifier R	(see nyee fyay)	to mean	R's
simplifier R	(sahn plee fyay)	to simplify	R's

© 2010

FRENCH VERB	PRONUNCIATION	ENGLISH MEANING	PAGE
simuler R	(see mew lay)	to simulate	R's
soigner R	(swah nyay)	to care for / to treat	R's
sombrer R	(sohn bray)	to sink	R's
sommeiller R	(saw may yay)	to doze	R's
songer	(sohn zhay)	to think / to daydream	A46
sonner R	(saw nay)	to ring	R's
sortir	(sawr teer)	to go out / to bring out	A27
souffrir	(soo freer)	to suffer	A52
souhaiter R	(sway tay)	to hope for	R's
souiller R	(soo yay)	to soil	R's
soulager	(soo lah zhay)	to relieve	A46
soulever	(soo lvay)	to lift	A44
souligner R	(soo lee nyay)	to underline	R's
soumettre	(soo meh truh)	to subdue / to subject	A48
soupçonner R	(soop saw nay)	to suspect	R's
soupeser	(soo puh zay)	to weigh up	A44
sourire	(soo reer)	to smile	A58
souscrire	(soo skreer)	to subscribe to	A28
sous-entendre #	(soo zawn tawn druh)	to imply	#'s
soustraire	(soo strehr)	to subtract	A35
soutenir	(soo tneer)	to support	A23
souvenir (se)	(soo vneer)	to remember	A23
spécialiser R	(spay syah lee zay)	to specialize	R's
spécifier R	(spay see fyay)	to specify	R's
standardiser R	(stawn dahr dee zay)	to standardize	R's
stationner R	(stah syaw nay)	to park	R's
stériliser R	(stay ree lee zay)	to sterilize	R's
stimuler R	(stee mew lay)	to stimulate	R's
stupéfier R	(stew pay fyay)	to astound	R's
subir *	(sew beer)	to undergo	*'s
submerger	(sewb mehr zhay)	to submerge	A46
subsister R	(sewb zee stay)	to subsist	R's
substituer R	(sewp stee tway)	to substitute	R's
subvenir	(sewb vuh neer)	to provide for	A23
succéder	(sewk say day)	to succeed	A32
sucer	(sew say)	to suck	A13
suer R	(sway)	to sweat	R's
suffire	(sew feer)	to be enough	A60
suggérer	(sewg zhay ray)	to suggest	A32
suivre	(sweev ruh)	to follow	A61
supplier R	(sew plee yay)	to implore	R's
supposer R	(sew poh zay)	to suppose	R's
surcharger	(sewr shahr zhay)	to overload	A46
surenchérir *	(sew rawn shay reer)	to bid higher	*'s
surfaire	(sew fehr)	to overrate	A37
surgeler	(sewr zhuh lay)	to deep-freeze	A44
surgir *	(sewr zheer)	to appear suddenly	*'s
surmonter R	(sewr mohn tay)	to overcome	R's
surpasser R	(sewr pah say)	to surpass	R's

© 2010

FRENCH VERB	PRONUNCIATION	ENGLISH MEANING	PAGE
surprendre	(sewr prawn druh)	to surprise	A9
surveiller R	(sewr vay yay)	to watch / to supervise	R's
survenir	(sewr vuh neer)	to occur	A23
survivre	(sewr vee vruh)	to survive	A65
susciter R	(sew see tay)	to arouse / to incite	R's
suspendre #	(sew spawn druh)	to hang up / to suspend	#'s
tacher R	(tah shay)	to stain	R's
tâcher R	(tah shay)	to try	R's
tailler R	(tah yay)	to cut	R's
taire (se)	(tehr)	to be silent	A62
taper R	(tah pay)	to hit / to tap / to type	R's
tâter R	(tah tay)	to feel	R's
taxer R	(tahk say)	to tax	R's
teindre	(tahn druh)	to dye	A12
teinter R	(tahn tay)	to tint / to tinge	R's
téléphoner R	(tay lay faw nay)	to phone	R's
téléviser R	(tay lay vee zay)	to televise	R's
témoigner R	(tay mwa nyay)	to testify	R's
tendre #	(tawn druh)	to tighten / to stretch	#'s
tenir	(tuh neer)	to hold	A23
tenter R	(tawn tay)	to attempt	R's
terminer R	(tehr mee nay)	to finish	R's
ternir *	(tehr neer)	to tarnish	*'s
terrasser R	(teh rah say)	to knock down	R's
terrifier R	(teh ree fyay)	to terrify	R's
téter	(tay tay)	to suck at	A32
tiédir *	(tyay deer)	to warm up	*'s
timbrer R	(tahn bray)	to stampf	R's
tirer R	(tee ray)	to pull	R's
tolérer	(taw lay ray)	to tolerate	A32
tomber R	(tohn bay)	to fall	R's
tondre #	(tohn druh)	to shear / to mow	#'s
tonner R	(taw nay)	to thunder	R's
tordre #	(tawr druh)	to twist	#'s
torpiller R	(tawr pee yay)	to torpedo	R's
tortiller R	(tawr tee yay)	to twist	R's
torturer R	(tawr tew ray)	to torture	R's
toucher R	(too shay)	to touch	R's
tourmenter R	(toor mawn tay)	to torment	R's
tourner R	(toor nay)	to turn	R's
tournoyer	(toor nwah yay)	to whirl	A30
tousser R	(too say)	to cough	R's
tracasser R	(trah kah say)	to bother	R's
tracer	(trah say)	to draw / to trace	A13
traduire	(trah dweer)	to translate	A63
trahir *	(trah eer)	to betray	*'s
traîner R	(treh nay)	to drag	R's
traire	(trehr)	to milk	A35
traiter R	(treh tay)	to treat	R's

© 2010

FRENCH VERB	PRONUNCIATION	ENGLISH MEANING	PAGE
transcrire	(trawn skreer)	to transcribe	A28
transférer	(trawns fay ray)	to transfer	A32
transformer R	(trawns fawr may)	to transform	R's
transmettre	(trawns meh truh)	to convey / to transmit	A48
transparaître	(trawn spah reh truh)	to show through	A18
transpirer R	(trawn spee ray)	to perspire	R's
transplanter R	(trawn splawn tay)	to transplant	R's
transporter R	(trawn spawr tay)	to carry / to transport	R's
traquer R	(trah kay)	to track down	R's
travailler R	(trah vah yay)	to work	R's
traverser R	(trah vehr say)	to cross	R's
trébucher R	(tray bew shay)	to stumble	R's
trembler R	(trawn blay)	to shake	R's
tremper R	(trawn pay)	to soak / to dip	R's
tricher R	(tree shay)	to cheat	R's
tricoter R	(tree kaw tay)	to knit	R's
trier R	(tree yay)	to sort	R's
triompher R	(tree yohn fay)	to triumph	R's
tripoter R	(tree paw tay)	to grope	R's
tromper R	(trohn pay)	to deceive	R's
troquer R	(traw kay)	to trade	R's
trotter R	(traw tay)	to trot	R's
troubler R	(troo blay)	to disturb / to cloud	R's
trouer R	(troo ay)	to make a hole in	R's
trouver R	(troo vay)	to find	R's
truffer R	(trew fay)	to stuff	R's
truquer R	(trew kay)	to fiddle	R's
tuer R	(too ay)	to kill	R's
tutoyer	(tew twah yay)	to address (so) as " tu "	A30
ulcérer	(ewl say ray)	to sicken / to ulcerate	A32
unifier R	(ew nee fyay)	to unify	R's
unir *	(ew neer)	to unite	*'s
urbaniser R	(ewr bah nee zay)	to urbanize	R's
uriner R	(ew ree nay)	to urinate	R's
user R	(ew zay)	to wear out	R's
usiner R	(ew zee nay)	to machine / to manufacture	R's
utiliser R	(ew tee lee zay)	to use / to exploit	R's
vacciner R	(vahk see nay)	to vaccinate	R's
vadrouiller R	(vah droo yay)	to roam	R's
vaincre	(vahn kruh)	to defeat / to overcome	A19
valoir	(vah lwahr)	to be worth	A56
vanter R	(vawn tay)	to praise	R's
varier R	(vah ryay)	to vary	R's
végéter	(vay zhay tay)	to vegetate / to stagnate	A32
veiller R	(vay yay)	to watch over	R's
vendanger	(vawn dawn zhay)	to harvest the grapes	A46
vendre #	(vawn druh)	to sell	#'s
venger	(vawn zhay)	to avenge	A46
venir	(vuh neer)	to come	A23

© 2010

FRENCH VERB	PRONUNCIATION	ENGLISH MEANING	PAGE
verdir *	(vehr deer)	to turn green	*'s
verdoyer	(vehr dwah yay)	to be green	A30
vérifier R	(vay ree fyay)	to verify	R's
vernir *	(vehr neer)	to varnish	*'s
verrouiller R	(veh roo yay)	to bolt / to lock	R's
verser R	(vehr say)	to pour	R's
vêtir	(veh teer)	to dress	A64
vexer R	(vehk say)	to offend / to upset	R's
vibrer R	(vee bray)	to vibrate	R's
vider R	(vee day)	to empty	R's
vieillir *	(vyeh yeer)	to age	*'s
violer R	(vyaw lay)	to rape / to violate	R's
virer R	(vee ray)	to transfer / to sack	R's
viser R	(vee zay)	to aim at	R's
visiter R	(vee zee tay)	to visit	R's
visser R	(vee say)	to screw on	R's
vitrifier R	(vee tree fyay)	to vitrify	R's
vitupérer	(vee tew pay ray)	to rail against	A32
vivifier R	(vee vee fyay)	to invigorate	R's
vivoter R	(vee vaw tay)	to struggle along	R's
vivre	(vee vruh)	to live	A65
vociférer	(vaw see fay ray)	to shout	A32
voiler R	(vwah lay)	to veil / to conceal	R's
voir	(vwahr)	to see	A66
voler R	(vaw lay)	to steal / to fly	R's
vomir *	(vaw meer)	to vomit	*'s
voter R	(vaw tay)	to vote	R's
vouer R	(voo ay)	to vow	R's
vouloir	(voo lwahr)	to want	A67
vouvoyer	(voo vwah yay)	to address (so) as " vous "	A30
voyager	(vwah yah zhay)	to travel	A46
vrombir *	(vrohn beer)	to roar	*'s
vulgariser R	(vewl gah ree zay)	to popularize	R's
yodler R	(yawd lay)	to yodel	R's
zébrer	(zay bray)	to streak	A6
zézayer	(zay zay yay)	to lisp	A33
zigzaguer R	(zeeg zah gay)	to zigzag	R's
zoner R	(zoh nay)	to hang about	R's

© 2010

ENGLISH TO FRENCH VERB INDEX

ENGLISH	FRENCH VERB	PRONOUNCIATION	PAGE
to abandon	abandonner R	(ah bawn daw nay)	R's
"	délaisser R	(day lay say)	R's
to abolish	abolir *	(ah baw leer)	*'s
to abort	avorter R	(ah vawr tay)	R's
to abound	abonder R	(ah bohn day)	R's
"	foisonner R	(fwa zaw nay)	R's
"	fourmiller R	(foor mee yay)	R's
to absolve	absoudre	(ap soo druh)	A26
to absorb	absorber R	(ap sawr bay)	R's
to abstain	abstenir (s')	(ap stuh neer)	A23
to abstract	abstraire	(ap strehr)	A35
to abuse	abuser R	(ah bew zay)	R's
to accelerate	accélérer	(ahk say lay ray)	A32
to accentuate	accentuer R	(ahk sawn tway)	R's
to accept	accepter R	(ahk sep tay)	R's
to accommodate	héberger	(ay behr zhay)	A46
to accompany	accompagner R	(ah kohn pah nyay)	R's
to accomplish	accomplir *	(ah kohn pleer)	*'s
to acculturate	acculturer R	(ah kewl tew ray)	R's
to accumulate	accumuler R	(ah kew mew lay)	R's
"	amonceler	(ah mohn slay)	A8
"	cumuler R	(kew mew lay)	R's
to accuse	accuser R	(ah kew zay)	R's
"	incriminer R	(ahn kree mee nay)	R's
to accustom	accoutumer R	(ah koo tew may)	R's
to acquire	acquérir	(ah kay reer)	A4
to act	agir *	(ah zheer)	*'s
to activate	actionner R	(ahk syaw nay)	R's
to adapt	adapter R	(ah dahp tay)	R's
to add	additionner R	(ah dee syaw nay)	R's
"	ajouter R	(ah zhoo tay)	R's
to add more	rajouter R	(rah zhoo tay)	R's
to address	adresser R	(ah dray say)	R's
to address (so) as " tu "	tutoyer	(tew twah yay)	A30
to address (so) as " vous "	vouvoyer	(voo vwah yay)	A30
to adhere to	adhérer	(ah day ray)	A32
to adjoin	adjoindre	(ahd zhwahn druh)	A12
to adjust	ajuster R	(ah zhew stay)	R's
to administer	administrer R	(ahd mee nee stray)	R's
to admire	admirer R	(ahd mee ray)	R's
to admit	admettre	(ahd meh truh)	A48
"	convenir	(kohn vuh neer)	A23
to adopt	adopter R	(ah dawp tay)	R's
to adore	adorer R	(ah daw ray)	R's
to adorn	parer R	(pah ray)	R's
to advance	avancer	(ah vawn say)	A13
to advise	conseiller R	(kohn say yay)	R's
"	recommander R	(ruh kaw mawn day)	R's
to advise against	déconseiller R	(day kohn say yay)	R's

© 2010

ENGLISH	FRENCH VERB	PRONOUNCIATION	PAGE
to affect	affecter R	(ah fehk tay)	R's
"	dérégler	(day ray glay)	A5
to affirm	affirmer R	(ah feer may)	R's
to afflict	affliger	(ah flee zhay)	A46
to age	vieillir *	(vyeh yeer)	*'s
to aggravate	aggraver R	(ah grah vay)	R's
to agitate	agiter R	(ah zhee tay)	R's
to agree	agréer R	(ah gray ay)	R's
to aim at	viser R	(vee zay)	R's
to air	aérer	(ayr ay)	A32
to alarm	alarmer R	(ah lahr may)	R's
"	effarer R	(ay fah ray)	R's
to alert	alerter R	(ah lehr tay)	R's
to allege	alléguer	(ah lay gay)	A32
to allot	lotir *	(law teer)	*'s
"	départir	(day pahr teer)	A27
to allow (sth) to settle	décanter	(day kawn tay)	R's
to almost do	faillir	(fah yeer)	A36
to alternate	alterner R	(ahl tehr nay)	R's
to amplify	amplifier R	(awn plee fyay)	R's
to amputate	amputer R	(awn pew tay)	R's
to amuse	amuser R	(ah mew zay)	R's
to anaesthetize	insensibilise R	(ahn sawn see bee lee zay)	R's
to analyze	analyser R	(ah nah lee zay)	R's
to anger	fâcher R	(fah shay)	R's
to animate	animer R	(ah nee may)	R's
to annex	annexer R	(ah nehk say)	R's
to annihilate	anéantir *	(ah nay awn teer)	*'s
to annotate	annoter R	(ah naw tay)	R's
to announce	annoncer	(ah nohn say)	A13
to annoy	agacer	(ah gah say)	A13
"	contrarier R	(kohn trah ryay)	R's
"	mécontenter R	(may kohn tawn tay)	R's
to answer	répondre #	(ray pohn druh)	#'s
to anticipate	anticiper R	(awn tee see pay)	R's
to appal	révolter R	(ray vawl tay)	R's
to appear	apparaître	(ah pah reh truh)	A18
"	comparaître	(kohn pah reh truh)	A18
"	paraître	(pah reh truh)	A18
to appear suddenly	surgir *	(sewr zheer)	*'s
to appease	apaiser R	(ah pay zay)	R's
to applaud	applaudir *	(ah ploh deer)	*'s
to apply	appliquer R	(ah plee kay)	R's
to appoint	nommer R	(naw may)	R's
to appreciate	apprécier R	(ah pray syay)	R's
to approach	approcher R	(ah praw shay)	R's
"	aborder R	(ah bawr day)	R's
to appropriate	approprier (s') R	(ah praw pree yay)	R's
to approve of	approuver R	(ah proo vay)	R's

© 2010

ENGLISH	FRENCH VERB	PRONOUNCIATION	PAGE
to argue	arguer R	(ahr gay)	R's
"	bagarrer R	(bah gah ray)	R's
to arm	armer R	(ahr may)	R's
to arouse	éveiller R	(ay vay yay)	R's
to arrange	arranger	(ah rawn zhay)	A46
"	disposer R	(dee spoh zay)	R's
to arrive	arriver R	(ah ree vay)	R's
to ask for	demander R	(duh mawn day)	R's
"	réclamer R	(ray klah may)	R's
to aspire	ambitionner R	(awn bee syaw nay)	R's
to assail	assaillir	(ah sah yeer)	A10
to assassinate	assassiner R	(ah sah see nay)	R's
to assemble	assembler R	(ah sawn blay)	R's
to assess	chiffrer R	(shee fray)	R's
to assign	assigner R	(ah see nyay)	R's
to assimilate	assimiler R	(ah see mee lay)	R's
to assist	assister R	(ah see stay)	R's
to associate	associer R	(ah saw syay)	R's
to associate with	fréquenter R	(fray kawn tay)	R's
to assume	assumer R	(ah sew may)	R's
to assume (a role)	revêtir	(ruh veh teer)	A64
to assure	assurer R	(ah sew ray)	R's
to astound	ébahir *	(ay bah eer)	*'s
"	stupéfier R	(stew pay fyay)	R's
to attach	attacher R	(ah tah shay)	R's
to attack	attaquer R	(ah tah kay)	R's
to attain	atteindre	(ah tahn druh)	A12
to attempt	tenter R	(tawn tay)	R's
to attest	attester R	(ah teh stay)	R's
to attract	attirer R	(ah tee ray)	R's
to attribute	attribuer R	(ah tree bway)	R's
to authorize	autoriser R	(oh taw ree zay)	R's
to avenge	venger	(vawn zhay)	A46
to avoid	éviter R	(ay vee tay)	R's
to wake (so) up	réveiller R	(ray vay yay)	R's
to award	décerner R	(day sehr nay)	R's
to balance	balancer	(bah lawn say)	A13
"	équilibrer R	(ay kee lee bray)	R's
to bandage	panser R	(pawn say)	R's
to banish	bannir *	(bah neer)	*'s
to ban	proscrire	(praw skreer)	A28
to baptize	baptiser R	(bah tee zay)	R's
to bargain-hunt	chiner R	(shee nay)	R's
to bark	aboyer	(ah bwah yay)	A30
to barricade	barricader R	(bah ree kah day)	R's
to base	baser R	(bah zay)	R's
to baste	faufiler R	(foh fee lay)	R's
to bathe	baigner R	(bay nyay)	R's
to be	être	(eh truh)	A34

ENGLISH	FRENCH	PRONOUNCIATION	PAGE
to be able to (can)	pouvoir	(poo vwahr)	A55
to be a complete disaster	foirer R	(fwah ray)	R's
to beat	battre	(bah truh)	A1
to be back in print	reparaître	(ruh pah reh truh)	A18
to be born	naître	(neh truh)	A51
to become	devenir	(duh vneer)	A23
to become infatuated	enticher (s') R	(awn tee shay)	R's
to become middle- class	embourgeoiser (s') R	(awn boorzh wah zay)	R's
to be crazy about	raffoler R	(rah faw lay)	R's
to be cooking	cuisiner R	(kwee zee nay)	R's
to be delirious	délirer R	(day lee ray)	R's
to be enough	suffire	(sew feer)	A60
to be equivalent to	équivaloir	(ay kee vah lwahr)	A56
to be faulty	clocher R	(klaw shay)	R's
to be furious	enrager	(awn rah zhay)	A46
to beg	mendier R	(mawn dyay)	R's
to begin	commencer	(kaw mawn say)	A13
"	amorcer	(ah mawr say)	13
"	débuter R	(day bew tay)	R's
to be green	verdoyer	(verh dwah yay)	A30
to be idle	chômer R	(shoh may)	R's
to be jubilant	pavoiser R	(pah vwah zay)	R's
to believe	croire	(krwahr)	A23
to bellow	beugler R	(buh glay)	R's
to belong to	appartenir	(ah pahr tuh neer)	A23
to be mistaken	méprendre (se)	(may prawn druh)	A9
to bend	courber R	(koor bay)	R's
"	déformer R	(day fawr may)	R's
"	fléchir *	(flay sheer)	*'s
to be necessary	falloir	(fahl wahr)	A38
to benefit from	bénéficier R	(baynay fee syay)	R's
to be next to	côtoyer	(koh twah yay)	A30
to be out of place	détonner R	(day taw nay)	R's
to besiege	assiéger	(ah syay zhay)	A57
to be silent	taire (se)	(tehr)	A62
to be suitable	convenir	(kohn vuh neer)	A23
to bet	parier R	(pah ryay)	R's
to betray	trahir *	(trah eer)	*'s
to be unfair to	défavoriser R	(day fah vaw ree zay)	R's
to be untidy	débrailler (se) R	(day brah yay)	R's
to bewilder	abasourdir *	(ah bah zoor deer)	*'s
to be worth	valoir	(vah lwahr)	A56
to bid higher	surenchérir *	(sew rawn shay reer)	*'s
to bite	mordre #	(mawr druh)	#'s
to blacken	noircir *	(nwahr seer)	*'s
to bleat	bêler R	(beh lay)	R's
to blend in	incorporer R	(ahn kawr paw ray)	R's
to blend	mélanger	(may lawn zhay)	A46
to bless	bénir *	(bay neer)	*'s

© 2010

ENGLISH	FRENCH VERB	PRONOUNCIATION	PAGE
to blind	aveugler R	(ah vuh glay)	R's
to blink	cligner R	(klee nyay)	R's
"	ciller R	(see yay)	R's
to block	bloquer R	(blaw kay)	R's
"	barrer R	(bah ray)	R's
to block with snow	enneiger	(awn neh zhay)	A46
to blow one's nose	moucher (se) R	(moo shay)	R's
to boil	bouillir	(boo yeer)	A16
to bolt	verrouiller R	(veh roo yay)	R's
to bolt down	boulonner R	(boo law nay)	R's
to bombard	bombarder R	(bohn bahr day)	R's
to boo	huer R	(wee ay)	R's
to border	border R	(bawr day)	R's
to bore	ennuyer	(aw nwee yay)	A30
to borrow	emprunter R	(awn pruhn tay)	R's
to botch	bâcler R	(bah klay)	R's
"	bousiller R	(boo zee yay)	R's
to bother	incommoder R	(ahn kaw maw day)	R's
"	tracasser R	(trah kah say)	R's
to bounce	rebondir *	(ruh bohn deer)	*'s
to brandish	brandir *	(brawn deer)	*'s
to brave	braver R	(brah vay)	R's
to bray	brairer	(brehr)	A35
to break	briser R	(bree zay)	R's
"	casser R	(kah say)	R's
"	péter	(pay tay)	A32
"	rompre #	(rohn pruh)	#'s
to breathe in	respirer R	(reh spee ray)	R's
to bring	amener	(ahm nay)	A44
"	apporter R	(ah pawr tay)	R's
to bring back	ramener	(rah mnay)	A44
"	rapporter R	(rah pawr tay)	R's
to bring nearer	rapprocher R	(rah praw shay)	R's
to bring out	sortir	(sawr teer)	A27
to bring together	réunir *	(ray ew neer)	*'s
to broadcast	retransmettre	(ruh trawns meh truh)	A48
"	diffuser R	(dee few zay)	R's
to brown	brunir *	(brew neer)	*'s
to bruise	contusionner R	(kohn tewz yaw nay)	R's
to brush	brosser R	(braw say)	R's
"	frôler R	(froh lay)	R's
to build	bâtir *	(bah teer)	*'s
"	construire	(kohn strweer)	A63
to bully	brimer R	(bree may)	R's
to bump into	bousculer R	(boo skew lay)	R's
to burn	brûler R	(brew lay)	R's
"	cramer R	(krah may)	R's
to burst	crever	(kruh vay)	A44
to burst out laughing	esclaffer (s')R	(eh sklah fay)	R's

© 2010

ENGLISH	FRENCH VERB	PRONOUNCIATION	PAGE
to bury	enfouir *	(awn fweer)	*'s
"	ensevelir *	(awn suh vuh leer)	*'s
"	enterrer R	(awn tay ray)	R's
to bustle about	affairer (s') R	(ah fay ray)	R's
to butter	beurrer R	(buh ray)	R's
to button	boutonner R	(boo taw nay)	R's
to buy	acheter	(ash tay)	A44
to buy back	racheter	(rash tay)	A44
to buzz	bourdonner R	(boor daw nay)	R's
to calculate	calculer R	(kahl kew lay)	R's
to call	appeler	(ah play)	A8
"	intituler R	(ahn tee tew lay)	R's
to call off	décommander R	(day kaw mawn day)	R's
to calm	calmer R	(kahl may)	R's
to camp	camper R	(kawn pay)	R's
to cancel	annuler R	(ah new lay)	R's
to capitulate	capituler R	(kah pee tew lay)	R's
to captivate	captiver R	(kahp tee vay)	R's
"	séduire	(say dweer)	A63
to capture	capturer R	(kahp tew ray)	R's
"	capter R	(kahp tay)	R's
to care for	soigner R	(swah nyay)	R's
to caress	caresser R	(kah ray say)	R's
to caricature	caricaturer R	(kah ree kah tew ray)	R's
to carry	porter R	(pawr tay)	R's
"	transporter R	(trawn spawr tay)	R's
to carry out	effectuer R	(ay fehk tway)	R's
"	exécuter R	(eg zay kew tay)	R's
to carve	découper R	(day koo pay)	R's
to cash	encaisser R	(awn kay say)	R's
to catalogue	cataloguer R	(kah tah law gay)	R's
to catapult	catapulter R	(kah tah pewl tay)	R's
to catch	attraper R	(ah trah pay)	R's
to catch up with	rattraper R	(rah trah pay)	R's
to categorize	discriminer R	(dee scree mee nay)	R's
to cause	causer R	(koh zay)	R's
to cause to swell	boursoufler R	(boor soo flay)	R's
to celebrate	fêter R	(fay tay)	R's
to censor	censurer R	(sawn sew ray)	R's
to centralize	centraliser R	(sawn trah lee zay)	R's
to centre	cadrer R	(kah dray)	R's
to certify	certifier R	(sehr tee fyay)	R's
to chafe	écorcher R	(ay kawr shay)	R's
to chain up	enchaîner R	(awn sheh nay)	R's
to challenge	défier R	(day fyay)	R's
to change	changer	(shawn zhay)	A46
to change surroundings	dépayser R	(day peh zay)	R's
to characterize	caractériser R	(kah rahk tay ree zay)	R's
to charge	inculper R	(ahn kewl pay)	R's

© 2010

ENGLISH	FRENCH VERB	PRONOUNCIATION	PAGE
to charm	charmer R	(shahr may)	R's
to charter	affréter	(ah fray tay)	A32
to chat	bavarder R	(bah vahr day)	R's
to chat up	draguer R	(drah gay)	R's
to cheat	tricher R	(tree shay)	R's
to cheer (so) up	ragaillardir *	(rah gah yahr deer)	*'s
to cheer	acclamer R	(ah klah may)	R's
to cherish	chérir *	(shay reer)	*'s
to chew	mâcher R	(mah shay)	R's
to chill	glacer	(glah say)	A13
to chisel	ciseler	(see zlay)	A44
to choose	choisir *	(schwa zeer)	*'s
to chop	fendre #	(fawn druh)	#'s
to circle	cercler R	(sehr klay)	R's
to circulate	circuler R	(seer kew lay)	R's
to circumcise	circoncire	(seer kohn seer)	A60
to circumscribe	circonscrire	(seer kohn skreer)	A28
to circumvent	circonvenir	(seer kohn vuh neer)	A23
to cite	citer R	(see tay)	R's
to claim	prétendre #	(pray tawn druh)	#'s
"	réclamer R	(ray klah may)	R's
"	revendiquer R	(ruh vawn dee kay)	R's
to clamp down on	sévir *	(say veer)	*'s
to clarify	clarifier R	(klah ree fyay)	R's
to classify	classifier R	(klah see fyay)	R's
to clean	décaper R	(day kah pay)	R's
"	nettoyer	(neh twah yay)	A30
to clean out	curer R	(kew ray)	R's
to clean up	assainir *	(ah say neer)	*'s
to clear a path	frayer	(freh yay)	A33
to clear off	déguerpir *	(day gehr peer)	*'s
to clear out	débarrasser R	(day bah rah say)	R's
to clear (sth) through customs	dédouaner R	(day dwah nay)	R's
to climb	grimper R	(grahn pay)	R's
to climb up	gravir *	(grah veer)	*'s
to cling to	cramponner R	(krawn paw nay)	R's
to close	clore	(klawr)	A17
"	fermer R	(fehr may)	R's
to close (again)	refermer R	(ruh fehr may)	R's
to cloud	troubler R	(troo blay)	R's
to clutter up	encombrer R	(awn kohn bray)	R's
to coat	enduire	(awn dweer)	A63
to coax	cajoler R	(kah zhaw lay)	R's
to code	coder R	(kaw day)	R's
to codify	codifier R	(kaw dee fyay)	R's
to coincide	coïncider R	(kaw ahn see day)	R's
to collaborate with	collaborer R	(kaw lah baw ray)	R's
to collapse	écrouler (s') R	(ay kroo lay)	R's
"	crouler R	(kroo lay)	R's

© 2010

ENGLISH	FRENCH VERB	PRONOUNCIATION	PAGE
to collapse	effondrer	(ay fohn dray)	R's
to collect	collectionner	(kaw lehk syaw nay)	R's
"	ramasser	(rah mah say)	R's
"	recueillir	(ruh kuh yeer)	A3
to colonize	coloniser	(kaw law nee zay)	R's
to colour	colorer	(kaw law ray)	R's
to colour in	colorier	(kaw law ryay)	R's
to combine	allier	(ah lyay)	R's
"	jumeler	(zhewm lay)	A8
to comb	peigner	(pay nyay)	R's
to come	venir	(vuh neer)	A23
to come back	revenir	(ruh vneer)	A23
to come back to life	renaître	(reh neh truh)	A51
to come from	provenir	(praw vneer)	A23
to come through	réchapper	(ray shah pay)	R's
to comfort	réconforter	(ray kohn fawr tay)	R's
to commemorate	commémorer	(kaw may maw ray)	R's
to comment	commenter	(kaw mawn tay)	R's
to commit	commettre	(kaw meh truh)	A48
to communicate	communiquer	(kaw mew nee kay)	R's
to commute	commeuer	(kaw mway)	R's
to compare	comparer	(kohn pah ray)	R's
to compel	astreindre	(ah strahn druh)	A12
to compensate	compenser	(kohn pawn say)	R's
"	dédommager	(day daw mah zhay)	A46
to compete	concourir	(kohn koo reer)	A21
"	disputer	(dee spew tay)	R's
to compete with	concurrencer	(kohn kew rawn say)	A13
to compile	compiler	(kohn pee lay)	R's
to complete	compéter	(kohn play tay)	A32
"	achever	(ah shvay)	A44
"	parachever	(pah rah shvay)	A44
to complicate	compliquer	(kohn plee kay)	R's
to compliment	complimenter	(kohn plee mawn tay)	R's
to compose	composer	(kohn poh zay)	R's
to compromise	compromettre	(kohn praw meh truh)	A48
to conceal	celer	(suh lay)	A44
"	voiler	(vwah lay)	R's
"	masquer	(mah skay)	R's
"	receler	(ruh slay)	A44
to concede	concéder	(kohn say day)	A32
to conceive	concevoir	(kohn suh vwahr)	A7
to concentrate	conentrer	(kohn sawn tray)	R's
to conceptualize	conceptualiser	(kohn sep twah lee zay)	R's
to concern	concerner	(kohn sehr nay)	R's
to conclude	conclure	(kohn klewr)	A41
to condemn	condamner	(kohn daw nay)	R's
to condense	condenser	(kohn dawn say)	R's
to condescend to	condescendre	(kohn day sawn druh)	R's

© 2010

ENGLISH	FRENCH VERB	PRONOUNCIATION	PAGE
to confer	conférer	(kohn fay ray)	A32
to confess	avouer R	(ah vway)	R's
to confide	confier R	(kohn fyay)	R's
to confirm	confirmer R	(kohn feer may)	R's
to confiscate	confisquer R	(kohn fee skay)	R's
to confront	affronter R	(ah frohn tay)	R's
to confuse	confondre #	(kohn fohn druh)	#'s
to congeal	figer	(fee zhay)	A46
to congratulate	féliciter R	(fay lee see tay)	R's
to conjugate	conjuguer R	(kohn zew gay)	R's
to connect	raccorder R	(rah kawr day)	R's
to connect up	brancher R	(brawn shay)	R's
to conquer	conquérir	(kohn kay reer)	A4
to consent	consentir	(kohn sawn teer)	A27
to conserve	conserver R	(kohn sehr vay)	R's
to consider	peser	(puh zay)	A44
to consist of	consister R	(kohn see stay)	R's
to console	consoler R	(kohn saw lay)	R's
to consolidate	consolider R	(kohn saw lee day)	R's
"	conforter R	(kohn fawr tay)	R's
to constitute	constituer R	(kohn stee tway)	R's
to construct	édifier R	(ay dee fyay)	R's
to consult	consulter R	(kohn sewl tay)	R's
to consume	consommer R	(kohn saw may)	R's
to contact	contacter R	(kohn tahk tay)	R's
to contain	contenir	(kohn tuh neer)	A23
"	renfermer R	(rawn fehr may)	R's
to contaminate	contaminer R	(kohn tah mee nay)	R's
to contemplate	contempler R	(kohn tawn play)	R's
"	méditer R	(may dee tay)	R's
to contest	contester R	(kohn teh stay)	R's
to continue	continuer R	(kohn tee nway)	R's
to contradict	contredire	(kohn truh deer)	A25
to contrast	contraster R	(kohn trah stay)	R's
to contravene	contrevenir	(kohn truh vuh neer)	A23
to contribute	contribuer R	(kohn tree bway)	R's
to control	contrôler R	(kohn troh lay)	R's
"	maîtriser R	(meh tree zay)	R's
to convene	convoquer R	(kohn vaw kay)	R's
to converse	converser R	(kohn vehr say)	R's
to convert	convertir *	(kohn vehr teer)	*'s
to convert into cash	monnayer	(maw neh yay)	A33
to convey	transmettre	(trawns meh truh)	A48
to convince	convaincre	(kohn vahn kruh)	A19
to cook	cuire	(kweer)	A63
to cook a bit more	recuire	(ruh kweer)	A63
to cool down	refroidir *	(ruh frwah deer)	*'s
to cool	rafraîchir *	(rah freh sheer)	*'s
to cooperate	coopérer	(koh aw pay ray)	A32

© 2010

ENGLISH	FRENCH VERB	PRONOUNCIATION	PAGE
to coop up	parquer R	(pahr kay)	R's
to coordinate	coordonner R	(koh awr daw nay)	R's
to copy	copier R	(kaw pyay)	R's
"	calquer R	(kahl kay)	R's
to cork	boucher R	(boo shay)	R's
to correct	corriger	(kaw ree zhay)	A46
to correspond	correspondre #	(kawr reh spohn druh)	#'s
to corrupt	corrompre #	(kaw rohn pruh)	#'s
to cost	coûter R	(koo tay)	R's
to cough	tousser R	(too say)	R's
to count	compter R	(kohn tay)	R's
to counterfeit	contrefaire	(kohn truh fehr)	A37
to cover	couvrir	(koov reer)	A52
"	recouvrir	(ruh koov reer)	A52
to crack	fêler R	(feh lay)	R's
to crack up	flancher R	(flawn shay)	R's
to cram	bourrer R	(boo ray)	R's
to crave	briguer R	(bree gay)	R's
to creak	grincer	(grahn say)	A13
to crease	froisser R	(frwah say)	R's
to create	créer R	(kray ay)	R's
to credit	créditer R	(kray dee tay)	R's
to criticize	critiquer R	(kree tee kay)	R's
"	blamer R	(blah may)	R's
to crochet	crocheter	(krawsh tay)	A44
to cross	croiser R	(krwah zay)	R's
"	franchir *	(frawn sheer)	*'s
"	traverser R	(trah vehr say)	R's
to cross out	biffer R	(bee fay)	R's
to crown	couronner R	(koo raw nay)	R's
to crucify	crucifier R	(krew see fyay)	R's
to crumple	chiffonner R	(shee faw nay)	R's
to crunch	croquer R	(kraw kay)	R's
to crush	écraser R	(ay krah zay)	R's
to cuddle	câliner R	(kah lee nay)	R's
to cultivate	cultiver R	(kewl tee vay)	R's
to cure	guérir *	(gay reer)	*'s
to cure (so's) addiction	désaccoutumer R	(day zah koo tew may)	R's
to curl	friser R	(free zay)	R's
to curse	maudire	(moh deer)	A47
to cut	couper R	(koo pay)	R's
"	tailler R	(tah yay)	R's
to cut back	restreindre	(reh strahn druh)	A12
to cut up	dépecer	(day puh say)	A13
"	découper R	(day koo pay)	R's
to damage	abîmer R	(ah bee may)	R's
"	dégrader R	(day grah day)	R's
"	détériorer R	(day tay ryaw ray)	R's
"	endommager	(awn daw mah zhay)	A46

© 2010

ENGLISH	FRENCH VERB	PRONOUNCIATION	PAGE
to damn	damner R	(dah nay)	R's
to dampen	doucher R	(doo shay)	R's
to dance	danser R	(dawn say)	R's
to dare	oser R	(oh zay)	R's
to darken	assombrir *	(ah sohn breer)	*'s
"	foncer	(fohn say)	A13
to dash forward	élancer (s')	(ay lawn say)	A13
to date	dater R	(dah tay)	R's
to date stamp	composter R	(kohn paw stay)	R's
to daydream	songer	(sohn zhay)	A46
to daze	hébéter	(ay bay tay)	A32
to dazzle	éblouir *	(ay bloo eer)	*'s
to deafen	abrutir *	(ah brew teer)	*'s
"	assourdir *	(ah soor deer)	*'s
to debauch	debaucher R	(day boh shay)	R's
to debilitate	débiliter R	(day bee lee tay)	R's
to debit	débiter R	(day bee tay)	R's
to deceive	berner R	(behr nay)	R's
"	tromper R	(trohn pay)	R's
"	mystifier R	(mee stee fyay)	R's
to decentralize	décentraliser R	(day sawn trah lee zay)	R's
to decide	décider R	(day see day)	R's
to decide between	départager	(day pahr tah zhay)	A46
to decimate	décimer R	(day see may)	R's
to decipher	déchiffrer R	(day shee fray)	R's
to declaim	déclamer R	(day klah may)	R's
to declare	déclarer R	(day klah ray)	R's
to decline	décliner R	(day klee nay)	R's
to declutch	débrayer	(day bray yay)	A33
to decode	décoder R	(day kaw day)	R's
to decorate	décorer R	(day kaw ray)	R's
"	orner R	(awr nay)	R's
to decorate with flowers	fleurir *	(fluh reer)	*'s
to decree	décréter	(day kray tay)	A32
to dedicate	dédicacer	(day dee kah say)	A13
"	dédier R	(day dyay)	R's
to deduce	déduire	(day dweer)	A63
to deduct	défalquer R	(day fahl kay)	R's
to deduct	prélever	(pray lvay)	A44
to deep-freeze	surgeler	(sewr zhuh lay)	A44
to deepen	approfondir *	(ah praw fohn deer)	*'s
to defeat	vaincre	(vahn kruh)	A19
to defend	défendre #	(day fawn druh)	#'s
to define	définir *	(day fee neer)	*'s
to deflate	dégonfler R	(day gohn flay)	R's
to defuse	désamorcer	(day zah mawr say)	A13
to degenerate	dégénérer	(day zhay nay ray)	A32
to degrade	avilir *	(ah vee leer)	*'s
to deign	daigner R	(day nyay)	R's

© 2010

ENGLISH	FRENCH VERB	PRONOUNCIATION	PAGE
to delay	attarder R	(ah tahr day)	R's
to delegate	déléguer	(day lay gay)	A5
to deliberate	délibérer	(day lee bay ray)	A32
to delight	enchanter R	(awn shawn tay)	R's
"	réjouir *	(ray zhweer)	*'s
"	ravir *	(rah veer)	*'s
to delight in	complaire	(kohn plehr)	A53
to deliver	livrer R	(lee vray)	R's
to demand	exiger	(eg zee zhay)	A46
"	revendiquer R	(ruh vawn dee kay)	R's
to demolish	démolir *	(day maw leer)	*'s
to demonstrate	démontrer R	(day mohn tray)	R's
to denature	dénaturer R	(day nah tew ray)	R's
to denigrate	dénigrer R	(day nee gray)	R's
to denounce	dénoncer	(day nohn say)	A13
to deny	démentir	(day mawn teer)	A27
"	dénier R	(day nyay)	R's
"	désavouer R	(day zah vway)	R's
"	disconvenir	(dee skohn vuh neer)	A23
"	nier R	(nyay)	R's
to depend on	dépendre #	(day pawn druh)	#'s
to depict	dépeindre	(deh pahn druh)	A12
to depreciate	déprécier R	(day pray syay)	R's
to depress	déprimer R	(day pree may)	R's
to deprive	priver R	(pree vay)	R's
to descend	descendre #	(deh sawn druh)	#'s
to describe	décrire	(day kreer)	A28
"	qualifier R	(kah lee fyay)	R's
to desensitize	désensibiliser R	(day sawn see bee lee zay)	R's
to desert	déserter R	(day zehr tay)	R's
to deserve	mériter R	(may ree tay)	R's
to designate	désigner R	(day zee nyay)	R's
to desire	désirer R	(day zee ray)	R's
to despise	dédaigner R	(day day nyay)	R's
"	mépriser R	(may pree zay)	R's
to destine	destiner R	(deh stee nay)	R's
to destroy	abattre	(ah bah truh)	A1
"	détruire	(day trweer)	A63
to detach	détacher R	(day tah shay)	R's
to detail	détailler R	(day tah yay)	R's
to detain	détenir	(day tuh neer)	A23
to detect	détecter R	(day tehk tay)	R's
"	déceler	(day slay)	A44
to determine	déterminer R	(day tehr mee nay)	R's
to detest	détester R	(day teh stay)	R's
to detoxify	désintoxiquer R	(day zahn tawks ee kay)	R's
to develop	développer R	(day vlaw pay)	R's
"	élaborer R	(ay lah baw ray)	R's
to devote	consacrer R	(kohn sah kray)	R's

© 2010

ENGLISH	FRENCH VERB	PRONOUNCIATION	PAGE
to devote	dédier R	(day dyay)	R's
to devote oneself to	dévouer R	(day vway)	R's
to devour	dévorer R	(day vaw ray)	R's
to dictate	dicter R	(deek tay)	R's
to die	décéder	(day say day)	A32
"	mourir	(moo reer)	A50
"	périr *	(pay reer)	*'s
to differ	différer	(dee fay ray)	A32
to dig	bêcher R	(bay shay)	R's
"	creuser R	(kruh zay)	R's
to digest	digérer	(dee zhay ray)	A32
to dilute	diluer R	(dee lway)	R's
"	délayer	(day lay yay)	A33
to diminish	mollir *	(maw leer)	*'s
to dine	dîner R	(dee nay)	R's
to dip	tremper R	(trawn pay)	R's
to direct	diriger	(dee ree zhay)	A46
to dirty	salir *	(sah leer)	*'s
to disabuse	détromer R	(day trohn pay)	R's
to disadvantage	désavantager	(day zah vawn tah zhay)	A46
to disappear	disparaître	(dee spah reh truh)	A18
to disappoint	décevoir	(day suh vwahr)	A7
to disapprove of	désapprouver R	(day zah proo vay)	R's
to discharge	destituer R	(deh stee tway)	R's
to disconcert	déconcerter R	(day kohn sehr tay)	R's
to discourage	décourager	(day koo rah zhay)	A46
to discover	éventer R	(ay vawn tay)	R's
"	découvrir	(day koov reer)	A52
to discuss	discuter R	(dee skoo tay)	R's
"	débattre	(day bah truh)	A1
to disentangle	démêler R	(day may lay)	R's
"	débrouiller R	(day broo yay)	R's
to disfigure	défigurer R	(day fee gew ray)	R's
to disguise	déguiser R	(day gee zay)	R's
"	farder R	(fahr day)	R's
to disgust	dégoûter R	(day goo tay)	R's
"	rebuter R	(ruh bew tay)	R's
to disinfect	désinfecter R	(day zahn fehk tay)	R's
to disinherit	déshériter R	(day zay ree tay)	R's
to disintegrate	désintégrer	(day zahn tay gray)	A5
"	désagréger	(day zah gray zhay)	A57
to dislocate	déboîter R	(day bwah tay)	R's
"	démettre	(day meh truh)	A48
to dismantle	démanteler	(day mawn tlay)	A44
to dismay	consterner R	(kohn stehr nay)	R's
to dismiss	éconduire	(ay kohn dweer)	A63
"	congédier R	(kohn zhay dyay)	R's
"	démettre	(day meh truh)	A48
to disobey	désobéir *	(day zaw bay eer)	*'s

© 2010

ENGLISH	FRENCH VERB	PRONOUNCIATION	PAGE
to disorganize	désorganiser R	(day zawr gah nee zay)	R's
to disorientate	désorienter R	(day zaw ryahn tay)	R's
to disown	désavouer R	(day zah vway)	R's
to disparage	décrier R	(day kree yay)	R's
to dispatch	dépêcher R	(day pay shay)	R's
"	expédier R	(ek spay dyay)	R's
to dispel	dissiper R	(dee see pay)	R's
to display	afficher R	(ah fee shay)	R's
"	déployer	(day plwah yay)	A30
to displease	déplaire	(day plehr)	A53
to disregard	méconnaître	(may kaw neh truh)	A18
to dissaude	dissuader R	(dee swah day)	R's
to disseminate	disséminer R	(dee say mee nay)	R's
to dissociate	dissocier R	(dee saw syay)	R's
to dissolve	dissoudre	(dee soo druh)	A26
to distend	distendre #	(dee stawn druh)	#'s
to distinguish	distinguer R	(dee stahn gay)	R's
to distort	distordre #	(dee stawr druh)	#'s
"	déformer R	(day fawr may)	R's
"	fausser R	(foh say)	R's
to distract	distraire	(dee strehr)	A35
to distresss	désoler R	(day zaw lay)	R's
to distribute	distribuer R	(dee stree bway)	R's
to disturb	déranger	(day rawn zhay)	A29
"	émouvoir	(ay moo vwahr)	A46
"	gêner R	(zheh nay)	R's
"	troubler R	(troo blay)	R's
to dive	plonger	(plohn zhay)	A46
to divert	détourner R	(day toor nay)	R's
"	dévier R	(day vyay)	R's
to divest	démunir *	(day mew neer)	*'s
to divide	diviser R	(dee vee zay)	R's
"	désunir *	(day zew neer)	*'s
to divorce	divorcer	(dee vawr say)	A13
to do	faire	(fehr)	A37
to dominate	dominer R	(daw mee nay)	R's
to do odd jobs	bricoler R	(bree kaw lay)	R's
to do one's utmost	ingénier (s') R	(ahn zhayn yay)	R's
to do someone's hair	coiffer R	(kwa fay)	R's
to double	doubler R	(doo blay)	R's
"	jumeler	(zhewm lay)	A8
to doubt	douter R	(doo tay)	R's
to do up	retaper R	(ruh tah pay)	R's
to downgrade	déclasser R	(day klah say)	R's
to doze	sommeiller R	(saw may yay)	R's
to draft	rédiger	(ray dee zhay)	A46
to drag	traîner R	(treh nay)	R's
to drain	désamorcer	(day zah mawr say)	A13
to draw	étirer R	(ay tee ray)	R's

© 2010

ENGLISH	FRENCH VERB	PRONOUNCIATION	PAGE
to draw	dessiner R	(day see nay)	R's
"	tracer	(trah say)	A13
"	dégainer R	(day geh nay)	R's
to dread	redouter R	(ruh doo tay)	R's
to dream	rêver R	(ray vay)	R's
to dress	habiller R	(ah bee yay)	R's
"	vêtir	(veh teer)	A64
to dress (so) again	rhabiller R	(rah bee yay)	R's
to drink	boire	(bwahr)	A15
to drive	conduire	(kohn dweer)	A63
to drizzle	bruiner R	(brwee nay)	R's
to drool	baver R	(bah vay)	R's
to drop	décroître	(day krwa truh)	A2
to drown	noyer	(nwah yay)	A30
to dry	essuyer	(ay swee yay)	A30
"	sécher	(say shay)	A5
to dry out	dessécher	(day say shay)	A5
to duck	esquiver R	(eh skee vay)	R's
to dump	déposer R	(day poh zay)	R's
to dust	dépoussiérer	(day poo syay ray)	A32
to dye	teindre	(tahn druh)	A12
to earn	gagner R	(gah nyay)	R's
to eat	becqueter	(behk tay)	A43
"	bouffer R	(boo fay)	R's
"	manger	(mawn zhay)	A46
to eclipse	éclipser R	(ay kleep say)	R's
to economize	économiser R	(ay kaw naw mee zay)	R's
to edit	éditer R	(ay dee tay)	R's
to educate	éduquer R	(ay dew kay)	R's
to elate	exalter R	(ehg zahl tay)	R's
to elect	élire	(ay leer)	A45
to electrify	électrifier R	(ay lehk tree fyay)	R's
to elide	élider R	(ay lee day)	R's
to eliminate	éliminer R	(ay lee mee nay)	R's
to emanate	émaner R	(ay mah nay)	R's
to emancipate	émanciper R	(ay mawn see pay)	R's
to embark	embarquer R	(awn bahr kay)	R's
to embarrass	embarrasser R	(awn bah rah say)	R's
to embellish	embellir *	(awn beh leer)	*'s
"	enjoliver R	(awn zhaw lee vay)	R's
to embitter	aigrir *	(ay greer)	*'s
to emboss	gaufrer R	(goh fray)	R's
to embrace	étreindre	(ay trahn druh)	A12
"	enlacer	(awn lah say)	A13
to embroider	broder R	(braw day)	R's
to emerge	émerger	(ay mehr zhay)	A46
to emigrate	émigrer R	(ay mee gray)	R's
to emit	émettre	(ay meh truh)	A48
to employ	employer	(awn plwah yay)	A30

© 2010

ENGLISH	FRENCH VERB	PRONOUNCIATION	PAGE
to empty	vider R	(vee day)	R's
to enclose	enclore	(awn klawr)	A17
"	joindre	(zhwahn druh)	A12
to encourage	encourager	(awn koo rah zhay)	A46
"	inciter R	(ahn see tay)	R's
to encroach upon	empiéter	(awn pyay tay)	A32
to endow	douer R	(dway)	R's
to engage	engager	(awn gah zhay)	A46
to engineer	ingénier (s') R	(ahn zhayn yay)	R's
to engrave	graver R	(grah vay)	R's
to engulf	engloutir *	(awn gloo teer)	*'s
to enhance	rehausser R	(ruh oh say)	R's
to enjoin	enjoindre	(awn zhwan druh)	A12
to enjoy	jouir *	(zhweer)	*'S
to enlarge	agrandir *	(ah grawn deer)	*'S
"	grossir *	(groh seer)	*'S
to enliven	égayer	(ay gay yay)	A33
to ennoble	anoblir *	(ah naw bleer)	*'s
to enrol	inscrire	(ahn skreer)	A28
to enslave	asservir *	(ah sehr veer)	*'s
to enter	entrer R	(awn tray)	R's
to entertain	distraire	(dee strehr)	A35
to enthuse	enthousiasmer R	(awn too zy ahs may)	R's
to entitle	intituler R	(ahn tee tew lay)	R's
to enumerate	énumérer	(ay new may ray)	A32
to envisage	envisager	(awn vee zah zhay)	A46
to envy	envier R	(awn vyay)	R's
to equal	égaler R	(ay gah lay)	R's
to erase	effacer	(ay fah say)	A13
"	gommer R	(gaw may)	R's
to escape	échapper R	(ay shah pay)	R's
"	évader (s') R	(ay vah day)	R's
to escort	escorter R	(eh skawr tay)	R's
to estimate	évaluer R	(ay vah lway)	R's
"	estimer R	(eh stee may)	R's
to evade	éluder R	(ay lew day)	R's
to evaporate	évaporer R	(ay vah paw ray)	R's
to evict	déloger	(day law zhay)	A46
"	expulser R	(ek spewl say)	R's
to evolve	évoluer R	(ay vaw lway)	R's
to exaggerate	exagérer	(ehg zah zhay ray)	A32
to exalt	exalter R	(ehg zahl tay)	R's
to examine	examiner R	(ehg zah mee nay)	R's
to exasperate	exaspérer	(ehg zah spay ray)	A32
to exceed	excéder	(ek say day)	A32
to exchange	échanger	(ay shawn zhay)	A46
to excite	exciter R	(ek see tay)	R's
to exclaim	exclamer (s') R	(eks klah may)	R's
"	écrier (s') R	(ay kree yay)	R's

© 2010

ENGLISH	FRENCH VERB	PRONOUNCIATION	PAGE
to exclaim	récrier (se) R	(ray kree yay)	R's
to exclude	exclure	(eks klewr)	A41
to excommunicate	excommunier R	(eks kaw mew nyay)	R's
to excuse	excuser R	(eks kew zay)	R's
to exempt	exonérer	(eg zaw nay ray)	A32
to exempt from	exempter R	(eg zawn tay)	R's
to exercise	exercer	(eg zehr say)	A13
to exhale	expirer R	(ek spee ray)	R's
to exhaust	épuiser R	(ay pwee zay)	R's
to exhibit	exposer R	(ek spoh zay)	R's
to exhilarate	griser R	(gree zay)	R's
to exile	exiler R	(eg zee lay)	R's
to exist	exister R	(eg zee stay)	R's
to expand	étoffer R	(ay taw fay)	R's
to expedite	expédier R	(ek spay dyay)	R's
to expire	expirer R	(ek spee ray)	R's
to explain	expliquer R	(ek splee kay)	R's
to explode	éclater R	(ay klah tay)	R's
"	exploser R	(ek sploh zay)	R's
to exploit	exploiter R	(ek splwah tay)	R's
"	utiliser R	(ew tee lee zay)	R's
to export	exporter R	(ek spawr tay)	R's
to express	exprimer R	(ek spree may)	R's
"	formuler R	(fawr mew lay)	R's
to exterminate	exterminer R	(ek stehr mee nay)	R's
to extract	extraire	(ek strehr)	A35
to exult	exulter R	(eg zewl tay)	R's
to eye up	lorgner R	(lawr nyay)	R's
to facilitate	faciliter R	(fah see lee tay)	R's
to fade	défraîchir *	(day fray sheer)	*'s
"	flétrir *	(flay treer)	*'s
to fade (colour)	déteindre	(day tahn druh)	A12
to fail	échouer R	(ay shway)	R's
"	mollir *	(maw leer)	*'s
"	rater R	(rah tay)	R's
to faint	évanouir (s') *	(ay vah nweer)	*'s
to fall	chuter R	(shew tay)	R's
"	tomber R	(tohn bay)	R's
to fall again	retomber R	(ruh tohn bay)	R's
to fall in love with	éprendre (s')	(ay prawn druh)	A9
to falsify	falsifier R	(fahl see fyay)	R's
to familiarize	familiariser R	(fah meel yah ree zay)	R's
to fart	péter	(pay tay)	A32
to fascinate	fasciner R	(fah see nay)	R's
"	passionner R	(pah syaw nay)	R's
to fast	jeûner R	(zhuh nay)	R's
to fasten	boucler R	(boo klay)	R's
to fatten	engraisser R	(awn gray say)	R's
to favour	favoriser R	(fah vaw ree zay)	R's

© 2010

ENGLISH	FRENCH VERB	PRONOUNCIATION	PAGE
to favour	avantager	(ah vawn tah zhay)	A46
"	privilégier R	(pree vee layzh yay)	R's
to fear	craindre	(krahn druh)	A12
to feed	alimenter R	(ah lee mawn tay)	R's
to feel	éprouver R	(ay proo vay)	R's
"	sentir	(sawn teer)	A27
"	ressentir	(ruh sawn teer)	A27
"	tâter R	(tah tay)	R's
"	estimer R	(eh stee may)	R's
to feign	feindre	(fahn druh)	A12
to ferment	fermenter R	(fehr mawn tay)	R's
to fiddle	truquer R	(trew kay)	R's
to fight	combattre	(kohn bah truh)	A1
"	bagarrer R	(bah gah ray)	R's
"	batailler R	(bah tah yay)	R's
to file	classer R	(klah say)	R's
"	ficher R	(fee shay)	R's
to file down	limer R	(lee may)	R's
to fill	combler R	(kohn blay)	R's
"	emplir *	(awn pleer)	*'s
"	garnir *	(gahr neer)	*'s
"	remplir *	(rawn pleer)	*'s
to fill (so) with despair	désespérer	(day zeh spay ray)	A32
to filter	filtrer R	(feel tray)	R's
to finance	financer	(fee nawn say)	A13
to find	trouver R	(troo vay)	R's
to finish	finir *	(fee neer)	*'s
"	terminer R	(tehr mee nay)	R's
to fish	pêcher R	(peh shay)	R's
to fit together	emboîter R	(awn bwah tay)	R's
to fix	fixer R	(feek say)	R's
"	dépanner R	(day pah nay)	R's
to flank	flanquer R	(flawn kay)	R's
to flatten	aplatir *	(ah plah teer)	*'s
"	faucher R	(foh shay)	R's
to flatter	flatter R	(flah tay)	R's
to flaunt	exhiber R	(eg zee bay)	R's
to flavour	parfumer R	(pahr few may)	R's
to flee	fuir	(fweer)	A39
to flirt	flirter R	(fluhr tay)	R's
to float	flotter R	(flaw tay)	R's
to flog	fouetter R	(fweh tay)	R's
to flood	inonder R	(ee nohn day)	R's
to flourish	fructifier R	(frewk tee fyay)	R's
to flow	couler R	(koo lay)	R's
to fly	voler R	(vaw lay)	R's
to foil	déjouer R	(day zhway)	R's
to fold	plier R	(plee yay)	R's
to follow	découler R	(day koo lay)	R's

© 2010

ENGLISH	FRENCH VERB	PRONOUNCIATION	PAGE
to follow	ensuivre (s')	(awn swee vruh)	A61
"	suivre	(sweev ruh)	A61
to foment	fomenter R	(faw mawn tay)	R's
to fool	abuser R	(ah bew zay)	R's
"	duper R	(dew pay)	R's
to forage about	fouiner R	(fwee nay)	R's
to forbid	interdire	(ahn tehr deer)	A42
to force	forcer	(fawr say)	A13
"	contraindre	(kohn trahn druh)	A12
"	obliger	(aw blee zhay)	A46
to forge	forger	(fawr zhay)	A46
to forget	désapprendre	(day zah prawn druh)	A9
"	oublier R	(oo blee yay)	R's
to forgive	pardonner R	(pahr daw nay)	R's
to formalize	formaliser R	(fawr mah lee zay)	R's
to form	former R	(fawr may)	R's
to found	fonder R	(fohn day)	R's
to free	dégager	(day gah zhay)	A46
to free oneself from	déprendre (se)	(day prawn druh)	A9
to freeze	congeler	(kohn zlay)	A44
"	geler	(zhuh lay)	A44
"	glacer	(glah say)	A13
to frighten away	effaroucher R	(ay fah roo shay)	R's
to frolic	ébattre (s')	(ay bah truh)	A1
"	batifoler R	(bah tee faw lay)	R's
to frost	dépolir *	(day paw leer)	*'s
to frost over	givrer R	(zhee vray)	R's
to frown	froncer	(frohn say)	A13
to frustrate	frustrer R	(frew stray)	R's
to fry	frire	(freer)	A60
to fulfil	réaliser R	(ray ah lee zay)	R's
to furl	ferler R	(fehr lay)	R's
to furnish	meubler R	(muh blay)	R's
to gallop	galoper R	(gah law pay)	R's
to gasp for breath	haleter	(ahl tay)	A44
to gather	froncer	(frohn say)	A13
"	rassembler R	(rah sawn blay)	R's
to generalize	généraliser R	(zhay nay rah lee zay)	R's
to get ahead of	devancer	(duh vawn say)	A13
to get back to	regagner R	(ruh gah nyay)	R's
to get engaged	fiancer	(fee awn say)	A13
to get even	revaloir	(ruh vah lwahr)	A56
to get out of control	déraper R	(day rah pay)	R's
to get out of the habit	déshabituer R	(day zah bee tway)	R's
to get over	franchir *	(frawn sheer)	*'s
to get plastered	cuiter R	(kwee tay)	R's
to get ready	apprêter R	(ah preh tay)	R's
to get used to	habituer R	(ah bee tway)	R's
to get worse	empirer R	(awn pee ray)	R's

ENGLISH	FRENCH VERB	PRONOUNCIATION	PAGE
to gild	dorer R	(daw ray)	R's
to give	donner R	(daw nay)	R's
to give back	rendre #	(rawn druh)	#'s
to give birth	accoucher R	(ah koo shay)	R's
"	enfanter R	(awn fawn tay)	R's
to give information	renseigner R	(rawn say nyay)	R's
to give up	céder	(say day)	A32
"	renoncer	(ruh nawn say)	A13
to glimpse	entrevoir	(awn truh vwahr)	A66
to glorify	glorifier R	(glaw ree fyay)	R's
to gnaw	ronger	(rohn zhay)	A46
to go	aller	(ah lay)	A6
to go mouldy	moisir *	(mwa zeer)	*'s
to go out	sortir	(sawr teer)	A27
to go out again	ressortir	(ruh sawr teer)	A27
to go up	monter R	(mohn tay)	R's
to gossip	jaser R	(zhah zay)	R's
to govern	gouverner R	(goo vehr nay)	R's
"	régir *	(ray zheer)	*'s
to graft	greffer R	(gray fay)	R's
to grant	accorder R	(ah kawr day)	R's
"	octroyer	(awk trwah yay)	A30
to gratify	gratifier R	(grah tee fyay)	R's
to greet	saluer R	(sah lway)	R's
to grieve	chagriner R	(shah gree nay)	R's
to grill	griller R	(gree yay)	R's
to grimace	grimacer	(gree mah say)	A13
to grind	broyer	(brwah yay)	A30
"	moudre	(moo druh)	A49
to grip	serrer R	(say ray)	R's
to groan	gémir *	(zhay meer)	*'s
to grope	tripoter R	(tree paw tay)	R's
to grow	croître	(krwah truh)	A2
"	pousser R	(poo say)	R's
"	grandir *	(grawn deer)	*'s
to group together	regrouper R	(ruh groo pay)	R's
to grow pale	pâlir *	(pah leer)	*'s
to grumble	maugréer R	(moh gray ay)	R's
"	rouspéter	(roo spay tay)	A32
to guarantee	garantir *	(gah rawn teer)	*'s
to guess	deviner R	(duh vee nay)	R's
to guide	guider R	(gee day)	R's
to gush out	jaillir *	(zhah yeer)	*'s
to hail	grêler R	(greh lay)	R's
to hallucinate	halluciner R	(ah lew see nay)	R's
to hammer	marteler	(mahr tuh lay)	A44
to handicap	handicaper R	(awn dee kah pay)	R's
to handle	manier R	(mah nyay)	R's
"	manipuler R	(mah nee pew lay)	R's

© 2010

ENGLISH	FRENCH VERB	PRONOUNCIATION	PAGE
to handle	manutentionner R	(mah new tawn syaw nay)	R's
to handle carefully	ménager	(may nah zhay)	A46
to hand out	dispenser R	(dee spawn say)	R's
to hang	pendre #	(pawn druh)	#'s
to hang about	zoner R	(zoh nay)	R's
to hang (sth) back up	raccrocher R	(rah kraw shay)	R's
to hang around	morfondre (se) #	(mawr fohn druh)	#'s
to hang up	suspendre #	(sew spawn druh)	#'s
"	accrocher R	(ah kraw shay)	R's
to happen	advenir	(ahd vuh neer)	A23
to harden	durcir *	(dewr seer)	*'s
to harm	nuire	(nweer)	A63
to harmonize	harmoniser R	(ahr maw nee zay)	R's
to harness	atteler	(aht lay)	A8
to harvest	moissonner R	(mwah saw nay)	R's
"	récolter R	(ray kawl tay)	R's
to harvest the grapes	vendanger	(vawn dawn zhay)	A46
to hasten	empresser (s') R	(awn pray say)	R's
"	hâter R	(ah tay)	R's
to hate	haïr	(ah eer)	A40
to haul	charrier R	(shah ryay)	R's
to haunt	hanter R	(awn tay)	R's
"	obséder	(awp say day)	A32
to have a premonition about	pressentir	(pray sawn teer)	A27
to have	avoir	(ah vwahr)	A14
to have lunch	déjeuner R	(day zhuh nay)	R's
to have to (must)	devoir	(duh vwahr)	A24
to heal	cicatriser R	(see kah tree zay)	R's
to hear	entendre #	(awn tawn druh)	#'s
to heat	chauffer R	(shoh fay)	R's
to heat up	réchauffer R	(ray shoh fay)	R's
to hedge	biaiser R	(bee yeh zay)	R's
to help	aider R	(ay day)	R's
"	secourir	(suh koo reer)	A21
to hesitate	hésiter R	(ay see tay)	R's
to hiccup	hoqueter	(awk tay)	A43
to hide	cacher R	(kah shay)	R's
"	dérober R	(day raw bay)	R's
"	ensevelir *	(awn suh vuh leer)	*'s
to hinder	entraver R	(awn trah vay)	R's
to hire	embaucher R	(awn boh shay)	R's
"	engager	(awn gah zhay)	A46
"	louer R	(loo ay)	R's
to hit	cogner R	(kaw nyay)	R's
"	frapper R	(frah pay)	R's
"	heurter R	(uhr tay)	R's
"	taper R	(tah pay)	R's
to hold	tenir	(tuh neer)	A23
to hold forth	discourir	(dee skoo reer)	A21

© 2010

ENGLISH	FRENCH VERB	PRONOUNCIATION	PAGE
to hold (so) up	retenir	(ruh tneer)	A23
to honk	klaxonner R	(klahk saw nay)	R's
to honour	honorer R	(aw naw ray)	R's
to hope	espérer	(eh spay ray)	A32
to hope for	souhaiter R	(sway tay)	R's
to horrify	horrifier R	(aw ree fyay)	R's
to house	loger	(law zhay)	A46
to humanize	humaniser R	(ew mah nee zay)	R's
to hum	chantonner R	(shawn taw nay)	R's
to humidify	humidifier R	(ew mee dee fyay)	R's
to humiliate	humilier R	(ew mee lyay)	R's
to hunt	chasser R	(shah say)	R's
to hurt	froisser R	(frwah say)	R's
"	meurtrir *	(muhr treer)	*'s
to hurtle down	dévaler R	(day vah lay)	R's
to hypnotize	hypnotiser R	(eep naw tee zay)	R's
to idealize	idéaliser R	(ee day ah lee zay)	R's
"	magnifier R	(mah nyee fyay)	R's
to identify	identifier R	(ee dawn tee fyay)	R's
to ignore	ignorer R	(ee nyaw ray)	R's
to illuminate	illuminer R	(ee lew mee nay)	R's
"	éclairer R	(ay klay ray)	R's
to illustrate	illustrer R	(ee lew stray)	R's
to imagine	imaginer R	(ee mah zhee nay)	R's
to imitate	imiter R	(ee mee tay)	R's
to immigrate	immigrer R	(ee mee gray)	R's
to immobilize	immobiliser R	(ee maw bee lee zay)	R's
to implicate	impliquer R	(ahn plee kay)	R's
to implore	implorer R	(ahn plaw ray)	R's
"	supplier R	(sew plee yay)	R's
to imply	sous-entendre #	(soo zawn tawn druh)	#'s
to import	importer R	(ahn pawr tay)	R's
to impoverish	appauvrir *	(ah poh vreer)	*'s
to impress	impressionner R	(ahn preh syaw nay)	R's
"	épater R	(ay pah tay)	R's
to imprint	empreindre	(awn prahn druh)	A12
to imprison	emprisonner R	(awn pree zaw nay)	R's
to improve	améliorer R	(ah may lyaw ray)	R's
"	bonifier R	(baw nee fyay)	R's
to improvise	improviser R	(ahn praw vee zay)	R's
to inaugurate	inaugurer R	(ee noh gew ray)	R's
to incite	inciter R	(ahn see tay)	R's
"	susciter R	(sew see tay)	R's
to include	inclure	(ahn klewr)	A41
"	comporter R	(kohn pawr tay)	R's
to incorporate	incorporer R	(ahn kawr paw ray)	R's
to increase	accroître	(ah krwah truh)	A2
"	augmenter R	(ohg mawn tay)	R's
"	majorer R	(mah zhaw ray)	R's

© 2010

ENGLISH	FRENCH VERB	PRONOUNCIATION	PAGE
to increase	renchérir *	(rawn shay reer)	*'s
to incriminate	incriminer R	(ahn kree mee nay)	R's
to incur	encourir	(awn koo reer)	A21
to indicate	indiquer R	(ahn dee kay)	R's
to indoctrinate	endoctriner R	(awn dawk tree nay)	R's
to infect	infecter R	(ahn fehk tay)	R's
to infer	induire	(ahn dweer)	A63
to inflate	enfler R	(awn flay)	R's
"	gonfler R	(gohn flay)	R's
to inflict	infliger	(ahn flee zhay)	A46
to influence	influencer	(ahn flew awn say)	A13
to inform	informer R	(ahn fawr may)	R's
"	avertir *	(ah vehr teer)	*'s
"	aviser R	(ah vee zay)	R's
to infringe	déroger	(day raw zhay)	A46
"	enfreindre	(awn frahn druh)	A12
to inhale	inhaler R	(ee nah lay)	R's
to inhale	aspirer R	(ah spee ray)	R's
to inherit	hériter R	(ay ree tay)	R's
to initiate	initier R	(ee nee syay)	R's
"	entamer R	(awn tah may)	R's
to injure	blesser R	(blay say)	R's
to innovate	innover R	(ee naw vay)	R's
to inoculate	inoculer R	(ee naw kew lay)	R's
to inpair	altérer	(ahl tay ray)	A32
to inquire	enquérir (s')	(awn kay reer)	A4
to insert	insérer	(ahn say ray)	A32
"	introduire	(ahn traw dweer)	A63
to insinuate	insinuer R	(ahn see nway)	R's
to insist	insister R	(ahn see stay)	R's
to inspect	inspecter R	(ahn spehk tay)	R's
to inspire	inspirer R	(ahn spee ray)	R's
to install	installer R	(ahn stah lay)	R's
to institute	instituer R	(ahn stee tway)	R's
to insult	insulter R	(ahn sewl tay)	R's
"	injurier R	(ahn zhewr yay)	R's
to integrate	intégrer	(ahn tay gray)	A5
to intensify	intensifier R	(ahn tawn see fyay)	R's
"	aviver R	(ah vee vay)	R's
"	redoubler R	(ruh doo blay)	R's
to intercede	intercéder	(ahn tehr say day)	A32
to interest	intéresser R	(ahn tay ray say)	R's
to interfere	immiscer (s')	(ee mee say)	A13
to interrogate	interroger	(ahn tehr raw zhay)	A46
to interrupt	interrompre #	(ahn tay rohn pruh)	#'s
to intertwine	entrelacer	(awn truh lah say)	A13
to intervene	intervenir	(ahn tehr vuh neer)	A23
to intoxicate	enivrer R	(awn nee vray)	R's
to intrigue	intriguer R	(ahn tree gay)	R's

© 2010 214

ENGLISH	FRENCH VERB	PRONOUNCIATION	PAGE
to introduce	introduire	(ahn traw dweer)	A63
"	présenter R	(pray zawn tay)	R's
to inundate	inonder R	(ee nohn day)	R's
to invade	envahir *	(awn vah eer)	*'s
to invalidate	infirmer R	(ahn feer may)	R's
to invent	inventer R	(ahn vawn tay)	R's
to invert	invertir *	(ahn vehr teer)	*'s
to investigate	enquêter R	(awn kay tay)	R's
to invest	investir *quêter R	(ahn veh steer)	*'s
to invigorate	vivifier R	(vee vee fyay)	R's
to invite	inviter R	(ahn vee tay)	R's
"	convier R	(kohn vyay)	R's
to invoice	facturer R	(fahk tew ray)	R's
to invoke	alléguer	(ah lay gay)	A5
"	invoquer R	(ahn vaw kay)	R's
to irritate	irriter R	(ee ree tay)	R's
"	énerver R	(ay nehr vay)	R's
to irritate	impatienter R	(ahn pah syawn tay)	R's
to isolate	isoler R	(ee zaw lay)	R's
to join	joindre	(zhwahn druh)	A12
to joke	blaguer R	(blah gay)	R's
to judge	juger	(zhew zhay)	A46
to jump	sauter R	(soh tay)	R's
to justify	justifier R	(zhew stee fyay)	R's
to keep	garder R	(gahr day)	R's
"	retenir	(ruh tneer)	A23
to kidnap	kidnapper R	(keed nah pay)	R's
to kill	tuer R	(too ay)	R's
to kiss	baiser R	(bay zay)	R's
"	embrasser R	(awn brah say)	R's
to knead	pétrir *	(pay treer)	*'s
to kneel	agenouiller (s') R	(ahzh noo yay)	R's
to knit	tricoter R	(tree kaw tay)	R's
to knock	cogner R	(kaw nyay)	R's
to knock down	terrasser R	(teh rah say)	R's
to knock out	assommer R	(ah saw may)	R's
to knock over	culbuter R	(kewl bew tay)	R's
to knock over	renverser R	(rawn vehr say)	R's
to know	connaître	(kaw neh truh)	A18
"	savoir	(sah vwahr)	A59
to label	étiqueter	(ay teek tay)	A43
to lace up	lacer	(lah say)	A13
to lambast	pourfendre #	(poor fawn druh)	#'s
to land	atterrir *	(ah tay reer)	*'s
to land on the moon	alunir *	(ah lew neer)	*'s
to languish	languir *	(lawn geer)	*'s
to last	durer R	(dew ray)	R's
to laugh	rigoler R	(ree gaw lay)	R's
"	rire	(reer)	A58

ENGLISH	FRENCH VERB	PRONOUNCIATION	PAGE
to lay	pondre #	(pohn druh)	#'s
to lay down	allonger	(ah lohn zhay)	A46
to lay off	debaucher R	(day boh shay)	R's
to laze about	fainéanter R	(fay nay awn tay)	R's
to lead	mener	(muh nay)	A44
to lead astray	égarer R	(ay gah ray)	R's
to lead to	entraîner R	(awn tray nay)	R's
"	induire	(ahn dweer)	A63
to leaf through	feuilleter	(fuhy tay)	A43
to lean	accoter R	(ah kaw tay)	R's
"	adosser R	(ah doh say)	R's
"	appuyer	(ah pwee yay)	A30
to lean	pencher R	(pawn shay)	R's
to lean on one's elbows	accouder (s') R	(ah koo day)	R's
to leap	bondir *	(bohn deer)	*'s
to learn	apprendre	(ah prawn druh)	A9
to leave	absenter (s') R	(ap sawn tay)	R's
"	laisser R	(lay say)	R's
"	partir	(pahr teer)	A27
"	quitter R	(kee tay)	R's
to leave again	repartir	(ruh pahr teer)	A27
to leave (so) breathless	essouffler R	(ay soo flay)	R's
to legalize	légaliser R	(lay gah lee zay)	R's
to legislate	légiférer	(lay zhee fay ray)	A32
to lend	prêter R	(preh tay)	R's
to lengthen	rallonger	(rah lohn zhay)	A46
to let	louer R	(loo ay)	R's
to let up	décolérer	(day kaw lay ray)	A32
to level	niveler	(neev lay)	A8
to liberate	libérer	(lee bay ray)	A32
"	délivrer R	(day lee vray)	R's
to lick	lécher	(lay shay)	A5
to lie	mentir	(mawn teer)	A27
to lift	lever	(leh vay)	A44
"	soulever	(soo lvay)	A44
to light	allumer R	(ah lew may)	R's
to lighten	éclaircir *	(ay klehr seer)	*'s
to lighten up	épanouir *	(ay pahn weer)	*'s
to like	aimer R	(ay may)	R's
to limit	limiter R	(lee mee tay)	R's
"	borner R	(bawr nay)	R's
to limp	boiter R	(bwa tay)	R's
to line	fourrer R	(foo ray)	R's
to link up	relier R	(ruh lyay)	R's
to liquefy	liquéfier R	(lee kay fyay)	R's
to liquidate	liquider R	(lee kee day)	R's
to lisp	zézayer	(zay zay yay)	A33
to listen to	écouter R	(ay koo tay)	R's
to live	vivre	(vee vruh)	A65

ENGLISH	FRENCH VERB	PRONOUNCIATION	PAGE
to live in	habiter R	(ah bee tay)	R's
to live together	cohabiter R	(koh ah bee tay)	R's
to load	charger	(shahr zhay)	A46
"	embarquer R	(awn bahr kay)	R's
to loaf around	flemmarder R	(fleh mahr day)	R's
to loathe	exécrer	(eg zay kray)	A5
to lock	verrouiller R	(veh roo yay)	R's
to look after	entretenir	(awn truh tuh neer)	A23
to look at	regarder R	(ruh gahr day)	R's
to look for	chercher R	(shehr shay)	R's
"	rechercher R	(ruh shehr shay)	R's
"	quêter R	(kay tay)	R's
to loosen	desserrer R	(day say ray)	R's
"	disjoindre	(dees zhwahn druh)	A12
"	relâcher R	(ruh lah shay)	R's
to lose	perdre #	(pehr druh)	#'s
to lose (sth) again	reperdre #	(ruh pehr druh)	#'s
to lose weight	maigrir *	(meh greer)	*'s
to love	aimer R	(ay may)	R's
to lower	abaisser R	(ah bay say)	R's
"	baisser R	(bay say)	R's
to lubricate	lubrifier R	(lew bree fyay)	R's
to machine	usiner R	(ew zee nay)	R's
to magnetize	aimanter R	(eh mawn tay)	R's
to maim	estropier R	(eh straw pyay)	R's
to maintain	maintenir	(mahn tuh neer)	A23
to make	faire	(fehr)	A37
"	fabriquer R	(fah bree kay)	R's
to make a feint	feinter R	(fahn tay)	R's
to make a hole in	trouer R	(troo ay)	R's
to make awkward	guinder R	(gahn day)	R's
to make drowsy	assoupir *	(ah soo peer)	*'s
to make fun of	railler R	(rah yay)	R's
to make indifferent	blaser R	(blah zay)	R's
to make (so) late	retarder R	(ruh tahr day)	R's
to make (so) lose interest	désintéresser R	(day zahn tay ray say)	R's
to make progress	progresser R	(praw gray say)	R's
to make puffy	bouffir *	(boo feer)	*'s
to make (so) redundant	licencier R	(lee sawn syay)	R's
to make rich	enrichir *	(awn ree sheer)	*'s
to make stupid	abêtir *	(ah bay teer)	*'s
to make tense	crisper R	(kree spay)	R's
to make things up	fabuler R	(fah bew lay)	R's
to make thinner	amaigrir *	(ah may greer)	*'s
to make tired	fatiguer R	(fah tee gay)	R's
to make (sth) uneven	déniveler	(day nee vlay)	A8
to make unstable	déséquilibrer R	(day zay kee lee bray)	R's
to malign	médire	(may deer)	A25
to manage	diriger	(dee ree zhay)	A46

ENGLISH	FRENCH VERB	PRONOUNCIATION	PAGE
to manage	gérer	(zhay ray)	A32
to manhandle	malmener	(mahl muh nay)	A44
to manipulate	manipuler R	(mah nee pew lay)	R's
to manoeuvre	manœuvrer R	(mah nuh vray)	R's
to manufactur	manufacturer R	(mah new fahk tew ray)	R's
"	façonner R	(fah saw nay)	R's
"	usiner R	(ew zee nay)	R's
to march	défiler R	(day fee lay)	R's
to mark down	démarquer R	(day mahr kay)	R's
to mark	marquer R	(mahr kay)	R's
to mark out	baliser R	(bah lee zay)	R's
to marry	marier R	(mah ryay)	R's
"	épouser R	(ay poo zay)	R's
"	convoler R	(kohn vaw lay)	R's
to massacre	massacrer R	(mah sah kray)	R's
to match	apparier R	(ah pah ryay)	R's
"	assortir *	(ah sawr teer)	8's
to match up	appareiller R	(ah pah ray yay)	R's
to materialize	matérialiser R	(mah tay ryah lee zay)	R's
to mean	signifier R	(see nyee fyay)	R's
to measure	mesurer R	(muh zew ray)	R's
to mechanize	mécaniser R	(may kah nee zay)	R's
to mediate	entremettre (s')	(awn truh meh truh)	A48
to meditate	méditer R	(may dee tay)	R's
to meet	rencontrer R	(rawn kohn tray)	R's
to meet up with	rejoindre	(ruh zhwahn druh)	A12
to melt	fondre #	(fohn druh)	#'s
to mend	raccommoder R	(rah kaw maw day)	R's
to mention	mentionner R	(mawn syaw nay)	R's
to meow	miauler R	(myoh lay)	R's
to mess up	cochonner R	(kaw shaw nay)	R's
to milk	traire	(trehr)	A35
to mimic	mimer R	(mee may)	R's
to mince	hacher R	(ah shay)	R's
to mine	miner R	(mee nay)	R's
to minimize	minimiser R	(mee nee mee zay)	R's
to mirror	refléter	(ruh flay tay)	A32
to mislead	fourvoyer	(foor vwah yay)	A30
to miss	louper R	(loo pay)	R's
"	manquer R	(mawn kay)	R's
to mistreat	maltraiter R	(mahl treh tay)	R's
to mistrust	méfier (se) R	(may fyay)	R's
to misunderstand	méconnaître	(may kaw neh truh)	A18
to mix	mêler R	(may lay)	R's
to mix up	brouiller R	(broo yay)	R's
to moan	geindre	(zhahn druh)	A12
"	lamenter (se) R	(lah mawn tay)	R's
to mobilize	mobiliser R	(maw bee lee zay)	R's
to mock	moquer R	(maw kay)	R's

© 2010

ENGLISH	FRENCH VERB	PRONOUNCIATION	PAGE
to mock	gausser (se) R	(goh say)	R's
to model	modeler	(mawd lay)	A44
to moderate	modérer	(maw day ray)	A32
to modernize	moderniser R	(maw dehr nee zay)	R's
to modify	modifier R	(maw dee fyay)	R's
"	remanier R	(ruh mahn yay)	R's
to monopolize	monopoliser R	(maw naw paw lee zay)	R's
"	accaparer R	(ah kah pah ray)	R's
to moo	meugler R	(muh glay)	R's
to mop up	éponger	(ay pohn zhay)	A46
to mortify	mortifier R	(mawr tee fyay)	R's
to motivate	motiver R	(maw tee vay)	R's
"	exhorter R	(eg zawr tay)	R's
to mourn	pleurer R	(pluh ray)	R's
to move	mouvoir	(moo vwahr)	A29
"	bouger	(boo zhay)	A46
"	déplacer	(day plah say)	A13
"	remuer R	(ruh mway)	R's
to move apart	écarter R	(ay kahr tay)	R's
to move away	éloigner R	(ay lwah nyay)	R's
to move back	reculer R	(ruh kew lay)	R's
to move deeply	émouvoir	(ay moo vwahr)	A29
"	bouleverser R	(boo lvehr say)	R's
to move in	emménager	(awn may nah zhay)	A46
to move to pity	apitoyer	(ah pee twah yay)	A33
to mow	faucher R	(foh shay)	R's
"	tondre #	(tohn druh)	#'s
to multiply	multiplier R	(mewl tee plee yay)	R's
to mumble	bredouiller R	(bruh doo yay)	R's
to murmur	murmurer R	(mewr mew ray)	R's
to mutate	muter R	(mew tay)	R's
to mutilate	mutiler R	(mew tee lay)	R's
to mutter	grogner R	(graw nyay)	R's
"	grommeler	(grawm lay)	A8
to muzzle	museler	(mew zuh lay)	A8
to mystify	mystifier R	(mee stee fyay)	R's
to nail down	clouer R	(kloo ay)	R's
to name	nommer R	(naw may)	R's
to narrate	narrer R	(nah ray)	R's
to need	falloir	(fahl wahr)	A38
to neglect	négliger	(nay glee zhay)	A46
to negotiate	négocier R	(nay gaw syay)	R's
to neigh	hennir *	(ay neer)	*'s
to nestle	blottir *	(blaw teer)	*'s
to nibble	grignoter R	(gree nyaw tay)	R's
to nod	hocher R	(aw shay)	R's
to normalize	normaliser R	(nawr mah lee zay)	R's
to note	constater R	(kohn stah tay)	R's
to note down	noter R	(naw tay)	R's

© 2010

ENGLISH	FRENCH VERB	PRONOUNCIATION	PAGE
to nourish	nourrir *	(noo reer)	*'s
to numb	engourdir *	(awn goor deer)	*'s
to number	numéroter R	(new may raw tay)	R's
to obey	obéir *	(aw bay eer)	*'s
to object	objecter R	(awb zhehk tay)	R's
to oblige	obliger	(aw blee zhay)	A46
to obliterate	oblitérer	(aw blee tay ray)	A32
to obscure	obscurcir *	(awp skewr seer)	*'s
to observe	observer R	(awp sehr vay)	R's
to obsess	obséder	(awp say day)	A32
to obtain	obtenir	(awp tuh neer)	A23
to occupy	occuper R	(aw kew pay)	R's
to occur	survenir	(sewr vuh neer)	A23
to offend	offenser R	(aw fawn say)	R's
"	outrager	(oot rah zhay)	A46
"	vexer R	(vehk say)	R's
to offer	offrir	(aw freer)	A52
"	proposer R	(praw poh zay)	R's
to omit	omettre	(aw meh truh)	A48
to open	ouvrir	(oov reer)	A52
to open a little	entrouvrir	(awn troo vreer)	A52
to open out	épanouir *	(ay pahn weer)	*'s
to operate (on)	opérer	(aw pay ray)	A32
to oppose	opposer R	(aw poh zay)	R's
to oppress	opprimer R	(aw pree may)	R's
to order	ordonner R	(awr daw nay)	R's
"	commander R	(kaw mawn day)	R's
to organize	organiser R	(awr gah nee zay)	R's
"	aménager	(ah may nah zhay)	A46
to oscillate	osciller R	(aw see lay)	R's
to outrage	outrager	(oot rah zhay)	A46
to overcome	surmonter R	(sewr mohn tay)	R's
"	vaincre	(vahn kruh)	A19
to overflow	déborder R	(day bawr day)	R's
to overload	surcharger	(sewr shahr zhay)	A46
to overrate	surfaire	(sew fehr)	A37
to overshadow	éclipser R	(ay kleep say)	R's
to overtake	dépasser R	(day pah say)	R's
to overwhelm	accabler R	(ah kah blay)	R's
to owe	devoir	(duh vwahr)	A24
to oxidize	oxyder R	(awk see day)	R's
to pace up and down	arpenter R	(ahr pawn tay)	R's
to pacify	pacifier R	(pah see fyay)	R's
to paint	peindre	(pahn druh)	A12
to palpate	palper R	(pahl pay)	R's
to palpitate	palpiter R	(pahl pee tay)	R's
to pamper	bichonner R	(bee shaw nay)	R's
"	choyer	(shwah yay)	A30
to panic	paniquer R	(pah nee kay)	R's

ENGLISH	FRENCH VERB	PRONOUNCIATION	PAGE
to panic	affoler R	(ah faw lay)	R's
to parachute	parachuter R	(pah rah shew tay)	R's
to parade	défiler R	(day fee lay)	R's
to paralyse	paralyser R	(pah rah lee zay)	R's
to parade	gracier R	(grah syay)	R's
to park	parquer R	(pahr kay)	R's
"	garer R	(gah ray)	R's
"	stationner R	(stah syaw nay)	R's
to participate	participer R	(pahr tee see pay)	R's
to pass	passer R	(pah say)	R's
"	écouler R	(ay koo lay)	R's
"	paver R	(pah vay)	R's
to patent	breveter	(bruh vtay)	A43
to pave	daller R	(dah lay)	R's
to pay	régler	(ray glay)	A5
to pay back	revaloir	(ruh vah lwahr)	A56
to pay for	payer	(pay yay)	A33
to pay off	rembourser R	(rawn boor say)	R's
to pay out	débourser R	(day boor say)	R's
to peak	culminer R	(kewl mee nay)	R's
to peck at	becqueter	(behk tay)	A43
to peel	éplucher R	(ay plew shay)	R's
to peel off	peler	(puh lay)	A44
"	décoller R	(day kaw lay)	R's
to penetrate	pénétrer	(pay nay tray)	A5
to perceive	percevoir	(pehr suh vwahr)	A7
"	apercevoir	(ah pehr suh vwahr)	A7
to perfect	parachever	(pah rah shvay)	A44
"	perfectionner R	(pehr fehk syaw nay)	R's
to perish	périr *	(pay reer)	*'s
to perforate	perforer R	(pehr faw ray)	R's
to permit	permettre	(pehr meh truh)	A48
to persecute	persécuter R	(pehr say kew tay)	R's
to persevere	persévérer	(pehr say vay ray)	A32
to persist	persister R	(pehr see stay)	R's
"	obstiner (s') R	(awp stee nay)	R's
"	acharner (s') R	(ah shar nay)	R's
to perspire	transpirer R	(trawn spee ray)	R's
to persuade	persuader R	(pehr swah day)	R's
to pervert	pervertir *	(pehr vehr teer)	*'s
to pester	harceler	(ahr suh lay)	A44
to petrify	pétrifier R	(pay tree fyay)	R's
to phone	téléphoner R	(tay lay faw nay)	R's
to photograph	photographier R	(faw toh grah fyay)	R's
to pick	cueillir	(kuh yeer)	A3
to pick up	relever	(ruh lvay)	A44
to pierce	percer	(pehr say)	A13
to pile up	entasser R	(awn tah say)	R's
to pinch	pincer	(pahn say)	A13

© 2010

ENGLISH	FRENCH VERB	PRONOUNCIATION	PAGE
to pity	plaindre	(plahn druh)	A12
to place	placer	(plah say)	A13
"	caser R	(kah zay)	R's
to plan	planifier R	(plah nee fyay)	R's
"	concerter R	(kohn sehr tay)	R's
"	projeter	(praw zhuh tay)	A43
to play	jouer R	(zhway)	R's
to play up	chahuter R	(shah ew tay)	R's
to plead	plaider R	(play day)	R's
to please	plaire	(plehr)	A53
to pledge	jurer R	(zhew ray)	R's
to plot	conspirer R	(kohn spee ray)	R's
"	machiner R	(mah shee nay)	R's
to plough	labourer R	(lah boo ray)	R's
to plunge	plonger	(plohn zhay)	A46
to poach	braconner R	(brah kaw nay)	R's
to point	braquer R	(brah kay)	R's
to point out	indiquer R	(ahn dee kay)	R's
"	remarquer R	(ruh mahr kay)	R's
"	signaler R	(see nyah lay)	R's
to poison	empoisonner R	(awn pwah zaw nay)	R's
to polish	astiquer R	(ah stee kay)	R's
"	polir *	(paw leer)	*'s
"	cirer R	(see ray)	R's
to pollute	polluer R	(pawl lway)	R's
to popularize	vulgariser R	(vewl gah ree zay)	R's
to populate	peupler R	(puh play)	R's
to possess	posséder	(paw say day)	A32
to post	poster R	(paw stay)	R's
to postpone	différer	(dee fay ray)	A32
to pour	répandre #	(ray pawn druh)	#'s
"	verser R	(vehr say)	R's
to pour out	déverser R	(day vehr say)	R's
to practise	pratiquer R	(prah tee kay)	R's
to praise	vanter R	(vawn tay)	R's
to pray	prier R	(pree yay)	R's
to preach	prêcher R	(pray shay)	R's
to precede	précéder	(pray say day)	A32
to predict	prédire	(pray deer)	A25
"	prévoir	(pray vwahr)	A66
to prefer	préférer	(pray fay ray)	A32
to prejudge	préjuger	(pray zhew zhay)	A46
to premeditate	préméditer R	(pray may dee tay)	R's
to prepare	préparer R	(pray pah ray)	R's
"	accommoder R	(ah kaw maw day)	R's
"	mijoter R	(mee zhaw tay)	R's
to prescribe	prescrire	(preh skreer)	A28
"	ordonner R	(awr daw nay)	R's
to present	présenter R	(pray zawn tay)	R's

© 2010

ENGLISH	FRENCH VERB	PRONOUNCIATION	PAGE
to preserve	préserver R	(pray zehr vay)	R's
to preside over	présider R	(pray zee day)	R's
to press	appuyer	(ah pwee yay)	A30
to presume	présumer R	(pray zew may)	R's
to prevail	prévaloir	(pray vah lwahr)	S56
to prevent	prévenir	(pray vneer)	A23
"	empêcher R	(awn pay shay)	R's
to print	imprimer R	(ahn pree may)	R's
to proceed	procéder	(praw say day)	A32
to proclaim	proclamer R	(praw klah may)	R's
to procrastinate	atermoyer	(ah tehr mwah yay)	A30
to procreate	procréer R	(praw kray ay)	R's
to produce	produire	(praw dweer)	A63
"	pondre #	(pohn druh)	#'s
to profit from	profiter R	(praw fee tay)	R's
to project	projeter	(praw zhuh tay)	A43
to prolong	prolonger	(praw lohn zhay)	A46
to promise	promettre	(praw meh truh)	A48
to promote	promouvoir	(praw moo vwahr)	A29
to pronounce	prononcer	(praw nohn say)	A13
"	énoncer	(ay nohn say)	A13
to proofread	relire	(ruh leer)	A45
to prop up	étayer	(ay tay yay)	A33
to protect	protéger	(praw tay zhay)	A57
"	préserver R	(pray zehr vay)	R's
to protest	protester R	(praw teh stay)	R's
to prove	prouver R	(proo vay)	R's
to provide	munir *	(mew neer)	*'s
"	nantir *	(nawn teer)	*'s
"	équiper R	(ay kee pay)	R's
to provide for	subvenir	(sewb vuh neer)	A23
to publish	publier R	(pew blee yay)	R's
to puff out	renfler R	(rawn flay)	R's
to pull	tirer R	(tee ray)	R's
to pull down	rabattre	(rah bah truh)	A1
to pull out	arracher R	(ah rah shay)	R's
to pulse	palpiter R	(pahl pee tay)	R's
to pump	pomper R	(pohn pay)	R's
to punctuate	ponctuer R	(pohnk tway)	R's
to punish	punir *	(pew neer)	*'s
"	châtier R	(shah tyay)	R's
to purify	purifier R	(pew ree fyay)	R's
to pursue	poursuivre	(poor swee vruh)	A61
to push	pousser R	(poo say)	R's
to push back	repousser R	(ruh poo say)	R's
to push in	enfoncer	(awn fohn say)	A13
to put	mettre	(meh truh)	A48
to put back	remettre	(ruh meh truh)	A48
to put (so) back to sleep	rendormir	(rawn dawr meer)	A27

ENGLISH	FRENCH VERB	PRONOUNCIATION	PAGE
to put down	déposer R	(day poh zay)	R's
"	poser R	(poh zay)	R's
to put (so) into debt	endetter R	(awn day tay)	R's
to put (so) off	échauder R	(ay shoh day)	R's
to put (sth) on	chausser R	(shoh say)	R's
to put on (a role/ appearance)	revêtir	(ruh veh teer)	A64
to put oneself to a lot of trouble	décarcasser (se) R	(day kahr kah say)	R's
to put on weight	grossir *	(groh seer)	*'s
to put out	éteindre	(ay tahn druh)	A12
to put out flags	pavoiser R	(pah vwah zay)	R's
to put right	redresser R	(ruh dray say)	R's
to put to bed	coucher R	(koo shay)	R's
to put together	grouper R	(groo pay)	R's
to put up	dresser R	(dray say)	R's
to qualify	qualifier R	(kah lee fyay)	R's
to quarrel	quereller (se) R	(kuh reh lay)	R's
to quench thirst	désaltérer	(day zahl tay ray)	A32
to question	questionner R	(keh styaw nay)	R's
"	contester R	(kohn teh stay)	R's
to quibble	chipoter R	(shee paw tay)	R's
to quiet down	assagir *	(ah sah zheer)	*'s
to quiver	frémir *	(fray meer)	*'s
to rail against	vitupérer	(vee tew pay ray)	A32
to rain	pleuvoir	(pluh vwahr)	A54
to raise	élever	(ay lvay)	A44
"	rehausser R	(ruh oh say)	R's
"	relever	(ruh lvay)	A44
to rally	rallier R	(rah lyay)	R's
to rant on	déblatérer	(day blah tay ray)	A32
to rape	violer R	(vyaw lay)	R's
to rate	coter R	(kaw tay)	R's
to rationalise	rationaliser R	(rah syaw nah lee zay)	R's
to re-emerge	resurgir *	(ruh sewr zheer)	*'s
to re-enter	rentrer R	(rawn tray)	R's
to reaccustom	réhabituer R	(ray ah bee tway)	R's
to reach	accéder	(ahk say day)	A32
"	parvenir	(pahr vuh neer)	A23
to react	réagir *	(ray ah zheer)	*'s
to read	lire	(leer)	A45
to readjust	rajuster R	(rah zhew stay)	R's
to realize	réaliser R	(ray ah lee zay)	R's
to reappear	reparaître	(ruh pah reh truh)	A18
to reappoint	renommer R	(ruh naw may)	R's
to rear up	cabrer R	(kah bray)	R's
to reason	raisonner R	(reh zaw nay)	R's
to reassure	rasséréner	(rah say ray nay)	A32
"	rassurer R	(rah sew ray)	R's
to reboil	recuire	(ruh kweer)	A63
to rebound	rebondir *	(ruh bohn deer)	*'s

© 2010

ENGLISH	FRENCH VERB	PRONOUNCIATION	PAGE
to recall	rappeler	(rah play)	A8
"	évoquer R	(ay vaw kay)	R's
to recapture	ressaisir *	(ruh seh zeer)	*'s
to recast	refondre #	(ruh fohn druh)	#'s
to receive	recevoir	(ruh svwahr)	A7
"	percevoir	(pehr suh vwahr)	A7
to receive Communion	communier R	(kaw mew nyay)	R's
to recite	réciter R	(ray see tay)	R's
to recognize	reconnaître	(ruh kaw neh truh)	A18
to reconcile	réconcilier R	(ray kohn see lyay)	R's
"	concilier R	(kohn see lyay)	R's
to reconquer	reconquérir	(ruh kohn kay reer)	A4
to reconstruct	reconstruire	(ruh kohn strweer)	A63
to recopy	recopier R	(ruh kaw pyay)	R's
to record	consigner R	(kohn see nyay)	R's
"	enregistrer R	(awn ruh zhee stray)	R's
to recover	recouvrir	(ruh koov reer)	A52
"	guérir *	(gay reer)	*'s
to recreate	recréer R	(ruh kree ay)	R's
to rectify	rectifier R	(rehk tee fyay)	R's
to recuperate	récupérer	(ray kew pay ray)	A32
to recycle	recycler R	(ruh see klay)	R's
to redden	rougir *	(roo zheer)	*'s
to rediscover	retrouver R	(ruh troo vay)	R's
to redo	refaire	(ruh fehr)	A37
to reduce	alléger	(ah lay zhay)	A57
"	démultiplier R	(day mewl tee plee yay)	R's
"	diminuer R	(dee mee nway)	R's
"	réduire	(ray dweer)	A63
to reduplicate	redoubler R	(ruh doo blay)	R's
to refer	référer	(ray fay ray)	A32
"	déférer	(day fay ray)	A32
to refine	raffiner R	(rah fee nay)	R's
to reflect	refléter	(ruh flay tay)	A32
"	réfléchir *	(ray flay sheer)	*'s
to reform	réformer R	(ray fawr may)	R's
to refresh	rafraîchir *	(rah freh sheer)	*'s
to refuel	ravitailler R	(rah vee tah yay)	R's
to refuse	refuser R	(ruh few zay)	R's
to refute	réfuter R	(ray few tay)	R's
to regenerate	régénérer	(reh zhay nay ray)	A32
to register	enregistrer R	(awn ruh zhee stray)	R's
to regret	regretter R	(ruh gray tay)	R's
"	repentir (se)	(ruh pawn teer)	A27
to rehabilitate	réhabiliter R	(ray ah bee lee tay)	R's
to reheat	réchauffer R	(ray shoh fay)	R's
to reign	régner	(ray nyay)	A5
to regain	regagner R	(ruh gah nyay)	R's
to reimbourse	rembourser R	(rawn boor say)	R's

© 2010

ENGLISH	FRENCH VERB	PRONOUNCIATION	PAGE
to reinforce	renforcer	(rawn fawr say)	A13
to reintegrate	réintégrer	(ray ahn tay gray)	A5
to reject	rejeter	(ruh zhtay)	A43
to rejoin	rejoindre	(ruh zhwahn druh)	A12
to rejuvenate	rajeunir *	(rah zhuh neer)	*'s
to relax	décontracter R	(day kohn trahk tay)	R's
"	délasser R	(day lah say)	R's
to release	débloquer R	(day blaw kay)	R's
"	détendre #	(day tawn druh)	#'s
"	lâcher R	(lah shay)	R's
to relegate	reléguer	(ruh lay gay)	A5
to relieve	soulager	(soo lah zhay)	A46
to relieve boredom	désennuyer	(day zaw nwee yay)	A30
to relight	rallumer R	(rah lew may)	R's
to relinquish	résigner R	(ray zee nyay)	R's
to relive	revivre	(ruh vee vruh)	A65
to relocate	déménager	(day may nah zhay)	A46
to remake	refaire	(ruh fehr)	A37
to remarry	remarier R	(ruh mahr yay)	R's
to remedy	remédier R	(ruh may dyay)	R's
to remember	souvenir (se)	(soo vneer)	A23
to remind	rappeler	(rah play)	A8
to remove	ôter R	(oh tay)	R's
"	dessaisir *	(day seh zeer)	*'s
"	enlever	(awn lvay)	A44
"	retirer R	(ruh tee ray)	R's
to render	crépir *	(kray peer)	*'s
to renew	renouer R	(ruh nway)	R's
"	renouveler	(ruh noov lay)	A8
to renounce	renier R	(ruhn yay)	R's
to renovate	rénover R	(ray naw vay)	R's
to rent	louer R	(loo ay)	R's
to reopen	rouvrir	(roo vreer)	A52
to reorganize	réorganiser R	(ray awr gah nee zay)	R's
to repaint	repeindre	(ruh pahn druh)	A12
to repair	réparer R	(ray pah ray)	R's
to repeal	abroger	(ah braw zhay)	A46
to repeat	répéter	(ray pay tay)	A32
to repeat a year	redoubler R	(ruh doo blay)	R's
to repel	rebuter R	(ruh bew tay)	R's
to repent	repentir (se)	(ruh pawn teer)	A27
to replace	remplacer	(rawn plah say)	A13
to represent	représenter R	(ruh pray zawn tay)	R's
"	figurer R	(fee gew ray)	R's
to reprint	réimprimer R	(ray ahn pree may)	R's
to reproduce	reproduire	(ruh praw dweer)	A63
to repudiate	répudier R	(ray pew dyay)	R's
to request	requérir	(ruh kay reer)	A4
to require	nécessiter R	(nay say see tay)	R's

ENGLISH	FRENCH VERB	PRONOUNCIATION	PAGE
to reread	relire	(ruh leer)	A45
to reroute	dérouter R	(day roo tay)	R's
to rescue	secourir	(suh koo reer)	A21
to resell	revendre #	(ruh vawn druh)	#'s
to resemble	ressembler R	(ruh sawn blay)	R's
"	apparenter R	(ah pah rawn tay)	R's
to reserve	réserver R	(ray zehr vay)	R's
to reshuffle	rebattre	(ruh bah truh)	A1
to reside	résider R	(ray zee day)	R's
"	demeurer R	(duh muh ray)	R's
to resign	démissionner R	(day mee syaw nay)	R's
to resist	résister R	(ray zee stay)	R's
to resole	ressemeler	(ruh suhm lay)	A8
to resolve	résoudre	(ray zoo druh)	A26
to resort to	recourir	(ruh koo reer)	A21
to restart	relancer	(ruh lawn say)	A13
to restore	rétablir *	(ray tah bleer)	*'s
to restrain	brider R	(bree day)	R's
to restructure	reconvertir *	(ruh kohn vehr teer)	*'s
to result from	résulter R	(ray zewl tay)	R's
to retail	revendre #	(ruh vawn druh)	#'s
to retie	renouer R	(ruh nway)	R's
to retract one's statement	dédire (se)	(day deer)	A25
to retrieve	récupérer	(ray kew pay ray)	A32
to return	retourner R	(ruh toor nay)	R's
to return home	rentrer R	(rawn tray)	R's
to return to	réintégrer	(ray ahn tay gray)	A5
to reveal	révéler	(ray vay lay)	A32
to revere	révérer	(ray vay ray)	A32
to reverse	inverser R	(ahn vehr say)	R's
to revise	réviser R	(ray vee zay)	R's
to revive	revivre	(ruh vee vruh)	A65
"	ranimer R	(rah nee may)	R's
to reward	récompenser R	(ray kohn pawn say)	R's
to rework	refondre #	(ruh fohn druh)	#'s
to rewrite	récrire	(ray kreer)	A28
to riddle with	cribler R	(kree blay)	R's
to ridicule	ridiculiser R	(ree dee kew lee zay)	R's
to ring	sonner R	(saw nay)	R's
to ring out	fuser R	(few zay)	R's
to ring out	résonner R	(ray zaw nay)	R's
to rip	déchirer R	(day shee ray)	R's
to ripen	mûrir *	(mew reer)	*'s
to rise up against	insurger (s')	(ahn sewr zhay)	A46
to risk	risquer R	(ree skay)	R's
to risk	hasarder R	(ah zahr day)	R's
to rival	rivaliser R	(ree vah lee zay)	R's
to roam	vadrouiller R	(vah droo yay)	R's
to roar	vrombir *	(vrohn beer)	*'s

© 2010

ENGLISH	FRENCH VERB	PRONOUNCIATION	PAGE
to roast	rôtir *	(raw teer)	*'s
to rock	bercer	(behr say)	A13
to rocket	fuser R	(few zay)	R's
to roll	rouler R	(roo lay)	R's
to roll up	retrousser R	(ruh troo say)	R's
to root	enraciner R	(awn rah see nay)	R's
to rot	pourrir *	(poo reer)	*'s
to round off	arrondir *	(ah rohn deer)	*'s
to rouse	ameuter R	(ah muh tay)	R's
to rub	frotter R	(fraw tay)	R's
to ruffle up	hérisser R	(ay ree say)	R's
to ruin	ruiner R	(rwee nay)	R's
"	bousiller R	(boo zee yay)	R's
to run	courir	(koo reer)	A21
to run away	enfuir (s')	(awn fwee eer)	A39
to run again	recourir	(ruh koo reer)	A21
to rush	accourir	(ah koo reer)	A21
to sacrifice	immoler R	(ee maw lay)	R's
to sadden	attrister R	(ah tree stay)	R's
to safeguard	sauvegarder R	(sohv gahr day)	R's
to sag	affaisser (s') R	(ah fay say)	R's
to sail	naviguer R	(nah vee gay)	R's
to sanctify	sanctifier R	(sahnk tee fyay)	R's
to satisfy	satisfaire	(sah tees fehr)	A37
"	contenter R	(kohn tawn tay)	R's
to save	sauver R	(soh vay)	R's
"	épargner R	(ay pahr nyay)	R's
to savour	déguster R	(day gew stay)	R's
to saw	scier R	(syay)	R's
to say	dire	(deer)	A25
to say again	redire	(ruh deer)	A25
to scald	échauder R	(ay shoh day)	R's
to scare	effrayer	(ay freh yay)	A33
to scatter	disperser R	(dee spehr say)	R's
"	éparpiller R	(ay pahr pee yay)	R's
to scent	parfumer R	(pahr few may)	R's
to scheme	manigancer	(mah nee gawn say)	A13
to scorn	bafouer R	(bah fway)	R's
to scrape (sth) clean	racler R	(rah klay)	R's
to scratch	gratter R	(grah tay)	R's
"	griffer R	(gree fay)	R's
to scrawl	griffoner R	(gree faw nay)	R's
to screw on	visser R	(vee say)	R's
to screw up	louper R	(loo pay)	R's
to search	fouiller R	(foo yay)	R's
to seduce	séduire	(say dweer)	A63
to see	voir	(vwahr)	A66
to see again	revoir	(ruh vwahr)	A66
to see (so) out	reconduire	(ruh kohn dweer)	A63

ENGLISH	FRENCH VERB	PRONOUNCIATION	PAGE
to seem	sembler R	(sawn blay)	R's
"	apparaître	(ah pah reh truh)	A18
"	paraître	(pah reh truh)	A18
to seize	saisir *	(say zeer)	*'s
to sell	écouler R	(ay koo lay)	R's
"	vendre #	(vawn druh)	#'s
to send	envoyer	(awn vwah yay)	A31
to send back	renvoyer	(rawn vwah yay)	A31
to send (so) to sleep	endormir	(awn dawr meer)	A27
to separate	séparer R	(say pah ray)	R's
"	disjoindre	(dees zhwahn druh)	A12
to serve	servir	(sehr veer)	A27
to set	sertir *	(sehr teer)	*'s
"	durcir *	(dewr seer)	*'s
to set fire to	enflammer R	(awn flah may)	R's
to set off	déclencher R	(day klawn shay)	R's
to set up	établir *	(ay tah bleer)	*'s
to sew	coudre	(koo druh)	A20
to sew up	recoudre	(ruh koo druh)	A20
to shake	ébranler R	(ay brawn lay)	R's
"	secouer R	(suh kway)	R's
"	trembler R	(trawn blay)	R's
to share	partager	(pahr tah zhay)	A46
to share out	répartir *	(ray pahr teer)	*'s
to sharpen	aiguiser R	(ay gee zay)	R's
to shave	raser R	(rah zay)	R's
to shear	tondre #	(tohn druh)	#'s
to shelter	abriter R	(ah bree tay)	R's
to shift	décaler R	(day kah lay)	R's
to shine	briller R	(bree yay)	R's
"	reluire	(ruh lweer)	A63
to shine brightly	resplendir *	(reh splawn deer)	*'s
to shiver	frissonner R	(free saw nay)	R's
"	grelotter R	(gruh law tay)	R's
to shock	choquer R	(shaw kay)	R's
to shoot	fusiller R	(few zee yay)	R's
to shore up	étayer	(ay tay yay)	A33
to shorten	abréger	(ah bray zhay)	A57
"	raccourcir *	(rah koor seer)	*'s
to shout	crier R	(kree yay)	R's
"	vociférer	(vaw see fay ray)	A32
to show	manifester R	(mah nee feh stay)	R's
"	montrer R	(mohn tray)	R's
to show again	remontrer R	(ruh mohn tray)	R's
to show off	frimer R	(free may)	R's
to show through	transparaître	(trawn spah reh truh)	A18
to shower someone	doucher R	(doo shay)	R's
to shred	déchiqueter	(day sheek tay)	A43
to shrink	rétrécir *	(ray tray seer)	*'s

© 2010

ENGLISH	FRENCH VERB	PRONOUNCIATION	PAGE
to shrug	hausser R	(oh say)	R's
to shut away	cloîtrer R	(klwah tray)	R's
to shut	rabattre	(rah bah truh)	A1
to shut in	enfermer R	(awn fehr may)	R's
to sicken	écœurer R	(ay kuh ray)	R's
"	ulcérer	(ewl say ray)	A32
to sign	signer R	(see nyay)	R's
to signal	signaler R	(see nyah lay)	R's
to silver	argenter R	(ahr zhawn tay)	R's
to simplify	simplifier R	(sahn plee fyay)	R's
to simulate	simuler R	(see mew lay)	R's
to sing	chanter R	(shawn tay)	R's
to singe	flamber R	(flawn bay)	R's
to sink	sombrer R	(sohn bray)	R's
to sin	pécher	(pay shay)	A5
to sit	siéger	(syay zhay)	A57
to sit at the table	attabler (s') R	(ah tah blay)	R's
to sit (so) down	asseoir	(ah swahr)	A11
to sketch	esquisser R	(eh skee say)	R's
to sketch out	ébaucher R	(ay boh shay)	R's
to skid	déraper R	(day rah pay)	R's
to skim (milk)	écrémer	(ay kray may)	A32
to skimp on	lésiner R	(lay zee nay)	R's
to skin	écorcher R	(ay kawr shay)	R's
"	dépouiller R	(day poo yay)	R's
to slander	calomnier R	(kah lawm nyay)	R's
to slap	gifler R	(zhee flay)	R's
to slash	balafrer R	(bah lah fray)	R's
to sleep	dormir	(dohr meer)	A27
to slim	amincir *	(ah mahn seer)	*'s
to slip	glisser R	(glee say)	R's
to slip on	enfiler R	(awn fee lay)	R's
to slit the throat of	égorger	(ay gawr zhay)	A46
to slow down	décélérer	(day say lay ray)	A32
"	freiner R	(freh nay)	R's
"	ralentir *	(rah lawn teer)	*'s
to smash	défoncer	(day fohn say)	A13
"	fracasser R	(frah kah say)	R's
to smear	barbouiller R	(bahr boo yay)	R's
to smell	sentir	(sawn teer)	A27
to smile	sourire	(soo reer)	A58
to smoke	fumer R	(few may)	R's
to sneeze	éternuer R	(ay tehr nway)	R's
to sniff	flairer R	(flay ray)	R's
"	renifler R	(ruh nee flay)	R's
to snore	ronfler R	(rohn flay)	R's
to snow	neiger	(neh zhay)	A46
to soak	tremper R	(trawn pay)	R's
to sob	sangloter R	(sawn glaw tay)	R's

© 2010

ENGLISH	FRENCH VERB	PRONOUNCIATION	PAGE
to sober (so) up	dégriser R	(day gree zay)	R's
to soften	adoucir *	(ah doo seer)	*'s
"	amollir *	(ah maw leer)	*'s
"	assouplir *	(ah soo pleer)	*'s
"	ramollir *	(rah maw leer)	*'s
to soil	souiller R	(soo yay)	R's
to solicit	racoler R	(rah kaw lay)	R's
to solve	élucider R	(ay lew see day)	R's
"	résoudre	(ray zoo druh)	A26
to sort	trier R	(tree yay)	R's
to sow	semer	(suh may)	A44
to space (sth) out	échelonner R	(aysh law nay)	R's
to spank	fessser R	(fay say)	R's
to sparkle	scintiller R	(sahn tee yay)	R's
to arouse	susciter R	(sew see tay)	R's
to speak	parler R	(pahr lay)	R's
to specialize	spécialiser R	(spay syah lee zay)	R's
to specify	spécifier R	(spay see fyay)	R's
"	préciser R	(pray see zay)	R's
to speed up	activer R	(ak tee vay)	R's
to spell	épeler	(ay play)	A8
"	orthographier R	(awr taw grah fyay)	R's
to spend	dépenser R	(day pawn say)	R's
to spice	épicer	(ay pee say)	A13
to spin	filer R	(fee lay)	R's
to spit out	cracher R	(krah shay)	R's
to splash	éclabousser R	(ay klah boo say)	R's
to splash back	rejaillir *	(ruh zhah yeer)	*'s
to split	craquer R	(krah kay)	R's
"	fendre #	(fawn druh)	#'s
to split	scinder R	(sahn day)	R's
to split in two	dédoubler R	(day doo blay)	R's
to spoil	gâter R	(gah tay)	R's
to spread	épandre #	(ay pawn druh)	#'s
"	diffuser R	(dee few zay)	R's
"	répandre #	(ray pawn druh)	#'s
to spread out	étaler R	(ay tah lay)	R's
to spy on	épier R	(ay pyay)	R's
"	espionner R	(eh spyaw nay)	R's
to squabble	chamailler R	(shah mah yay)	R's
to squander	gaspiller R	(gah spee yay)	R's
to squat	accroupir (s') *	(ah kroo peer)	*'s
to squeeze out	épreindre	(ay prahn druh)	A12
to squint	loucher R	(loo shay)	R's
to stagger	chanceler	(shawn slay)	A8
to stagnate	croupir *	(kroo peer)	*'s
"	végéter	(vay zhay tay)	A32
to stain	tacher R	(tah shay)	R's
to stammer	balbutier R	(bahl bew syay)	R's

© 2010

ENGLISH	FRENCH VERB	PRONOUNCIATION	PAGE
to stamp	affranchir *	(ah frahn sheer)	*'s
"	timbrer R	(tahn bray)	R's
to standardize	standardiser R	(stawn dahr dee zay)	R's
to start	commencer	(kaw mawn say)	A13
"	débuter R	(day bew tay)	R's
to start again	recommencer	(ruh kaw mawn say)	A13
to start up	démarrer R	(day mah ray)	R's
to starve	affamer R	(ah fah may)	R's
to stay	rester R	(reh stay)	R's
to steal	dérober R	(day raw bay)	R's
"	voler R	(vaw lay)	R's
to sterilize	stériliser R	(stay ree lee zay)	R's
to stick	coller R	(kaw lay)	R's
to stifle	étouffer R	(ay too fay)	R's
to stimulate	stimuler R	(stee mew lay)	R's
to sting	picoter R	(pee kaw tay)	R's
to stop	arrêter R	(ah ray tay)	R's
"	cesser R	(say say)	R's
"	interrompre #	(ahn tay rohn pruh)	#'s
to straighten	dégauchir *	(day goh sheer)	*'s
to strain	distendre #	(dee stawn druh)	#'s
to strangle	étrangler R	(ay trawn glay)	R's
to streak	zébrer	(zay bray)	A5
to strengthen	affermir *	(ah fehr meer)	*'s
"	endurcir *	(awn dewr seer)	*'s
"	fortifier R	(fawr tee fyay)	R's
"	raffermir *	(rah fehr meer)	*'s
to stretch	étendre #	(ay tawn druh)	#'s
"	tendre #	(tawn druh)	#'s
to strike (someone)	asséner	(ah say nay)	A32
to strike down	foudroyer	(foo drwah yay)	A30
to strip	dépouiller R	(day poo yay)	R's
to strive	efforcer (s')	(ay fawr say)	A13
to stroll	flâner R	(flah nay)	R's
to struggle	lutter R	(lew tay)	R's
to struggle along	vivoter R	(vee vaw tay)	R's
to study	étudier R	(ay tew dyay)	R's
to stuff	farcir *	(fahr seer)	*'s
"	fourrer R	(foo ray)	R's
"	truffer R	(trew fay)	R's
to stumble	broncher R	(brohn shay)	R's
"	trébucher R	(tray bew shay)	R's
to stun	étourdir *	(ay toor deer)	*'s
"	ahurir *	(ah ew reer)	*'s
to stutter	bégayer	(bay gay yay)	A33
to subdue	soumettre	(soo meh truh)	A48
to subject	assujettir *	(ah sew zheh teer)	*'s
"	soumettre	(soo meh truh)	A48
to submerge	submerger	(sewb mehr zhay)	A46

© 2010

ENGLISH	FRENCH VERB	PRONOUNCIATION	PAGE
to subscribe	abonner R	(ah baw nay)	R's
to subscribe to	souscrire	(soo skreer)	A28
to subside	affaisser (s') R	(ah fay say)	R's
"	décroître	(day krwa truh)	A2
to subsist	subsister R	(sewb zee stay)	R's
to substitute	substituer R	(sewp stee tway)	R's
to subtract	soustraire	(soo strehr)	A35
"	retrancher R	(ruh trawn shay)	R's
to succeed	succéder	(sewk say day)	A32
"	aboutir *	(ah boo teer)	*'s
"	réussir *	(ray ew seer)	*'s
to suck	sucer	(sew say)	A13
to suck at	téter	(tay tay)	A32
to suffer	souffrir	(soo freer)	A52
"	pâtir *	(pah teer)	*'s
to suffocate	asphyxier R	(ahs feek syay)	R's
to suggest	suggérer	(sewg zhay ray)	A32
"	proposer R	(praw poh zay)	R's
to sulk	bouder R	(boo day)	R's
to summarize	résumer R	(ray zew may)	R's
to supervise	encadrer R	(awn kah dray)	R's
"	surveiller R	(sewr vay yay)	R's
to supply	fournir *	(foor neer)	*'s
to support	soutenir	(soo tneer)	A23
to suppose	supposer R	(sew poh zay)	R's
to surface	dégauchir *	(day goh sheer)	*'s
to surpass	surpasser R	(sewr pah say)	R's
to surprise	surprendre	(sewr prawn druh)	A9
"	étonner R	(ay taw nay)	R's
to surround	cerner R	(sehr nay)	R's
"	entourer R	(awn too ray)	R's
to survive	survivre	(sewr vee vruh)	A65
to suspect	soupçonner R	(soop saw nay)	R's
to suspend	suspendre #	(sew spawn druh)	#'s
to swallow	avaler R	(ah vah lay)	R's
to swarm about	grouiller R	(groo yay)	R's
to swear at	injurier R	(ahn zhewr yay)	R's
to sweat	suer R	(sway)	R's
to sweep up	balayer	(bah lay yay)	A33
to swim	nager	(nah zhay)	A46
to swing	balancer	(bah lawn say)	A13
"	osciller R	(aw see lay)	R's
to swipe	rafler R	(rah flay)	R's
to switch off	éteindre	(ay tahn druh)	A12
to sympathize	compatir R	(kohn pah teer)	R's
to tack	louvoyer	(loo vwah yay)	A30
to take	prendre	(prawn druh)	A9
to take (so) aback	interloquer R	(ahn tehr law kay)	R's
to take a census of	recenser R	(ruh sawn say)	R's

© 2010

ENGLISH	FRENCH VERB	PRONOUNCIATION	PAGE
to take advantage	profier R	(praw fee tay)	R's
to take a sample of	prélever	(pray lvay)	A44
to take away	emmener	(awn mnay)	A44
"	emporter R	(awn pawr tay)	R's
"	remporter R	(rawn pawr tay)	R's
to take back	reprendre	(ruh prawn druh)	A9
to take (sth) back	remmener	(rawn mnay)	A44
to take (so/sth) back down	redescendre #	(ruh deh sawn druh)	#'s
to take (so/sth) back up	remonter R	(ruh mohn tay)	R's
to take down	décrocher R	(day kraw shay)	R's
"	démonter R	(day mohn tay)	R's
to take (sth) down	descendre #	(deh sawn druh)	#'s
to take for a walk	balader R	(bah lah day)	R's
"	promener	(praw mnay)	A44
to take out again	ressortir	(ruh sawr teer)	A27
to take over	emparer (s') R	(awn pah ray)	R's
to take refuge	réfugier (se) R	(ray few zhee ay)	R's
to take the top off	décapsuler R	(day kahp sew lay)	R's
to take (so/sth) up	monter R	(mohn tay)	R's
to tally	cadrer R	(kah dray)	R's
to tame	apprivoiser R	(ah pree vwa zay)	R's
"	dompter R	(dohn tay)	R's
to tan	bronzer R	(brohn zay)	R's
to tap	taper R	(tah pay)	R's
to tarnish	ternir *	(tehr neer)	*'s
to taste	goûter R	(goo tay)	R's
to tax	taxer R	(tahk say)	R's
to teach	apprendre	(ah prawn druh)	A9
"	enseigner R	(awn say nyay)	R's
"	instruire	(ahn strweer)	A63
to teach to read and write	alphabétiser R	(ahl fah bay tee zay)	R's
to televise	téléviser R	(tay lay vee zay)	R's
to tell	conter R	(kohn tay)	R's
"	dire	(deer)	A25
"	raconter R	(rah kohn tay)	R's
to tell off	engueuler R	(awn guh lay)	R's
"	gronder R	(grohn day)	R's
to tempt	allécher	(ah lay shay)	A5
to tenderize	attendrir *	(ah tawn dreer)	*'s
to terminate	résilier R	(ray zee lyay)	R's
to terrify	terrifier R	(teh ree fyay)	R's
"	épouvanter R	(ay poo vawn tay)	R's
to test	expérimenter R	(ek spay ree mawn tay)	R's
to testify	attester R	(ah teh stay)	R's
"	témoigner R	(tay mwa nyay)	R's
to thank	remercier R	(ruh mehr syay)	R's
to thaw	dégeler	(day zhlay)	A44
to think	penser R	(pawn say)	R's
"	réfléchir *	(ray flay sheer)	*'s

© 2010

ENGLISH	FRENCH VERB	PRONOUNCIATION	PAGE
to think	songer	(sohn zhay)	A46
to thin out leaves	effeuiller R	(ay fuh yay)	R's
to thrash about	démener (se)	(day muh nay)	A44
to thread	fileter	(feel tay)	A44
to threaten	menacer	(muh nah say)	A13
to throw	jeter	(zhuh tay)	A43
"	lancer	(lawn say)	A13
to throw (sth) again	relancer	(ruh lawn say)	A13
to throw into confusion	désemparer R	(day zawn pah ray)	R's
to thunder	tonner R	(taw nay)	R's
to tick	cocher R	(kaw shay)	R's
to tickle	chatouiller R	(shah too yay)	R's
to tie	nouer R	(nway)	R's
to tie around	ceindre	(sahn druh)	A12
to tie up	ficeler	(fee slay)	A8
"	lier R	(lyay)	R's
to tighten	raidir *	(reh deer)	*'s
"	tendre #	(tawn druh)	#'s
to tilt	incliner R	(ahn klee nay)	R's
"	pencher R	(pawn shay)	R's
to tinge	teinter R	(tahn tay)	R's
to tint	teinter R	(tahn tay)	R's
to tire	fatiguer R	(fah tee gay)	R's
to tolerate	tolérer	(taw lay ray)	A32
to tone	raffermir *	(rah fehr meer)	*'s
to topple over	basculer R	(bah skew lay)	R's
to torment	tourmenter R	(toor mawn tay)	R's
to torpedo	torpiller R	(tawr pee yay)	R's
to torture	torturer R	(tawr tew ray)	R's
to touch	toucher R	(too shay)	R's
to tow	remorquer R	(ruh mawr kay)	R's
to trace	tracer	(trah say)	A13
to track down	traquer R	(trah kay)	R's
"	dépister R	(day pee stay)	R's
to trade	troquer R	(traw kay)	R's
to train	dresser R	(dray say)	R's
"	entraîner R	(awn tray nay)	R's
to trample	piétiner R	(pyay tee nay)	R's
to transcribe	transcrire	(trawn skreer)	A28
to transfer	transférer	(trawns fay ray)	A32
"	virer R	(vee ray)	R's
to transform	transformer R	(trawns fawr may)	R's
"	muer R	(moo ay)	R's
to translate	traduire	(trah dweer)	A63
to transmit	transmettre	(trawns meh truh)	A48
to transplant	transplanter R	(trawn splawn tay)	R's
to transport	transporter R	(trawn spawr tay)	R's
"	acheminer R	(ah shuh mee nay)	R's
to trap	piéger	(pyay zhay)	A57

ENGLISH	FRENCH VERB	PRONOUNCIATION	PAGE
to travel	voyager	(vwah yah zhay)	A46
to travel all over	parcourir	(pahr koo reer)	A21
to treat	traiter R	(treh tay)	R's
to treat (patient)	soigner R	(swah nyay)	R's
to trim	rogner R	(raw nyay)	R's
to trip	buter R	(bew tay)	R's
to triumph	triompher R	(tree yohn fay)	R's
to trot	trotter R	(traw tay)	R's
to truss up	ligoter R	(lee gaw tay)	R's
to trust	confier R	(kohn fyay)	R's
"	fier (se) R	(fyay)	R's
to try	tâcher R	(tah shay)	R's
"	essayer	(ay say yay)	A33
to try one's best	évertuer (s') R	(ay vehr tway)	R's
to try to persuade	baratiner R	(bah rah tee nay)	R's
to tumble	dégringoler R	(day grahn gaw lay)	R's
to turn	tourner R	(toor nay)	R's
to turn blue	bleuir *	(bluh eer)	*'s
to turn green	verdir *	(vehr deer)	*'s
to turn over	retourner R	(ruh toor nay)	R's
to turn pale	blêmir *	(blay meer)	*'s
to turn yellow	jaunir *	(zhoh neer)	*'s
to twinkle	clignoter R	(klee nyaw tay)	R's
to twist	tortiller R	(tawr tee yay)	R's
"	tordre #	(tawr druh)	#'s
to type	taper R	(tah pay)	R's
to ulcerate	ulcérer	(ewl say ray)	A32
to unbind	délier R	(day lyay)	R's
to unblock	déboucher R	(day boo shay)	R's
to unbutton	déboutonner R	(day boo taw nay)	R's
to undergo	subir *	(sew beer)	*'s
to underline	souligner R	(soo lee nyay)	R's
to undermine	miner R	(mee nay)	R's
to understand	comprendre	(kohn prawn druh)	A9
to undertake	entreprendre	(awn truh prawn druh)	A9
to undo	défaire	(day fehr)	A37
"	dénouer R	(day nway)	R's
to undress	déshabiller R	(day zah bee yay)	R's
"	dévêtir	(day veh teer)	A64
to unfold	déplier R	(day plee yay)	R's
to unharness	dételer	(dayt lay)	A8
to unify	unifier R	(ew nee fyay)	R's
to unite	unir *	(ew neer)	*'s
"	conjoindre	(kohn zhwahn druh)	A12
to unlearn	désapprendre	(day zah prawn druh)	A9
to unleash	déchaîner R	(day shay nay)	R's
to unload	débarquer R	(day bahr kay)	R's
"	décharger	(day shahr zhay)	A46
to unpack	dépaqueter	(day pahk tay)	A43

ENGLISH	FRENCH VERB	PRONOUNCIATION	PAGE
to unpack	déballer R	(day bah lay)	R's
to unplug	débrancher R	(day brawn shay)	R's
to unravel	dénouer R	(day nway)	R's
to unroll	dérouler R	(day roo lay)	R's
to unscrew	dévisser R	(day vee say)	R's
to unshackle	désentraver R	(day zawn trah vay)	R's
to unstitch	découdre	(day koo druh)	A20
to untie	déficeler	(day fee slay)	A8
to unveil	dévoiler R	(day vwah lay)	R's
"	inaugurer R	(ee noh gew ray)	R's
to unwind	détordre #	(day tawr druh)	#'s
to update	actualiser R	(ak twa lee zay)	R's
to uproot	déraciner R	(day rah see nay)	R's
to upset	navrer R	(nah vray)	R's
"	vexer R	(vehk say)	R's
"	dérégler	(day ray glay)	A5
to urbanize	urbaniser R	(ewr bah nee zay)	R's
to urinate	uriner R	(ew ree nay)	R's
to use	utiliser R	(ew tee lee zay)	R's
to vaccinate	vacciner R	(vahk see nay)	R's
to vanish	disparaître	(dee spah reh truh)	A18
to variegate	barioler R	(bahr yaw lay)	R's
to varnish	vernir *	(vehr neer)	*'s
to very	varier R	(vah ryay)	R's
"	diversifier R	(dee vehr see fyay)	R's
to vegetate	végéter	(vay zhay tay)	A32
to veil	voiler R	(vwah lay)	R's
to venture	aventurer R	(ah vawn tew ray)	R's
"	hasarder R	(ah zahr day)	R's
to verify	vérifier R	(vay ree fyay)	R's
to vibrate	vibrer R	(vee bray)	R's
to violate	violer R	(vyaw lay)	R's
to visit	visiter R	(vee zee tay)	R's
to vitrify	vitrifier R	(vee tree fyay)	R's
to vomit	vomir *	(vaw meer)	*'s
"	dégueuler R	(day guh lay)	R's
to vote	voter R	(vaw tay)	R's
to vow	vouer R	(voo ay)	R's
to wage war	guerroyer	(gayr wah yay)	A30
to wait for	attendre #	(ah tawn druh)	#'s
"	patienter R	(pah syawn tay)	R's
to walk	marcher R	(mahr shay)	R's
to walk (so) back home	raccompagner R	(rah kohn pah nyay)	R's
to wander	errer R	(eh ray)	R's
to want	vouloir	(voo lwahr)	A67
to ward off	parer R	(pah ray)	R's
to warm up	échauffer R	(ay shoh fay)	R's
"	tiédir *	(tyay deer)	*'s
to warm (sth) up	dégourdir *	(day goor deer)	*'s

© 2010

ENGLISH	FRENCH VERB	PRONOUNCIATION	PAGE
to warn	avertir *	(ah vehr teer)	*'s
"	prévenir	(pray vneer)	A23
to warp	déjeter	(day zhuh tay)	A43
"	gauchir *	(goh sheer)	*'s
to wash	laver R	(lah vay)	R's
to waste	gâcher R	(gah shay)	R's
to waste away	dépérir *	(day pay reer)	*'s
to watch	surveiller R	(sewr vay yay)	R's
to watch out for	guetter R	(gay tay)	R's
to watch over	veiller R	(vay yay)	R's
to water	abreuver R	(ah bruh vay)	R's
"	arroser R	(ah roh zay)	R's
"	larmoyer	(lahr mwah yay)	A30
to weaken	affaiblir *	(ah feh bleer)	*'s
"	amoindrir *	(ah mwahn dreer)	*'s
to wean	sevrer R	(suh vray)	R's
to wear out	avachir *	(ah vah sheer)	*'s
"	user R	(ew zay)	R's
to wedge	caler R	(kah lay)	R's
"	coincer	(kwahn say)	A13
to weigh	peser	(puh zay)	A44
to weigh down	alourdir *	(ah loor deer)	*'s
to weigh up	soupeser	(soo puh zay)	A44
to welcome	accueillir	(ah kuh yeer)	A3
to wet	mouiller R	(moo yay)	R's
to whirl	tournoyer	(toor nwah yay)	A30
to whisper	chuchoter R	(shew shaw tay)	R's
to whistle	siffler R	(see flay)	R's
to whiten	blanchir *	(blawn sheer)	*'s
to widen	élargir *	(ay lahr zheer)	*'s
to wind	enrouler R	(awn roo lay)	R's
to win	gagner R	(gah nyay)	R's
"	remporter R	(rawn pawr tay)	R's
to win over	rallier R	(rah lyay)	R's
to wipe	essuyer	(ay swee yay)	A30
to withdraw	retirer R	(ruh tee ray)	R's
"	désister (se) R	(day zee stay)	R's
to wobble	branler R	(brawn lay)	R's
to work	fonctionner R	(fohnk syaw nay)	R's
"	travailler R	(trah vah yay)	R's
to worry	angoisser R	(awn gwa say)	R's
"	inquiéter	(ahn kyay tay)	A32
to wrap up	envelopper R	(awn vlaw pay)	R's
to wreck	détraquer R	(day trah kay)	R's
"	saccager	(sah kah zhay)	A46
to wring	essorer R	(ay sawr ray)	R's
to write	écrire	(ay kreer)	A28
to write down	inscrire	(ahn skreer)	A28
to write up	rédiger	(ray dee zhay)	A46

ENGLISH	FRENCH VERB	PRONOUNCIATION	PAGE
to yawn	bâiller R	(bah yay)	R's
to yell	hurler R	(ewr lay)	R's
to yell out	brailler R	(brah yay)	R's
to yield a profit	fructifier R	(frewk tee fyay)	R's
to yodel	yodler R	(yawd lay)	R's
to zigzag	zigzaguer R	(zeeg zah gay)	R's

Recommendations for learning French

Please check these out.

Michel Thomas method French CDs.
These CDs will be a god send as they teach you how to speak French in the most easiest and natural way possible. You just listen and learn without trying to learn. There are 4 CD courses from beginner right up to advanced. Michel also teaches other languages.
Here is the website: www.michelthomas.com/learn-french.php

Go and have a look, there is a sample audio that you can listen to.

Here are the two websites that I think you would benefit greatly from visiting:

www.ielanguages.com
They have loads of info with audio (from beginner to advanced) and flash cards to learn with. This site also teaches other languages.

www.lawlessfrench.com
This website is a bit like the site above in that it has soo much to offer for learning French (from beginner to advanced). Laura Lawless runs this site and you can subscribe to her newsletter that is sent twice a week (Tuesday and Friday) which will deliver to you the latest lessons and features right to your inbox.

© 2010

Made in United States
Troutdale, OR
06/21/2024